Chin Hsiao-Fen

JOHN BOWE

Us: Americans Talk About Love

John Bowe has contributed to the *New Yorker*, the *New York Times Magazine*, GQ, the *American Prospect*, PRI's *This American Life*, *McSweeney's*, and others. He is the coeditor of *Gig: Americans Talk About Their Jobs*, the coscreenwriter of the film *Basquiat*, and the author of the book *Nobodies: Modern American Slave Labor and the Dark Side of the New Global Economy*.

He is a recipient of the J. Anthony Lukas Work-in-Progress Award; the Sydney Hillman Award for journalists, writers, and public figures who pursue social justice and public policy for the common good; the Richard J. Margolis Award, dedicated to journalism that combines social concern and humor; and the Harry Chapin Media Award for reportage of hunger- and poverty-related issues.

He lives in New York.

ALSO BY JOHN BOWE

*Nobodies: Modern American Slave Labor and the
Dark Side of the New Global Economy*

Gig: Americans Talk About Their Jobs (coeditor)

US

US

AMERICANS
TALK ABOUT
LOVE

EDITED BY JOHN BOWE

With Marisa Bowe and Clancy Nolan

FABER AND FABER, INC.

An affiliate of Farrar, Straus and Giroux

New York

Faber and Faber, Inc.

An affiliate of Farrar, Straus and Giroux

18 West 18th Street, New York 10011

Distributed in Canada by D&M Publishers, Inc.

Printed in the United States of America

First edition, 2010

Excerpt from "The Road Home" on page vii is from *Rumi: The Book of Love: Poems of Ecstasy and Longing*, translations and commentary by Coleman Barks, HarperOne, 2005.

Library of Congress Cataloging-in-Publication Data

Us : Americans talk about love / edited by John Bowe.— 1st ed.

p.   cm.

ISBN 978-0-86547-929-6 (pbk : alk. paper)

1. Man-woman relationships—United States—Case studies.

2. Love—United States—Case studies.   I. Bowe, John.

HQ801.U458 2010

305.3—dc22

2009040396

Designed by Michelle McMillian

www.fsgbooks.com

1   3   5   7   9   10   8   6   4   2

The names and identifying characteristics of some of the individuals interviewed for this book have been changed.

For Dum Dum

*An ant hurries along a threshing floor
with its wheat grain, moving between huge stacks
of wheat, not knowing the abundance
all around. It thinks its one grain
is all there is to love.*

—*Rumi, "The Road Home"*

CONTENTS

Ten Years to Twenty Years

PREFACE

The Spanish philosopher Ortega y Gasset, in an essay called "On Love: Aspects of a Single Theme," compares falling and staying in love to the obsessive devotion of the spiritual seeker. "The mystic," he writes, "speaks about the 'presence' of God. Does he imagine it? No, he *conjures* it through prayer, meditation, and constant address; it is never permitted to vanish from his thoughts and thereby takes on a very real life of its own. For the lover, his beloved also possesses a constant presence."

Ortega y Gasset describes the energies of a lover as "a flow, a stream of spiritual matter . . . a psychic radiation which proceeds from the lover to the beloved. It is not a single discharge, but a current." It is this flow of willed address and conjuring, of creation, as often errant as lovely, that is the subject of *Us*.

At the heart of the compact between two lovers is mystery code that, for anyone else, reads as kabbala-like, indecipherable gibberish. And yet, for the lovers, it's transformative, life-affirming, redeeming. It could well be a ghost. It doesn't matter a bit.

We all have the power to make others feel terrible or wonderful, to tolerate them, to like and to love them. When we choose the latter, even imperfectly and sporadically, it's one of the highest gifts we can bestow. We become, in a sense, magicians, transforming the dust of mundane reality with supernatural powers. Why are we not magicians more often? How can we be better magicians?

Us is a collection of oral reports from across the United States, describing the many ways romantic love is sparked, pursued, won, and lost. The stories range from poetic, inspiring, erotic, and heartbreaking to hilarious, preposterous, and sometimes disgusting. *Us* aims as an ensemble to do justice to the array of voices in our country, celebrating their earnestness, openness, optimism, vulgarity, humor, religiosity, sexuality, and generosity.

Love is one of the universal goals we share. It is a true bastion of absolute freedom. No one can tell us whom to love or how to love. We may do whatever we like, arrive at any arrangement we deem satisfying. Imperfect, irreducible, inexpressible, amazing, pathetic, frustrating, seldom gracefully executed, this is what we have, this is who we are. This is how we use our greatest gift.

Neither my coeditors nor I can claim any special expertise about love. Our skill, we hope, is listening: encouraging subjects to express honestly not what they think love is supposed to be but how they actually experience and live it.

We sought to arrange our interviews in a collection readers would find compelling, entertaining, meaningful, and—at least sometimes—enlightening. As a friend described them after reading a few samples, "They're like psychic bonbons." This is because each interview reads like a complete short story, conveying a worldview, a regional perspective, a surprisingly intense glimpse into another life unimaginably different from our own.

What is love for an American? To Jack Babineaux, of Hammond, Louisiana, love is "like two people each reaching for the french fries at the bottom of the McDonald's bag. They have the exact same thought . . . But one of them is going to let the other one have it." Celia Menendez, of San Antonio, Texas, describes her high school love gone wrong as being "like Crystal Pepsi . . . this really great idea. And then it didn't really work out." Orlando's Fritz Baecker speaks for many of us when he describes the difference between being alone and being in love as "like, wow, wow, wow."

We learned from our investigations that love means intercepting your partner when you hear her cocking the pump shotgun to kill herself. Love is smoking crystal meth together and marveling at visions of nitrogen. Love is healing after infidelity. Love is acceptance. Love is listening. Love is not being able to live without the other person. And according to several men and women we met, love means being able to fart without embarrassment.

From the snowy pine forests of Vermont to the plains of Oklahoma, from the strip malls of Florida to the waters of Puget Sound, from illiterate Guatemalan immigrants, go-go dancers, hormone-crazed monster truck drivers, stolid, green-visored accountants, we learned that love is someone who lets you be you. Love is someone who changes you and makes you better. Love is security. Love is friendship. Love is passion. Love is feeling like a schoolgirl. Love is giving. Love is getting. Love is an action. Love is a state of mind. Love is a decision. Love is a spiritual state, derived from God. Love is an arrangement of brain chemicals, oxytocin and endorphins. Love is every day. Love is once in a lifetime. And when it's all over, we find ourselves shopping at Rite Aid, box of Tucks in hand, sobbing at the realization that our beloved hemorrhoid sufferer is gone forever.

How we aspire to love, how our love actually measures up to our declarations—there are few more indelible measures of a person's emotional life. And yet, what is love actually made of? What we learned from these people is that successful love is most often a series of simple actions, performed repeatedly in varying forms: listen, affirm, accept, support, commit, share, be honest, forgive. Easy—except 50 percent of all first marriages in America end in failure.

One of the first questions people asked when we told them about our project was "How do you find these people?" In many ways, we revived the methodologies and the talented team of *Gig: Americans Talk About Their Jobs*, an oral history I coedited ten years ago. The process then and now began with a mass e-mail, followed by hundreds of conversations with friends, colleagues, relatives, and people referred to us from all over the country. We asked each contact to sift through his or her mental and social Rolodex for subjects who identify as happy, sad, black, Asian, Hispanic, rich, poor, and so on, until we began to feel we had a trove of interviews at least somewhat representative of the incredible diversity of the United States.

An old friend of mine from Minneapolis responded, "My wife's family is friends with a couple who were married, then

divorced, then married. Is that interesting?" My mother, who
works as an interpreter, knew the girlfriend of Thomas, a Cambodian immigrant, former monk, and virgin who, at twenty-six
years old, was forced to marry—at gunpoint. Another friend,
with a fundamentalist Christian background, recruited the Liberty University graduate and Delaware pastor Brad Kellum,
whose thoughts about love, God, and the orgasm are illumi-
nating.

We ran eight of our earliest interviews on the web magazine
Salon.com, and many readers responded with their own stories.
We heard from cheating housewives and heartbroken teens. Ads
placed on Craigslists around the country yielded Louise Mac-
Gregor, a mother and banker twenty-nine years into a perfectly
functional marriage—which she left for the high school boyfriend she could never forget.

They also yielded Jack Talbert, from Manhattan, Kansas, a
highly motivated interviewer who rounded up at least a dozen
subjects, one of whom included our longest-loving entrant,
Fred White.

The fearless and indefatigable young Diana Briggs found me
through my last book's website. She rented a car and made three
long trips through the Rocky Mountain states, Appalachia, and
the Mississippi Delta. Through her efforts, we met Marty Ed-
wards, a seamstress plying her trade in a picture-postcard Western town square in Oklahoma; and Deanna Rueda, a homeless
woman in the Hispanic neighborhood of Austin, Texas, interviewed at a bus stop bench near I-35.

The message of *Us* is not that love is wonderful or horrible,
or even that we are necessarily better people when we love
(indeed, many of us become monstrous). Our aim was to avoid

theorizing and hypothesizing altogether and simply document a representative sampling of Americans (or foreigners living on American soil), in all their variety, carrying on about romantic love. Every interview began with the same question: "Please tell me about the person whom you have loved the most."

Because our emphasis was on love, not relationships, our table of contents lists not the length of each relationship but the length of time since the subject first realized, "I'm in love." If there is an observation that becomes crystal clear in *Us*, it is this: the subjects who loved for six months, two years, five years are very different from those who loved for fifty or sixty years. Is it a generational thing? Perhaps in part. But after we had interviewed hundreds of people about love, one thing became incontrovertible: whether they had always been this way or learned to become so, people who have been in love a long time have an aptitude for selflessness. Growing old with someone else seems to correspond with less "me" and more "we."

We selected our stories on the basis of whether or not the interview augmented our understanding of romantic love. For this reason we excluded discussions of love for God, country, pets, or golf. We eliminated unnecessary details that didn't pertain to love: if a person was black, white, poor, wealthy, or the decathalon gold medal winner in the 1984 Olympics, if that fact didn't enhance our discussion of love, it fell to the cutting room floor.

We edited the interviews with an eye toward highlighting each person's unique preoccupations and insights. Accounts too similar to one another or insufficiently clear about their subjects' feelings and opinions about romantic love, no matter how fascinating or moving parts of them might be, were passed over in favor of those that offered a salient and fresh story, theme, or element of love. Within each interview we sought to the utmost to preserve the voice and speaking manner of the subject, while removing an enormous number of "ums," "I means," "y'knows," and "likes" for the purpose of maintaining our readers' sanity.

Our approaches to love are so often obscured by conditions and expectations, prior experience, popular culture, sentimentality, and delusion. On the one hand, there are the theories and prescriptions; on the other, there's the real thing. It's astonishing how little they have in common sometimes. We hear, and we feel, and we supposedly *know* that love is supposed to do such and such. Well, no. It does what you'll find in these stories.

While we rigorously avoided editorial intrusion into the views of our subjects, the spirit of this book as a whole has long been guided by an idea from the Upanishad, a two-thousand-year-old Hindu religious text: "Who sees all beings in his own Self, and his own Self in all beings, loses all fear."

At their best, these pages allow us to safely paratroop into the physical, emotional, and spiritual landscape of our fellow Americans. We may enjoy, admire, or recoil from what we learn from them. But my hope is that by traveling into the emotional reality of others who often are quite different from ourselves, we can expand our engagement with, and in fact love for, those around us. I can say that it has worked for me. The process of getting to know the people in *Us* has made me feel infinitely warmer toward humanity.

US

KAYLA JAMES, AGE 5

BELLINGHAM, WASHINGTON

"He had a lot of cool toys, and I really liked the toys."

Well, I was born, and Mommy took me over to his house to make some friends, and me and Lukey wanted to play with each other every day, and we gotted to do it. And that's how we got along.

I'm just in kindergarten. I knew him since preschool. Actually, I met him before preschool. I woke up and I got dressed for preschool and then I went to preschool and he's like, umm—he said this funny thing, I can't remember. He's like, "A-busha!" He was really funny.

He had a lot of cool toys, and I really liked the toys when I was little and he had all of the little working things. He really had great hair and he really had a fish on his clothes 'cause he liked to go fishing with his grandfather. And I had a princess on mine, because I liked princesses.

I felt happy that I made a friend, and me and him kept, like "UHH NNNN MMM NNN! I want that toy!" And we kept pulling the toy!

He was very nice to me and when I was born he let me drive in his little thing and that made me get along and like him. And he said nice things, like "I'm sorry, I didn't mean to hurt your feelings."

We played pirates, and we went on a treasure hunt. We went past some houses, we found this little statue of a lion, and we were pretending that the owner had a bunch of animals that were mean to people except the owners. We were both doing it. We went really far, we went to the street, we tried to walk to the mailbox to see if there was any gold inside.

He took the map. I was the captain. And he said the captain doesn't always hold the map. But the captain *always* holds the map!

He knew the way back to the house and he left me, and I'm like, "Luke, where did you go? I gotta find him!" And I was like, "Luke! Luke!" I kept on screaming "Luke!"

He used to have good table manners. He ate with his fork and spoon. Now he has bad table manners. 'Cause when I was four I came over for a playdate to have dinner and we had macaroni and cheese and I ate with my spoon and he ate with his hands. And his hands got all cheesy. And then like, "Okay, you're not having good table manners in front of girls." And— his dad—and he got in trouble. He had to go sit in the bathroom.

He's a little bit mean and a little bit nice. When I went to his playdate, he didn't let me drive his little red golf cart, and it really used to have a lot of *High School Musical* songs on it.

He lied to me. He said he could hold his breath for three days and three nights. And he really didn't do it. That's impossible.

And he said he could—he said he could go like this (*crosses eyes*) for two nights and two days. But if you do that for two nights and two days, your eyes will stay like that.

He lied about um . . . I was being mean every day, but I really wasn't. I mean bossy every day. But I wasn't. I used to, but now I'm not. And he said that on Monday. But I wasn't on Monday. When the school year started is when I stopped.

I felt sad that he lied to me—he was the first friend I knew.

I like talking! (*laughs*)

One time he tried to read a book, and he went like, "A-busha-shesha-yeah-a-sheeshay-sheeshay-shyah!" He was reading this book that Ms. Bennett read! (*laughs*) And I'm like, "What in the heck did you just say?" Ow! I just bit my tongue!! Um, yeah. You should have seen Lukey when he was reading! "A-busha-shesha-yeah-a-sheeshay-sheeshay-shyah!" (*laughs*)

I'm turning six on April 3! Can you believe that?

Love means that you're in love with somebody and you think he's cute or she's cute. That feeling of love is um . . . that you really love them. It's in your heart. God puts it there. God is actually inside of our heart so he put the love inside when he was inside. You can create it by . . . umm . . . thinking someone is cute.

No more questions!

One Month to **Five** Years

JACK BABINEAUX, AGE 27

HAMMOND, LOUISIANA

"A wedding is like love porno."

I've always been against marriage. I mean, not marriage—just weddings. A wedding is like love porno. With a regular porno you're watching other people havin' sex. And in a wedding people are watching you making a big production out of your being in love. I don't know. I like to live and breathe for each day. I don't need a big special event to make the fact that I love someone all official. No, bein' in love's somethin' that happens every day.

If I had to close my eyes and imagine what love looks like I guess it'd be like two people each reaching for the french fries at the bottom of the McDonald's bag. Because they have the exact same thought at the exact same time. Each one of 'em wants the last of those fries. But one of them is going to let the other one have it. That's love. Just that moment.

Or maybe it's like two people sleeping in a car on a long road trip. And one person wants to drive but the other one won't let him. It was actually on a road trip when I realized I was in love with my last girlfriend. I was twenty-three then. I'm twenty-seven now. We drove from Hammond, Louisiana, to Seagrove Beach in Florida, near Destin. We just went out there with no place to stay—just drove and drove. Went to Wal-Mart and stole a tent, put it on the rack under the cart, underneath all the food and shit, and just walked out with it.

When we got there, we were just like, "Fuck it, we'll sleep wherever." So we pulled up to a public beach and got underneath a blanket. We were all like smoking weed and drinking and fucking when this other couple came up to us. This girl had like nubby fingers, she didn't have complete hands. There was cob at the knuckle. She and her boyfriend were wasted. And they were like, "You can crash with us," whatever. It was this dude's uncle's apartment. We stayed in their bedroom and they stayed on the couch.

Yeah, it was nice. We were just fuckin', fuckin', fuckin'. And we were so drunk that, when I got up to take a pee, I couldn't find my way to the door. So I tried to pee in a beer can and it didn't really work. Anyway, a little later, while we were havin' sex, I pulled out and shot it right in her mouth. Bam. That's when I fell in love. That was the magical moment! (*laughs*) No, but not really, I just remembered that. It really did happen but that wasn't the love moment.

It's actually hard to say when that was. It was really that whole road trip. We were really together, you know? We were one with a common cause. We were out there for like ten days with nowhere to go, no money, nothing. And that was probably only like three weeks after we met each other.

Honestly, I think that when you fall in love you pretty much know right away. You just know. And then, as far as keepin' it going, it's just waking up each morning on the same page. There's not really much more to it than that.

I get kinda goofy when I meet someone I really like. There's a whole other side that I don't show to anybody else. I mean, I'm a mean dancer when I'm in love with somebody. You know, I sing little songs. And that's my true side really. I can't be that way with anybody else. So I guess that's also really what it's all about. Love brings out the true sides of people.

I've been in love twice. The first time was when I was sixteen, during high school in Algiers. She was five six, thin, about 110 pounds, brunette, brown eyes—kind of looked like a model. What's that chick, from the new *Star Wars*? Natalie Portman. Kind of looked like her. She was a very straitlaced person, very determined, she knew exactly what she wanted—the complete opposite of me. I'm a Sid and Nancy kind of guy. Sid Vicious. Kurt Cobain. I like intense feelings. But she was chill.

The other girl, the road trip one, was the complete opposite from the first one. She was crazy. We were best friends—almost like the same person. We moved in together probably a week after meeting each other. At first I actually didn't like her. She's very brash. I didn't like her for the same reasons people don't like me. But that first night—we obviously slept together the first night we met—we had sex for about three hours, all the way through both *White Albums*—the Beatles.

She was about five six, blonde hair. She kinda looked like Scarlett Johansson. Funny because she probably weighed more than me. I wasn't all that healthy at the time; I probably weighed 130 and she probably weighed 150. We thought we were going to get married. But we screwed up after a few more weeks. I mean, we both had some type of jealous streak. Jealousy is a terrible thing. She kissed some other people. She told me. I punched the wall and broke my hand. At least she was honest. And then I was working in New Orleans and she was going to school in Baton Rouge. The long distance just killed it—kills everything.

Some people get married when they're young and some people don't. I don't know. I would never ask anyone to marry me. Just do it. Not talk about it. Want to get married right now? I don't plan.

Yeah, just be thankful for what you got. Some people never fall in love. I have this theory that my third time's a charm. I had the one girl who was almost complete opposite of me and the one girl who was exactly like me. So I figure the third one will be—might—may or may not be the true one? I don't know. It's hard to say.

My parents have been married since they were eighteen and sixteen, and now they're in their . . . I don't know, in their fifties? For them it's like they've had to spend every day with the same fuckin' person for thirty years. I don't know how they keep it from being boring, besides using a strap-on. (laughs) My dad is a sailor. He loves his boat. And my mom, I don't know, she's an Oprah-phile. So they have their interests.

As for me, I think my next girlfriend's gotta be somebody who likes to walk. If you like to stand still, I'm not your guy—both in a literal and figurative sense. I mean, I could see myself having a country house, way out on the water somewhere. Having a boat and going somewhere from there. But I could never imagine living in a fucking suburb—you know, raising some spawn. I'm gonna be wherever you find me.

I've wanted every girlfriend I've had to be the last one. But I wasn't the greatest person. I fucked up. I fucked up and lost people and learned. So I'm gonna have to wait for the next girl for things to work out right. Another one. One more. I think I'm ready. I think I've learned a lot.

CELIA MENENDEZ, AGE 17

SAN ANTONIO, TEXAS

"I'm the kind of girl who pines."

This is the first time I've ever been in love and I'm still feeling miserable. Terribly awful and miserable.

His name is Rob. I have known him going on for three and half years now. The way I met him, it was the third day of freshman year and we have last names that are close alphabetically so we're always in the same sort of advisories, etcetera. And I had noticed him and thought, "Oh, that guy's kind of cute."

And then I'm sitting there talking with some people and suddenly, he's like, "Hey, Celia, right?"

I'm like, "Yes."

And he was like, "You have the tiniest ears I've ever seen on someone your age!"

And I was like, "What are you talking about?"

He's like, "Look how freaking tiny your ears are!"

So everybody, like, in that general vicinity—and it's the third day of freshman year, and I'm so nervous, I'm so shy, and I have all these people staring at me—they measure my ear to their ears and like, "Oh, my God, your ears are so small!" I had never noticed it. And so I was just really freaked out. That's how I first met him.

So I tell my friend, "I met this kind of cute guy. You should meet him," because I wanted to see what she thought.

So she met him, and then the next day she's like, "So how much do you like him? Because I think we might like each other." And he said the same thing to me—that he liked her.

So they did the little freshman date-for-a-week thing. Afterward we all find out she's a crazy bitch, and he's like, "I can't believe you set me up with her!"

And I was like, "Shut up! I told her I liked you, and she was a crappy friend and dated you. Don't blame me for you being a dumbass and her being a whore!" So, that was awkward.

So . . . I'm in the second half of my senior year now, but at the beginning of my junior year, he and I had calculus together with a couple of other people that we knew, and so we talk and I mean, hang out. And so one day he calls me and he was like, "Celia, do you think you can do me a favor?"

I was like, "Sure."

He's like, "Do you think you could gauge and see if Amalia might be into me?" Amalia is another friend of ours.

And I said, "Sure. I can find out."

Through that, we started to become a lot better friends. We had been friends but never very close. And right about that time, my parents got separated, and my mom and my brother and I ended up moving two miles from where he lives.

I don't know how it happened, but I just kind of started liking him. Just one day, I like realized, I was like, "Wow. Oh, crap, I like him. How do I handle this?" It was really awful. I didn't want it to happen.

Because I'm the kind of girl who pines. I'll like a guy for forever and ever and just wait and hope that he'll come out. Like my ex-boyfriend. I liked him for months after we broke up. Months.

I think part of the reason that I get so hung up is that I'm waiting for my liking them to overlap with them liking me. I've always been very unlucky on that count. I have complete weirdos liking me, like total creepers, or nice guys who I'm just not interested in. Or I like a guy, but he doesn't like me. And it just never overlaps well.

I like having a boyfriend and being in a relationship. Part of it is just like, as a hormonal teenage girl, that's kind of something that I want. I start to want it even more when there's, like, a specific person and it's, like, wow.

I did think Rob was attractive. I think he's one of the funniest people I've ever met, and we have a lot in common, and I think all of those things attracted me to him. But, like, if you asked me to pinpoint one single thing or, like, pinpoint when I started liking him or exactly why, I couldn't tell you.

I told a friend of mine who, of course, through the gossip chain, told his cousin, who was a year ahead of us. So one day Rob's giving me a ride home and his cousin is in the car in front of us, and she calls him, and he always has his phone on a really high volume. And she's like, "Hey, Rob."

And he was like, "Yes."

And she was like, "You know that girl in the car with you?"

And he was like, "Yes."

And she's like, "Well, she has a really big thing for you."

I was mortified. I thought I was going to die. I was so embarrassed and he dropped me off at home and I almost cried. It was really awful. So things were awkward with us for a couple of days. Obviously.

Then I started to get kind of suspicious. He was spending a lot of time with a friend of mine who had a boyfriend. A lot of time. And I said, "Look, Sadika, I think Rob has a thing for you." She says, "No, no, we're totally just friends."

And then of course like two days later he tells her, "I don't think we can be friends anymore, because I have feelings for you, and you're in a relationship."

But she says, "No, no, we have to be friends. I can't bear to not have you as a friend." So even though he likes her, and even though she has a boyfriend, and even though he hates her boyfriend and has always hated her boyfriend long before he had a thing for her, she decided they needed to stay friends.

And this put me in an awkward position because, for one, he likes my best friend, and for another thing, I like him. And suddenly, she tells me, "Noah and I are going to break up. I think I'm going to date Rob."

I was just devastated. I was horrified. I had liked him for . . . I don't know, a few months at this point. She had known it and she had encouraged it the whole time. And then she and her boyfriend started having problems, and suddenly Rob is the white knight who comes and makes everything better.

I was really angry with him, but I wasn't going to stop being friends because, as I established, I pine, and I was just hoping that maybe he would wake up one day and be like, "You know, the Sadika thing is okay, but things with Celia could really be better." I kept hoping that like one day, he would figure it out.

So one day she and Noah get in a big fight and then she tells me, "I don't know if I could be that passionately upset with somebody unless I love them."

I was like, "So what does that mean?"

And she was like, "It means I'm going to get back together with Noah."

I'm like, "What about Rob?"

And she's like, "Well," and she explained to me that she felt like Rob and her wouldn't work, that he was going to try to change her, that they just didn't fit—all these things.

This was a year ago.

Of course, she and Rob stopped speaking, and he's all like, "I've always loved you and you broke my heart and blah blah blah and . . ."

And then he calls me, and he's like, "You want to hang out this afternoon?"

I'm like, "Yeah, sure." But I'm like, "Oh, so he called me because he has nobody to spend time with today."

A lot of the time throughout our friendship and his whole thing with Sadika, I had this complex about being his backup plan. You know, like she had classes at community college, so he would call me to hang out and grab dinner. If she was busy at lunch, he would ask if I wanted to go to lunch. If she was busy on the phone, he would call me. I was always his Plan B.

But I was crazy about him, so I put up with it. And I would always make this resolution, you know, like, "No. No more. I'm not going to put up with this crap anymore. I'm not going to put up with this Plan B." But I always would.

So for a couple of weeks, he didn't have Sadika to attend to, so me and him hung out a lot more. And one weekend we were watching a movie at my house, and I'm kind of like leaning on him, I don't know. We were kind of like cuddled up on the couch.

And I don't know. We're talking, and then I look up, and then he kisses me. And now I'm just like going crazy, and I'm flipping the fuck out. Part of me is like, "Celia, this is bad. This is really, really bad." And part of me is like, "Shut up." And then part of me was like, "No, no, this is really bad."

So then, I don't know. I was just too nervous to address it. I didn't know what to do. I didn't want to ruin the whole thing. I thought it was a really fragile situation and I was worried that I would miss it, that I would miss that overlap.

But the next weekend, we hung out, and I was like, "So where is this going? I don't want to be your consolation prize, but I also don't want to lose this."

And he was like, "Well, we saw what happened just recently with me and Sadika being friends. I guess maybe we should be kind of careful about this." And I was like, "I guess you're right."

And so we just kind of went on nondates. I had to keep reassuring my parents they were not dates. We were like in the weird gray areas as to whether we were together or whether we were dating or whether this was just, like, fooling around.

We both really like the band CAKE. Like as a couple, we never had a song, but we had a band. And just all the time, we listened to CAKE. People would get annoyed with us when they'd get in his truck and he'd be playing CAKE, and I'd be like, "We can't change it. Like it's not allowed."

So CAKE had a concert at Southwestern University, and he and I and a couple of other people went, and it was fun. And afterward, a friend of his asked him, "So are you and Celia dating?" And he tells her, "Yes."

I didn't want to discuss it with anybody because, I mean, Megan, my best friend in the entire world, hates him with all her being. My mom—well, she never really expressed feelings about whether she liked him or disliked him; I'm pretty sure she did not like him, but I don't know. My dad really hated him. He would be like, "He's just a stupid boy, he isn't a stand-up guy." So it caused a lot of arguments with my dad.

But I just . . . I always wanted to be talking to him and I always wanted to be with him, more so than I ever have with anybody else. And I think that's how I knew that I was maybe starting to fall in love with him.

Sometimes I would be like, "Am I in love with him? No, I'm not in love with him. Well, maybe I am. How do I know if I'm in love with him?"

I would measure it against other people I knew who were in love. Like I'd look at Sadika and Noah and say, "They're in love."

But what does that mean for me? They get into fights all the time and break up and get back together like four times a week. So I knew that that wasn't something that I wanted to measure off of.

I used to think it was based on time. I thought that after a while, either I was in love with him or I wasn't, and that was it. But then it became an issue of "How do I know when that time is?"

So then I felt like, hey, I put up with all his bullshit. Always—no questions asked. It's unconditional. I overlook things that no other person would. He would be dramatic. He would be stupid. He would blow me off. I mean, there were a million things. I would never have stayed up on the phone until one in the morning, just talking about nothing, with anyone else—even my best, best friends. But him, even if I couldn't physically be with him, I could sit on the phone with him for hours. I think it's part of the reason I failed calculus.

But it was nice. It was like finally not only do you have somebody who wants to spend time with you, but they're actually physically attracted to you. And that makes you feel good. I would see him in the hallways and be like, "I get to make out with him this afternoon." Or I would see a girl that I didn't like and I'm like, "Ha-ha, she doesn't have a boyfriend." And it's partially smugness, and also I guess pride. Because for me, I didn't usually get to be that girl who had a boyfriend and was happy with him and had good chemistry and everything. I was usually the awkward girl who liked the guy and he didn't like her back.

I would talk to Sadika a lot about what was going on with Rob. I don't know why I did this. I guess because she's one of my closest friends, and my other best friend didn't want to hear about it. But I think it caused two things.

One, it made her think about what she was missing. I think it made her think that Rob is all that and a bag of chips, and that he was so much better than her current boyfriend. And later, when they finally decided they could be friends again, she kind of knew how I was feeling all the time. I would tell her, you know, like, "Rob was flirting with Megan today, and it really annoyed me," or, you know, "He still won't tell his parents we're dating."

Because he never told his parents we were dating. And after

the whole feeling like his Plan B thing, that just made it worse. There had been a point when he was spending time with Sadika that his parents had said, "Look, we want to meet her whether you admit you're dating her or not." He wasn't even technically dating her, and he was more open with his parents about her, than with me, a girl he's actually dating. It was really hard for me.

So. Times goes on. We go to prom and it's great.

Then it's the summer and I had a job teaching middle schoolers. Things are going okay. I don't see Rob a lot, because I'm working twelve-hour days. And then I find out that he's hanging out with Sadika.

He's like, "Yeah, Sadika and me and Jimmy"—that's somebody's cousin—"are going to grab lunch tomorrow." You know, or, "I was talking to Sadika yesterday, and she and I were thinking that we should all do this, this, and this."

And I was just like, "Okay." Of course I'm not going to tell him who he can and he can't be friends with. That's silly. But it's just weird, because they had gone from basically not speaking at the end of the school year to suddenly being friends. Like, how does that happen? And why didn't I hear this from him?

And then the final straw came when he picked me up from work and he was late, and we only had half an hour to hang out and go grab an ice cream before he had to be home for something. And I'm talking with Sadika later, and she's like, "Rob and I watched this and this and this."

And I was like, "When did y'all watch that?"

And she was like, "The other day."

And I'm like, "That wouldn't happen to be Monday, would it?"

And she's like, "Yes, we hung out Monday evening."

I mean, technically he didn't lie to me. He had to go "do something," but he didn't tell me he was hanging out with the girl he used to be in love with. You know, allegedly "used to be," because now I'm wondering, "Well, is he still in love with her?"

So I'm freaking out. I'm freaking out. But I don't want to say anything because I don't want to seem like that desperate, pathetic girlfriend. Plus I'm really bad about confrontations.

And then, on the Fourth of July, a bunch of us decide we're going to go drink. So we're at some park in the woods. It was dark. It's so like teen slasher–like, I half expected somebody in a hockey mask is going to kill us, it was so sketchy.

It's me, Rob, Sadika, and a couple of other friends of ours, and Rob's cousin, who's in from out of town. He's a complete idiot. I hate this guy so much.

Rob has stolen this liquor from his parents, this crazy crap— none of it is good. Some sort of like pineapple, rum, and coconut. It's awful and I have hardly any because I just can't down it.

Basically, the night goes on, and Rob's drunk. So we're sitting, waiting for him to sober up enough to drive by the time we all need to get home.

And he's like, "Celia, I have something to tell you."

And I'm like, "Okay."

He's like, "So I used to have these really small controlled moments where I had feelings for Sadika. But not anymore. They're done. And I just . . . I don't want you to worry about it. They're done."

Well, of course I worry about it. He was one of my best

friends before we dated! I knew everything about his feelings for Sadika, and everything they did, and how he told her, you know, "I'll love you forever," and everything. And I got really freaked. But I wasn't going to have an argument with him right then. He's drunk and there were other people. It was just not a good time.

I was pissed off because he lied to me. He had said he was going to be fine to drive and he wasn't, and I was stupid enough to go along with it. So I called him and left him this really long, angry message, because I'm passive-aggressive, and I don't like confrontations. And that's how I handle things.

We didn't talk about it. We pretended nothing had happened. We went out, we saw a movie. That was Saturday.

And then Monday came and some friends said, "Look, you should talk about it. Ask him what's going on. Talk about what this means, because obviously he was scared to talk to you about it."

So I call him that night and he doesn't answer. So I start to leave him this message and I just like break down in the middle of the message, and I'm sobbing and freaking out and yelling at the phone about how I feel like I was being made a fool of and how I spent all this time on this relationship, and how I was really, really crazy about him, and I told him, "You know, sometimes I think I might be in love with you, Rob. And then you go and pull shit like this." I remember that exact phrase.

That was the first time I had ever vaguely mentioned to him that I might be in love with him. So I'm screaming in the phone about how mad I am at him and I'm crying—and then the message like hangs up on me. So I leave another message, and I continue yelling at him.

And after, I'm like I don't know if that was a good idea. That was either a good way to get this across or a very, very bad way. I'm nervous as hell, and I'm sitting around my house, and my phone rings, and it's him.

He was like, "What the hell are you freaking out about?" And I explained, and he was like, "Well, the only reason that I said anything Friday night was because I had been hearing from Sadika that you were uncomfortable with us hanging out alone and not telling you."

And basically he talked me down, and suddenly I wasn't angry anymore.

So this was, I guess, Monday night. Then Thursday night, a friend who moved away a couple of years ago came into town, so we all went to hang out with her, and he was acting really strange. I felt like he was avoiding me, and I was like, "This is weird," but then I thought I was imagining it, so I let it go.

Friday, I went to dinner with a friend of mine, and I talked about my relationship briefly. And I kind of had this revelation, you know, I think I'm in love with Rob. I guess it's like what Sadika said: I couldn't be this angry and passionate about him if I didn't love him.

And as I was considering this on my way home, I was like, "I really want to call him. I really want to see him tonight and tell him I'm sorry and that I think I might be in love with him. I need to see him tonight."

And then he calls me! And he says, "Hey, can I see you tonight?" And I was like, "Oh, my God, that's so weird. I wanted to call you. I really wanted to talk to you about something." He's like, "I'll swing by."

So he swung by. This is like eleven thirty and I go outside to see him and he kind of gives me this awkward hug and doesn't kiss me, and it was like, "Oh, no."

Whenever we would talk outside my house, we would go sit in the back of his truck. So we go to the back of his truck and he kind of reaches out his hand to help me up, and I don't really accept his hand, because I'm already knowing something bad is going to happen.

There was like this really heavy, awful ten seconds, and he was like, "I don't think this is going to work." And I just looked at him, and I was like, "No." He was like, "Yes. I really don't think this is going to work."

And I was like, "Rob, that is such complete bullshit. Like, why, exactly, will this not work? Because I have just come to this revelation today, and you're telling me this won't work."

And he says, "Well, you know, we moved really fast from being like best friends to a relationship, and I think we just know too much about each other for us to be able to trust each other, and you're really attractive, and you're really funny, and you're really great, and I thought it could work as a relationship, but I just feel like it's hard for us to move from friends to relationship. And this has nothing to do with the whole Sadika thing at all," which of course makes me think it has to do with everything with the Sadika thing.

He left. I gave him all his stuff including this sweatshirt of his that I wore like every single moment. And actually, he wore that sweatshirt a couple of months ago to school, and it made me really miserable the whole day. It was the perfect sweatshirt. It was the perfect size. It was hard for me to see him wearing that sweatshirt because it no longer has an association with me. Now it's just a sweatshirt.

And he left with all his stuff and that was it. I was really upset, obviously. Kind of devastated.

I didn't talk to him at all. I think I sent him an e-mail once asking for my stuff.

We have pretty much all the same friends at this point in time. So I hear things that happen with him, but I don't actually see him.

And then I finished reading this book he had recommended. It's part of the Dark Tower series by Stephen King, and because we have such similar taste in pretty much everything, he got me hooked on these and I love them, and so I wanted to talk to somebody about them.

I think this was partially me reaching out to him. I sent him an e-mail, and I was like, "I love this book. It was great. You're right. Here's what I loved about it. Here's what really bothered me about it." And then at the end, I was like, "I don't think you should reply to this e-mail. I don't think that's healthy, and I think that me sending you this e-mail in the first place was a really bad idea, but I need to talk to somebody."

And then, of course, he sends an e-mail back after I explicitly say don't.

And I got angry. First he scoops out my heart out like a cantaloupe, and then he goes and sends me back an e-mail after I asked him, "Please don't."

So I sent him an angry, angry e-mail, really angry. And he didn't answer. Obviously.

So fast-forward three weeks, it's the end of my summer job. We had a big party, and I don't usually drink but I did drink a little bit. And one thing I found, including and since then, is that when I drink, I like to talk on the phone.

All my friends were like, "Celia, you can't call him. Please don't call him. Do we need to take your phone away?"

And I was like, "No, no. I'm a big girl. I don't need you to take my phone away."

And then everybody leaves, and the drunken, stupid part of my brain is like, "This is our chance." I'm searching through my phone contacts, and part of me is like, "This is bad." But most of me is like, "Shut up." So I start calling him, and the phone rings and then I'm just like, "Oh, my God, I'm calling Rob. This is so stupid!" And I hang up.

And then it rings, and it's Rob. And this was like three in the morning. And I'm like, "Hey, Rob. I'm really sorry. I'm drunk. I'm really, really, really sorry."

And he was like, "What? Hello?"

Like he's just woken up. So I say it a little slower, "Rob, it's Celia. I'm sorry. I'm drunk. I shouldn't have called you. I'm sorry."

And he was like, "Okay, do you want to call me tomorrow and we can talk?"

And I was like, "Well, yes, I . . . no, no I can't call you, Rob." And then before I could finish, I just hung up because finally the rational part of my brain had taken over.

And that was probably one of the single most mortifying moments of my life. If I could take back one thing that happened with him, that would probably be it. It didn't do anything, except to show that I was still definitely not over it. I was definitely not handling it maturely.

So. I didn't talk to him for months. I wasn't okay. I wasn't okay at all. He was all ready to be friends, and I wasn't ready to be friends at all.

We didn't have any classes together, so I didn't have to see him that often, and eventually, I was like okay, we're good. It was hard not to be friends with him. But I kind of forced myself into being friends with him again.

He and Sadika had been hanging out a lot. She and Noah had broken up again. I was really suspicious, but I wasn't going to jump to any conclusions, because I knew that she's my friend, and he and I are starting to get back to normal, and if something was going on with them, they would definitely tell me. They would have to tell me because, you know, everybody is as honorable and truthful as I think they should be.

So time goes on. He and I are like fluctuating in our awkwardness. Sometimes I call him up or shoot him an e-mail, and sometimes we'll talk at school and I'll just feel like wow, that was the most awkward exchange ever. Like wow, this really, really sucks! I'm still in love with this guy, and he's walking around every day, half the time acting like I don't exist.

And of course, I'm pining. And the pining is always worse after a relationship. Because before, you imagine how good it's going to be with this person. But afterward, you know exactly how good it was, like exactly all the good times you had.

Eventually, mutual friends let something slip that they shouldn't have or I hear a snippet of conversation between him and Sadika. I'll see him get really jealous when she's hanging out with some other guy and I'll see her getting all uppity when he hangs out with a bunch of underclassmen girls. So there's a very long period, like from October to New Year's, where Sadika and I didn't talk and Rob and I talked like three times because I'm finally catching on to their BS.

Then New Year, there's a party, and we all get drunk and

Rob and Sadika are there, and I'm drunk and I'm like, "Sadika?"

And she's like, "What?"

And I was like, "I love you. I miss you."

And she was like, "Oh, my God. I love you and miss you too." And in our drunkenness, we make up. We decided that we were going to be friends again and all is going to be great.

And so I said, "Look, I was just upset because I thought something was going on with you and Rob. There's nothing going on with you and Rob though, right?"

And she says, "No, there's not."

And I figured, "Oh, God, she's that drunk, she wouldn't even remember to lie to me. Okay, we're good."

And then I see Rob later at the party and I'm like, "Rob?"

And he's like, "Yes, Celia?"

And he's really drunk and I said, "Can we just be okay again? Can we just be friends? Because I really need us to be friends, Rob. Like I really want us to be . . ." I don't know how many times I said the word "friend."

And he said, "Yeah, no, let's be friends!"

And a friend of mine finally told me, "Look, Celia, I really hate lying to you. They're dating and they're also having sex, and they're planning on telling you a few weeks before prom so it's not a surprise to you when they show up at prom together."

That was really hard to hear because (a) she had lied to me, just point-blank lied to me, and (b) I don't know, I mean . . . I don't know why their having sex would bother me. Maybe because just they like reached a level of intimacy that Rob and I never actually got to.

But if I go to prom, it's going to be really awful seeing them.

And it's such a high school cliché that I'm mad at myself for being so upset.

We haven't spoken ever since. We're done.

When you go into a relationship, you kind of have to expect that your heart might get broken. But I shouldn't have had to deal with having one of my best friends basically be a complete liar and date my ex-boyfriend behind my back.

So we haven't really spoken. He's been walking around looking like a complete ass in this hat he's been wearing for the last couple of months. He's been growing his hair out and wearing long sleeves and he looks like a heroin junkie. He just looks so bad and so tired, and she just looks so bad and so tired, and they've both been skipping school a lot because they're second-semester seniors, and they think they can get away with anything.

But I feel like he's not happy because he's realizing his grades aren't good enough for getting into a college that he's smart enough to be at. It's just bringing him down.

And the thing is, I feel bad for him. I want to be there and be like, "Babe, it's okay. You'll be fine. You'll figure out something." But I can't even talk to him.

I see them. I passed them together in the halls like four times the other day. It's really hard.

So suddenly it's losing that friend who I could go to for anything, who would, if I got in a fight with my mom, gladly drop what he was doing and come pick me up. I lost a friend who on his way home from study sessions would, you know, bring me and my mom baklava so that she would let me sit outside with him for an hour and talk. It's losing that friend I could tell anything to.

He was one of the first people I told that my parents are getting separated, and he helped me move some of my stuff into my house.

It sounds silly, but now I don't have the time to tell anybody why it's so hard for me when my parents get in a really huge stupid fight. It's like when my computer crashed and I had everything on it. I don't have the time and energy to go back and try to rebuild it. If I tried to tell, say, Megan, who's my best friend, who really hates Rob, if I tried to explain all the background information to her, I would feel like I was burdening her. With Rob, since I always put up with everything from him and listened to him bitch and moan, I told him everything. I felt like it came with the job.

I think the hardest part is knowing that theoretically we were perfect. We have the same sense of humor. We have the same likes and dislikes. We have the same pet peeves. We have the same interests.

Theoretically, everything was perfect. And then it wasn't. And that's really hard, because I had never had somebody that I thought I'd fit that well with.

I guess the best way to describe us is like Crystal Pepsi. Like, we were this really, really great idea. And then it didn't really work out.

I think about that "better to have loved and lost than never to have loved at all," and I don't know how I feel about that. I don't know. Maybe I'm still so miserable I can't appreciate it fully. But maybe it's just not true.

DEANNA RUEDA, AGE 38

AUSTIN, TEXAS

"Oh, my gosh! Oh, my God! He just drives me nuts!
He does! He drives me nuts!"

He's homeless. We're both homeless. I met him at the ARCH. Austin Research Center for the Homeless. It's downtown in Austin.

I loved him from the first day I saw him. He was cute. He's sexy. I don't know, I invited him for lunch. To Friday's.

He wasn't, like, ready to jump on my bones. He's quiet. He listened to me. He's a real good listener. He listens. He's . . . he's . . . he hurts, you know.

We get on the bus. We go everywhere. Wherever God lets us lay our heads down. He comes to church with me or I go with him. We're always together. It's romantic.

We have fun, we have fun, we have fun. Oh, I just love him so much. I do.

He has been through a lot with me, and me with him. And just being there for me. I went to drug rehab. I did seventeen days. It was Christian based—I focused on God and everything. And prayed for him. I couldn't stop thinking about him all along. I didn't eat. I came back, I mean he was right here. Right there. It's like, destined.

I've been with him four months, going on five. A little before Christmas.

Oh, my gosh. And it's awesome, because he's, like, everything that I wanted in a person—but yet, not quite: I'm a Christian, and he doesn't know the Lord is good. So. But he's getting there. He goes with me to church. He's real. He's real with me.

Me and him, every time we leave each other, I'm not with nobody else, and he's not either. And he doesn't desire nobody else and I don't desire nobody else either. I do good things for him, you know. I think that it goes both ways, you know what I'm saying?

For Valentine's Day, I took him to the Roadhouse. I got his hair cut. And I took him to go get margaritas. And ate some fajitas. Took him to the hotel. And that was the first time. I paid $250 for a room. I wanted him to feel special. I wanted him to remember. And regardless if we were never together, I wanted him to remember that he had a good time.

So what he do, he goes and panhandles. He asks this . . . He tells them. I don't know what he tells them, but I stay here and wait for him. He just says, "Wait here." He doesn't want me in and out of cars. He says, you know, just wait for me. So you don't have to do . . . he does it for you. So that we can go . . . do whatever we need to do.

Juan is hardheaded. I like that, because it gives you more destiny. It gives you more drive to move forward. It's sexy. It's exciting! It is! It's exciting because he's . . . you know, full of adrenaline. But it's hard, because he makes me cry. Because he doesn't want me sometimes. He's like, "I want to go do this! I want to go do that!"

I'm just, you know. I don't know. I just . . . I don't know. I just . . . I don't know.

Oh, my God! He just . . . he drives me nuts. He drives me nuts. *Oh, my gosh!* Oh, my God! Yes! He's just . . . oh, I don't know what to say!

He's a butt! He's a butt!

He's like . . . men, they're just . . . oh! They just, they just don't listen! They just, you know, they listen to you, but then you just, you know, they're just . . . they're just over, you know? They just have a mind of their own! It's frustrating. It is! It is! It is!

He just drives me nuts! He does! He drives me nuts! I have tried to get him to leave. I tell him, "Let's go. Let's get somewhere else. Somewhere just to have, you know, inner peace . . . within ourselves."

I don't like being out here, trying to find where to sleep and stuff. I desire a home. I desire my career. I desire my life. I desire my kids coming back to me. I desire him being with me. You know, not him thinking I'm over here doing this and doing that. That's not who I am. I'm not like that.

I'm like, "Don't do that to me anymore. It hurts, you know." I don't like being out here! I don't know nobody here. I get scared! And he knows that. And he's like, "Okay." You know, he's sticking with me.

I have to tell him, "Look, do you understand where I come from?" I am not these persons that you think that you want to be with. I'm a home mother. I got kids. I was married for fourteen years to a shrimper in Galveston. He wanted somebody else. Yes. So I got a divorce. I have six girls. Twenty-one, seventeen, fifteen, fourteen, and twelve. I got twins. I placed them up for adoption, my kids. I wouldn't want them out here and I don't want them to see me out here neither. My twins are in England. Yes, I wanted the best for them.

I'm thirty-eight. And I miss being a home wife, cooking, cleaning, and doing whatever. I'm a very good woman. I don't cheat on anybody. I'm old-fashioned and I just stay. I mean, you don't find any women like that are truly in love with some person and one person only.

I just never had much trouble as I do with him. I told him, "I cannot believe that I'm actually out here with you. My family doesn't like this." You know. And he's like, "Are you crazy? Why *are* you out here?" (*cries*)

Because I love him. Because I love him! And you gonna do anything for love. And loving him, I mean for me, I gave up a lot. I gave up my apartment. I gave up my life, I gave up my GED. I gave up a good life where I could get off the streets. I just put it on the back burner for him. He doesn't want to get off the streets. He just likes to be free.

I love him so much. You know? I want him to have the best. I don't want him to be out here doing this. I want him to see what it is to work, to do good, and live a productive life. (*cries*) Not to be out here, you know? Being here, there's just so much struggles.

A couple of days ago my little niece got murdered. She was in a drug addiction. They buried her yesterday.

I'm scared now because my little niece is twenty-three years old. She didn't ask anybody to take her life. You know what I'm saying? Do whatever you got to do to people, but don't take their lives. Life is precious.

A lot of people don't understand about relationships with people. I think that if you have a destiny with somebody, that destiny continues and continues and you build a relationship. That should go right. But sometimes it doesn't. And it's really hard these days to actually find somebody that would really care for you—and mean it. Some are out there just to use you and just do whatever they want.

I always tell him, "I love you, I love you, I love you." I say, "I really do love you." Because I know when I love somebody. It's when I get butterflies in my stomach. And you're constantly thinking about them and passionate and, I don't know, just connected, and you don't eat and you just . . . you just feel like a schoolgirl!

You know, what I want, it's like everybody else: the house, the white picket fence, kids, two kids, and a dog and a cat. I mean that's ordinary for Americans these days. It would be just like being in a home where you just live life. Just everyday life. And not worryin' about where you're going to sleep, what you're going to eat, how you're going to take a bath, where are you going to go, and are you going to get hurt or not.

And in my dream, it'd be being compatible in a relationship where you're just in a right state of mind. With God. And not worrying about anything. It'd be for him to just hold me. And hug me. And to just stand still. And just . . . just be at ease. Push everything to the side. Push everything to the side. And just . . . be at peace.

SHAMARA BLAINE, AGE 22

DAYTON, OHIO

"If you knew you met the right one, why would you wait?"

Brandon and I met on www.myyearbook.com back in March of 2007. The message I sent him was, "You're cute and you look pretty nice, would you like to chat?" At first it was just how he looked, and in all his pictures, his smile and just how he presented himself. Once we started talking, I was more attracted to his personality, his sense of humor, and how he talked to me and treated me.

His profile said he was dating someone. He said he really couldn't handle her anymore because she cannot deal with him being in the navy. Even though I really had no clue about someone being in the navy, with this war in Iraq, I have had friends over there, and some have died also, so I had known a little bit about military guys and life. I had just told him that I was here for him if he needed to talk about anything.

He was grateful because he never had someone say they were just there for him. Brandon's mother and him does not speak because of his childhood past, how she pawned him off to his stepfather. Then when his stepfather was beating him, Brandon tried to call his mother to help. She never did. I do not think I should go into detail about that because it's more his story than mine.

We started talking on March 2nd, and by the 10th he was single. My mother knew I really liked him, so she was on my father's MySpace and sent him a message with my number. He asked me to be his girlfriend and I immediately asked why. I usually never date online. He told me a list of reasons. Most of the reasons were because I always made him laugh, I always listened to him. Plus I was the only one in his life at the time that wanted to be there for him. And I said yes.

He just seemed like a completely different guy than I have ever dated before. I felt like I had spent years just waiting around for the right one. When Brandon came along I knew it was him. I even got to the point where every night I cried because we was not together. There was just something there. My mother called it the fireworks; I called it love from the start even though I do not believe in love at first sight.

After we'd been talking for more than a year, I went to Jacksonville, Florida, with my parents on April 30, 2008, to meet him. I had never been out of Ohio except for West Virginia. The first thing Brandon did when he laid eyes on me was jumped out of the car and run right up to me and kissed me and hugged me. I actually have pictures of this because my mother and father love taking pictures. It felt like we have known each other our entire lives, and we both are from Ohio—our towns are just thirty minutes away from each other. On May 3, 2008, he had my parents take us to Jacksonville Beach. We walked down the beach and he asked if I wanted to sit down, so we did.

We went to a little corner store in St. Augustine earlier that day that had just odds and ends and trinkets and just weird stuff in there, and I picked this old wooden box. It has a sailboat in it, and it looked really old. We took it to the beach with us and while we were sitting, we found small seashells to put inside of it, like little seashells that were smaller than my fingertips, and we just sat and talked and watched the waves.

And then he stood up and took my hands and lifted me up to walk closer to the waves. You know how when you're teaching little babies to walk and how you pick 'em up and they feel like they're about to fall back down—that's how I felt. I knew what was about to happen. My parents knew, he had their permission already. But I was shaking so much, I had to hide that by saying I was cold. He wrapped his arms around me and held me for about ten minutes. And then he got on his knee and asked "Will you . . . ?"

Before he could get the rest out I had dropped to my knees crying and said, "Of course!" It's still a big joke between him and I. He says, "You're not going to cry if I ask you, 'Will you . . . get some coffee?' " I always laugh.

That little box was filled with the sand from where his knee was when he asked me to marry him. I love that box. It sits on my headboard and when I move to Florida soon it will be going with me.

He wanted to be married before his deployment. So he came up to Ohio on June 30 and we got married on July 5.

When we met, I was twenty years old and he was nineteen. We have had a lot of people say we are crazy because we got married so fast. But honestly, if you knew you met the right one, why would you wait? We get along great, and we know everything there is to know about each other, and the days we spend together are the best days ever.

I have been through lots of boyfriends that treated me like I was nothing. See, I have a muscle disease. I've been in and out of a walker and wheelchair since 2004, my senior year of high school. In 2005 I was diagnosed with fibromyalgia. Sometimes I can't walk. It depends on my stress levels because a lot of stress will put me into a flare-up. I can work out a little bit but I have to watch how far I push myself. 'Cause then I'll be in my wheelchair.

I was the good kid in high school. And then after high school—I don't want to blame my muscle disease for me going into drugs but I don't want to blame something else, because I really don't know what's to blame for me doing all that, smoking weed, drinking alcohol.

I dated a lot of guys and they were just all different. Most of them had tattoos. I love tattoos. I met this guy named Raymond and he had tattoos all over his forehead, all over his body, basically. I remember his pickup line, it was so stupid. He said his name was Raymond, and he asked my name and I said Shay, because that's my nickname. He said, "Oh, Ray and Shay, we go together." He made crystal meth and he was into cocaine.

One day he had a bag of cocaine and took his finger and put it in the bag and put it in my mouth and he had a knife and he basically put it up to me and told me that I don't need to tell anyone about this and I should try it. So I tried it and then I just didn't stop for like six months.

I don't know if I liked it, but it got me away from everything. It made me feel more alive than I normally did, because with my muscle disease I hardly have energy at all. But when I

was doing these drugs I was nonstop on the go, never slept. I
used to weigh 300 pounds and I was down to 150 by the time
I overdosed the first time.

I got pregnant by him and he beat me to where I lost the
kid. It was horrible. I can't believe I put myself into those situations. I guess I got mixed up with the wrong people. It helped
me figure out what I wanted in life and what I don't want in life
and especially in guys.

I haven't been back to drugs yet. I'm basically drug free for
once in my life. It's so different now. I don't party. I don't even
have a way to find drugs, which is really good, but I don't have
any need for them or any want for them.

When I met Brandon I had literally given up on love and
trying to find that soul mate. Our childhoods were similar.
When we started talking, there was no pauses; we talked about
everything, from music to just our favorite things to do. With
Brandon I'm more me than I ever was.

I am random at times. To cheer my husband up all I have to
do is say "rubber ducky" or "peekaboo," and he is laughing. He
loves how I can be serious and take care of business when
needed, but most of the time I'd rather laugh and be a kid.
Brandon's motto is, "You can only be a kid once, but you can
always be a kid at heart."

Brandon is like that. He is the only man in my life that has
actually taken time to get me. He pays attention to everything I
have to say. He accepts me as I am and no one in this world has
ever done that before. Not even my own family. He told me I
am the only one that notices that his eyes change several colors.
I have never tried to change him in any way. He truly is the love
of my life.

My parents are happy for me and Brandon. When they took me down to Florida to meet him, I was really worried about them not liking him. Because my parents have never liked anyone I have ever dated. Well, after hours of meeting Brandon they loved him. We went out to dinner and spent days together. At the end of the week we was playing cards and my mother was already calling him "son."

In December or January, he'll be deployed. His deployments are supposed to be six months, but they may be longer. They say he will not be going on a full-blown war zone. Honestly I do not know how any woman can put up with the person they love being away from them for a while. Two days before the wedding we sat down and I literally asked him if he thought I could do this, and not just me but him also. I literally had him crying, and I cried also. It was supposed to be one of the best weeks of our lives, but we talked about it all, about the deployments and everything.

We have plans on how we are going to be able to put up with it all, how we keep communication alive, and how now, with how computers are, we can talk to each other online.

We want to at least try to start our family. I am not on birth control anymore, and well, him and I are both changing our diets and stopped smoking so we can try to have a baby sometime.

August 2008: I'm in Florida now. I'm sitting on base now waiting for 0900 hours so I can go get my military ID. Then it's official! I'm a navy wife. My parents are here and, well, they are stressing us both out. It's horrible having them here because there's almost ten people in a two-bedroom apartment. I cannot wait to just have my home and hubby to myself!

We talked. I'm not going to stay here in Florida alone. I'll be back in Ohio while he's deployed. My parents don't want me to be down here alone and not have anybody to help me when I'm sick.

Me and him actually went to St. Augustine together alone. And that was a fun trip. We went to Ripley's Believe It or Not! museum. They have these hand wax sculptures. You take your hands, dip 'em in ice, and then dip 'em in wax ten times and do it like twice. Well, me and him got our hands done together and did in sign language "I love you" with both of our hands, and we got that and it's sitting on top of my entertainment center right now.

I have a tattoo that I want to get fixed. I told him I wanted to get an anchor with our wedding date on it because we had a beach theme reception and he's also in the navy. And then last night I was watching *Miami Ink* and he's like, "Well, can I get an anchor also with our wedding date?" And I'm like, "If you want to." And he's like, "I love it." And he's like, "That's just the symbol for us." And I'm like, "Awww."

Yesterday was our one-month anniversary and it was amazing even though we was moving still. But a country CD and candles and him whispering "I love you" made it great. But also something else. I haven't told him yet and it's way too soon to know, but mornings I'm nauseated and I'm tired a lot and just some other little things. A friend is telling me to go get a pregnancy test! I'll let you know. Have a great day!

I'll TTYL.

I probably started planning how I was going to propose to Anne maybe a month and a half before.

I'd always had elaborate ideas—like take her on a plane to some city that she loved—but I also knew that I had zero money. I stressed over it a bit, but I figured the best time would be when we went back to Michigan for the Christmas holiday. We'd have a chance to celebrate with all of our families and whatnot. And it just kind of worked out with my work schedule and her work schedule.

I flew back five days before she did to get a few things into place.

She was flying in on a Saturday night. So I called her parents and asked if I could pick her up from the airport. They're like, "Oh, yeah, you could ride with us to the airport." I was like, "Actually, I was thinking about just wanting to pick her up myself. I would save you a trip." Her mother says, "We'd love the drive with you. It will be awesome." I was like, "I don't think you're getting it!"

So I had to drive an hour out of the way just to go to her parents' place to drive another two and a half hours to the airport, which was ridiculous. But on the way down, I stopped off at the old farmhouse that she grew up in, in Romeo.

I stopped at these people's house and knocked on the door. I was like, "I know you don't know me. But I was wondering if it would be all right if I took my girlfriend here just to show her the farmhouse." She hadn't seen it since she was twelve years old. And it would just be a special place where we could take some pictures.

Well, the lady just freaked out. She was like, "No. I don't know you." She wouldn't even open the door for me. I was talking through the screen. I said, "This is going to be part of the engagement. Her family owned this farm before you." She thought we wanted to go in the house and look through, and I was like, no just around the barns, that kind of stuff. She finally agreed. So, anyway, I got to her parents' place, and I had flowers and a card. I get in the backseat; her mom is talking nonstop. I'm feeling like an idiot, like I'm in junior high!

Anne had no clue that I was going to be at the airport. She came down on the escalator and I'm standing next to this huge crowd of people and she kind of walks right in front of me and I step out and gave her flowers and she just freaked out, tears in her eyes. Then we get back in the car and drive back to her parents' place.

Early the next morning I told her that we needed to get going because we were going to have lunch with my parents. On the way out I asked her if we could stop off at the farmhouse she grew up in. She's like, "Oh, my gosh, I'd love to go there."

So we pulled up and get out, and she insists we go up to the door. I'm like, "Crap!" If we go up to the door the owner is going to be like, "Congratulations!" I was just like, "God, please don't allow anybody to answer the door." And luckily nobody did.

The minute we started walking around she started sharing stories of her childhood, memories of her grandparents, memories of being on the farm and her playing. It was really sweet just to hear her heart. We were in one of the barns where she spent a lot of time, and I pulled out this scroll wrapped with a red ribbon. The paper is homemade, which I made specifically, and then I burned the edges around to make them look tattered. It said "I love you" at the top.

We had never said "I love you" to each other. I had told her that when I said it, I would really mean it. I said, "I brought you here for a specific reason. That reason is to tell you how much I love you."

So I read this to her:

> *Annabelle, I've waited nearly a year and a half to fully expose my heart to you by saying these three simple words. Although these words were often on the tip of my tongue, ready to burst from my heart to yours, I chose to save them for the right moment and place that you would have no doubt in your mind that I truly mean it when I say "I love you." Why here? Why now?*
>
> *When I picture you as a little girl playing house in the milk house of your grandparents' farm, I imagine this*

being the first place where you began to dream of the boy that would someday tell you that he loved you. I may not look, act, or be anything like that boy in your dreams so many years ago, but I am the man standing before you now who has fallen in love with the woman that you have become.

Then it just has a quote at the bottom that says:

Falling in love consists merely of uncorking the imagination and bottling the common sense.

We started dating two and a half years ago. When we first met, she just wasn't in a place that I was ready to be in a relationship with her, just where she was with the Lord. I don't think I was either, to be honest. But as she began a relationship with the Lord, I watched her relax and watched her become the person who she is today and who I fell in love with.

She is one of the most genuine people that I know. She has one of the most incredible, serving hearts. I just knew, watching, that she was the one. I was definitely attracted to her and I think that's something that the Lord develops. I was captivated by her. And she loved me like no one else has ever loved me before. She truly was generally interested in me, wouldn't allow me to just get off with not saying much. She really wanted to hear who I was, what makes me who I am.

I had wanted to tell her for so long. I'd explained that when girls are more pursuant than I am it's almost like a turnoff, especially when they jump to a stage that I'm not ready for; it kind of freaks me out.

She was just like, "I love you so much." She said, "I've been waiting for a year to say this to you. But I wanted to give you the freedom to say it first, and allow you to pursue me." She really honored me by allowing me to take it in that step. It was really sweet.

But then I was like, "You know, we've really got to get going." We jumped back in the car. We started driving, and she fell asleep. I texted my brother and said, "Okay, I need you to call in half an hour and just tell me I need to pick up something."

She was awake when my brother called. He said, "Hey, I need you to stop by our old pastor's house and pick up a Pampered Chef order."

I'm like, "Pampered Chef order?"

He's like, "Yeah, Mom ordered this Pampered Chef for Christmas."

Anne had no clue. We drop by the church where my pastor lives, and I say, "I could run in and grab this real quick or, if you wanted, we could even go inside the church. It's Sunday, maybe it's open and you could see where I grew up."

It's a very small, ancient church like from the fifties, forties, you know, wooden pews and all that. We walk in, and I'm sharing memories of growing up. We sat down on the steps where the pulpit was, and I pulled out a second scroll.

On the top it says "Will." And it has a watermark of a church and on the back it shares a verse:

Now we show the disciples the full extent of his love.
"You don't know now what I am doing, but it will
become clear enough later. I've given you an example to
follow. Do as I have done to you."

It's John 13.

And the quote at the bottom is, "Lord grant me that I might not so much seem to be loved as love someone else."

So I gave this to her and she was like, "What is this about?"

I said I want us to talk about what the Lord's will is for our relationship. Is this something that we're supposed to be pursuing or not? I told her that I wanted to pray together. I told her that my will and hope for our relationship was that it be centered not only on loving each other but also on serving one another and out of that love that we would serve others. I reached around underneath the pulpit and pulled out a basin of water and a towel and asked her if I could wash her feet.

It's just the symbol, an example of the love the Lord gave to show the full extent of His love. This was completely new. She had never had anybody wash her feet. I shared my heart about why I wanted to do it: so that our relationship would be sealed, so we could serve one another, and so that we could go out and do that to others.

So I got down and washed her feet, and shared different things about our relationship that I loved. She's crying once again, just really overwhelmed. I'm drying off her feet. We're sitting there and she's crying. I said, "Would you like to wash mine?"

She's like, "Oh, yeah, I'm so sorry." Later she's like, "I couldn't believe I didn't offer that." So anyway, we washed each other's feet and we prayed.

Then I was like, "We really need to get going. I've wasted enough time on this."

We got back in the car and she says, "Can I ask you a question?"

I'm like, oh crap, she's going to totally ask, "What about the Pampered Chef order?" I said, "It would honor me if you didn't."

She's like, okay. She didn't ask how did the basin of water get there, or how was it still warm. I asked her later if she knew by that point, and she said maybe, but that she didn't want to get her hopes up. We were driving these back roads and after a while, I pulled off on this dirt road and said, "Do you trust me?"

And she said, "Of course I trust you."

And I was like, "Well, I need you to bundle up in everything you have in your bag."

Well, it's a full-on blizzard outside. Wind blowing sideways, snow coming down. It was cold. I had made sure she brought her snowboarding outfit, so we bundle up and drive a little bit further to McBain, to the farm I grew up on.

In the car, I gave her this next scroll. On the top it says "Who you are to me from A to Z," and it has a watermark of a horse and just different words to describe her, each one beginning with a different letter:

> *Adventure, beauty, compassionate, devoted, elegant, faithful, genuine, hospitable, inspiring, job filled, kind, and loving, motherly, nurturing, optimistic, pure, quiet spirit, radiant, supportive, trustworthy, unfading beauty, voluptuous, warm, extreme, youthful, and zealous.*

And then on the bottom it says:

> *Your godly life will speak to them far better than any words. They will be won over by watching your pure*

godly behavior. Don't be concerned about outer beauty that depends on fancy hairstyles, expensive jewelry, or beautiful clothes. You should be known for the beauty that comes from within; the unfading beauty of a gentle quiet spirit which is so precious to God.

That's 1 Peter 3:1–4.

It was a verse I felt like the Lord wanted me to share with her, about not only what the Lord thinks of her, but what I think of her. We get out and we're walking toward the horses. She loves horses. There's this trailer alongside of the road that had a couple horses in it and she's like, "Oh, my gosh, they have these horses in the trailer and there's a blizzard out. What are they thinking?"

And I was like, "I don't know, let's go over there and look." And I opened up the back of the trailer and there's two saddled horses. And I said these are for us. It was hysterical, because we had all these clothes on and how are we going to get onto these horses! But we jumped on.

So, anyway, we ride out into the pastures. I built a tree stand in one of the trees when I was twelve, and it was still there, which was sweet. Anne and I were sitting here on horseback in the middle of the pasture, looking up at my old tree stand. I said, "This is a place I spent hours, by myself in the wilderness in complete silence, just dreaming about that girl I would some-day marry."

And I pull out another scroll. It says "Marry" on the top of it with a watermark of a tree. I handed this one to her, and she was just shaking at this point. Like, I can't do it! Like, giving it back. It said:

*I can remember the first time that I was asked that ever
lucid question, I was in the woods that day shooting stuff
with my BB gun with some buddies of mine when one of
them looked over with a huge grin on his face and asked
us to describe the perfect girl, or the one we would like to
marry someday. Strangely enough the answer has with-
stood this test of time, for it was the same today as it was
years ago when I was a young boy.*

*I simply said, I will know her when I see her across
the room and see how she genuinely loves those around
her. Though I was laughed at and made fun of years ago
with this response I knew it would be true today as I
watched you across the room. Annabelle, you are the one
who has captured my heart.*

Then a verse again:

*Love the Lord your God with all your heart, all your
soul, all your mind, and all your strength. And the second
is equally as important: Love your neighbor as yourself.*

That's Mark 12:30–31.

Once we entered the woods, it was unreal. It was just like
the Lord quieted the wind. There was no wind, the snow was
just kind of trickling down, there was deer running in front of
us. She turned to me and said, "Is this a fairy tale?"

It was just gorgeous, the most beautiful thing we ever went
through. I asked her to get off her horse, and tied up the horses
to a tree. Underneath that tree was this garbage bag that was
covered with sticks and all the snow. They'd been out there for

four days, and I didn't know what the weather was going to be like, but I knew Anne well enough to know that if we were outside for that long, she would start to get cold. I opened this bag, and there was a sleeping bag that I wrapped her up in. There was a propane heater that I cranked on and sat her next to. She was like, "You know me so well."

I had a bottle of wine in there, and around the bottle was this last scroll. It said, "Will you marry me?"

I got down on my knees. She was just bawling at this point, hysterical. It was really sweet. I then read this to her:

> As God's children, we are promised that if we delight ourselves in Him that He will give us the desires of our heart. Since a young boy growing up on my father's farm, my greatest desire has always been to find the one God set aside for me to love for the rest of my life. Each Thanksgiving Day, I would reiterate this desire on a prayer request slip of paper asking that God reveal her to me. I remember as far back as my freshman year in high school beginning to pray for that person each night, even though I didn't know her name.
>
> I prayed that God would protect her, watch over her, shower her with his love, and let her know that she was thought of from afar. I began throwing spare change in a jar nearly 10 years ago in the hope of one day being able to make the most meaningful purchase of my life. Annabelle, my prayers have been heard, and my coins have been spent. Would you be God's fulfilled promise to me by taking this ring and saying "yes" to my heart's desire for you to be my wife?

And at the bottom it says:

> *Take delight in the Lord and He will give your heart's desires. Commit everything you do to the Lord. Trust him and he will help you.*

That's Psalms 37:4–5.

I asked her to marry me. She said, "Yes, yes! Of course! Yes." She's just bawling. I pulled out a Bible. Engraved on the front was "Anne VanHaitsma." And tied to a ribbon in the middle of the Bible was the ring.

It was symbolic of us, with two rows of raw diamonds—all different kinds of raw diamonds. Then there's two polished diamonds right in the center of it. They're real small. But it was symbolic of us two in the rough. I've always told her that she's a diamond in the rough to me. Anyway, I pulled out the wine but the cork was frozen and I couldn't get it open. She was like, "No worries, I'm freezing anyway." So we just hopped back on the horses and rode back to the farm.

We were engaged for six months and then got married. A lot of friends have said that first year of marriage is going to be really hard. It's been really natural for us. I wouldn't say that there are many things that we're really struggling with. Of course there are little things, like my work and balancing that. Sometimes when I get home I just want to shut off. But she knows my heart well enough that when we need it, she's saying let's engage here, let's talk about this.

My definition of love has always been that God is love, God created us out of love, He created us to have a relationship with each other. The way that I've experienced love has radically changed since I met Anne because I never knew that I'd ever be able to experience the fullness of the Father's love. I mean, I know that it's given me a picture of the Father that I never dreamed of. I always thought about the day that I would propose to her. It is something you can make really quick, but I wanted to drag it out. I wanted to integrate things for her that were most precious to her in life, to make it a day that she was going to remember.

DOMINIC SCLAFANI, AGE 30

TUCSON, ARIZONA

"He's like, 'She's going to eat you alive.'
And I go, 'Yes, I know.'"

I like people who play. People who are fun and who punch me at random moments and who do weird shit. The first time I met Chyna, we were at a rave. She bit me. I was totally into it. I'm like, "Fucking bite me harder!" And she got all excited and I got all excited, because I like being bitten and scratched up. That was orgasmic. When we left, people were actually frightened of the way I looked. She had torn me apart from my forehead to my waist. I mean, forget just blood—I was bruised and bleeding. And I was singing out, I was so happy about it.

I was living on the border of Newport Beach and Costa Mesa, California. I was in college, studying philosophy, which I found out later was a mistake. I'm much more into psychology. I was working at a sushi bar in Huntington Beach where it was expected that you drink on the job. Korn and Orgy and all those bands used to come in. It was a party restaurant. I was having a lot of fun—nineteen and doing coke probably three times a week, just getting into Ecstasy. I got a whole new group of friends. Chyna was a part of that scene.

Chyna ended up getting together with my best friend, Randy. I've known Randy since we were eight. Anyway, it was cool the way it worked out, because this way, I still got to see Chyna without having to deal with her bullshit. Honestly, she was a kind of a pain in the ass sometimes.

Chyna's mom was a drug addict and Chyna was abused by her mom's boyfriend. She never had a clean slate to begin with. But Chyna was really smart and a good survivor. She was a beautiful, beautiful girl—about five one, a great mix of Chinese and Native American. And she was—well, by this time we were doing speed, so she was about 102 pounds. But she was strong as shit. She'd punch Randy. He'd be like, "Ow," and I'd always think, "Fuck, I wouldn't be saying 'Ow!' I'd be saying 'Again!' " (laughs)

When Randy and I moved to Huntington Beach, Chyna just kind of tagged along. Thing is, she wasn't working, wasn't cleaning the house, she wasn't giving anything, just living off of me and Randy. And it started to feel like we were both her boyfriend. She had Randy, the guy she went to bed with, and she had me, who provided most of the money and drugs and fun stuff. But Randy never understood how to keep her under control. I was like, "Dude, you gotta man up if you're gonna deal with her." But he was such a puppy. And slowly over the months, she started seducing me. I mean slow.

Chyna smoked a lot of meth. One night I tried some. It was fucking fantastic. All of a sudden I had a ten-day week. I could get all my schoolwork done. I could do my shift at the restaurant every night and have plenty of energy for my band. My

grade point average immediately jumped up. Randy started doing it too. But eventually he was like, "I don't want to do this
anymore." He'd come out at seven in the morning and there I
am, fucking having been up all night. And instead of he and
Chyna having sex, she starts staying up with me, doing meth. So
Randy starts getting pissy.

Now this is where she's gifted. She tells Randy things, then
she comes to me and tells me things slightly differently. She
starts fighting with Randy more, and she makes it look like it's
his fault. So now their whole relationship starts going to shit.

To clear his head, Randy went out of state for two weeks.
And that was it. Chyna made her move. Walked into my room
at two in the morning. And I'm like, "Okay, what? Are you
cold?" Because I didn't . . . I was totally not suspecting it. And
she's basically naked in my bed kind of thing, and I'm like, "Oh,
oh, oh, okay. Shit. Yes."

At first I thought, "Well, maybe this isn't such a big deal."
But it was. It was like finishing something off that should've
been taken care of a long time ago, when she clawed me up at
the rave—just kind of a completion of that experience. Very
soon into it, I realized I wasn't just having sex with her. I was
starting our relationship. And I knew it. It wasn't like we just
had this little fling and I was going to let her go back to my best
friend. No, we've really crossed this boundary. She's mine now.

So Randy comes back. I'm a Southern man. I can't lie to my
best friend. I had to tell him. By this time I'm totally into
Chyna. I loved her, and I believed in the relationship. So I
looked at Randy and said, "I like your girlfriend." Well, he
totally flipped out. He threw a fit. He was like, "You got to
stop! You got to stop this shit right now!"

I got down on my knees, took off my glasses and put them in my pocket. Hands behind my back. Like I said, I'm from the South. It's etiquette for someone to punch you if you sleep with their girlfriend. I said no, it's not going to stop. I told him to hit me. But he didn't hit me. He destroyed the house instead, which I ended up having to pay for. I would rather he broke my nose. I mean, I was kind of insulted. And I still had insurance at that time.

But you know, all I could do is say, "I'm fucking sorry, it crept up on me."

He's like, "She's going to eat you alive."

And I go, "Yes, I know."

And he goes, "Yes. You're fucked."

Chyna and I both moved out right away. She had another place to stay. I started sleeping in my car because I didn't want to go back into the house. Randy was my best friend and I was just experiencing so much sorrow and guilt. For the record, Randy and I are still friends. But after all this shit went down, our friendship was done for around two years. At the time, though, there was really no other choice. This shit was really happening.

So by this point, I'd busted up a friendship, I dropped out of college, I was addicted to speed, and I was going to get used and abandoned by the person I'd done it for. I mean, I knew it. And so with all this knowledge, I figured, ah fuck it, let's do it anyway. Just, you know, like the end of *Eternal Sunshine of the Spotless Mind*. What else are we going to do?

Eventually we decided to move out to Tucson, Arizona, where my mom lives. When we first got out there, we stayed at her house. My mom got sick of us pretty quick. So Chyna and

I both got jobs at this local restaurant and moved out to our own place. Since we weren't at my mom's house, we started doing even more meth.

Chyna and I always had this instant physical intensity as a couple. I have a really strong stomach and chest, so she just punched me whenever she wanted to, as hard as she could. She bloodied me up pretty good all the time—not just during sex. She was just really affectionate and passionate and fun and smart.

We played music all day long and all night long. We loved the same music, and that's a really big one for me: Tool, Radiohead, Zero 7, Tricky, stuff like that—experimental stuff, from Pink Floyd to The Mars Volta. I don't think there was a single band that we had static on—ever. We'd get high together and experience the music physically. I'd play DJ, changing the music every few songs, and we'd just sit there and soak the music in, really like studying the notes, losing ourselves to it, then coming back, seeing the world, seeing ourselves and the music in a different way. Which is really kind of an intimate experience.

We used to do art when were on speed. We'd be drawing, just one piece for about thirty hours. We'd keep switching the CDs to make sure we got the mood right. We were always very in tune with everything, from the rhythm to, you know, the undertones of the vocal intonations, where it becomes visual, where you can see the person singing the lines, like they're onstage, like they're doing theater for themselves. Chyna could access the music at a holy, deep level, the same way I was able to.

We loved the same lines. We heard the same things in the songs. She was better at that than probably any girlfriend I've had, and it was really attractive to me, because music is . . . I don't say, like, "It's my life," because that would assume that it's still outside of me. And she would attach to it the same way.

Due to being on the same drug we could do a lot of the same things. There's a reducing valve in the brain for sight, which is why you normally can't see oxygen, nitrogen, things in the air. But after you're sleep deprived for thirty-six hours, it goes away, so all of a sudden you think you're hallucinating, but what you're seeing is really there. So we'd get fucked up, and I'd start playing with energy, and by playing with energy I mean I'd intend certain hot spots of magnetism and basically create a ball out of it, and then not say anything and have her try to watch it and follow it around the room. It can be done. Magnetics are intense. And she was very open to that, which is nice because most of my girlfriends haven't been into that. Even most of my friends aren't. We did a lot of that. And also, like, using body energy to play around. We were very much in tune with each other's bodies. There were no boundaries between the two of us.

But the speed was making me crazy. Chyna and I were both doing lots of it. I'm stealing from work, I'm supporting the habit for the both of us. I did it for almost two years and I could tell when I crossed a line with it. I noticed the second when it was like, okay, I can't do this anymore.

When we stopped all that stuff it got different. The timing was off. We'd be tired, uninterested. Even three days without, you get really, really tired. It feels like taking tranquilizers all day long. And it's not that the speed was the predication for our sexual relationship, but the lack of it definitely hurt it. We didn't adjust very well, because I had to get drunk instead. Drunk boys, you know, we go to sleep. After a long day we go to sleep. We're not as affectionate.

I'm one of the one hundred that quits cold turkey, just goes nope, I'm done. She couldn't do that, apparently. She had a detox freak-out, and she kept on doing speed. We had a fight. She tore everything off the wall. So Chyna didn't quit. And she was nuts.

I don't fight. I've had seven girlfriends, and I've never fought with any of them. But Chyna could get me every time. Her favorite line was, "Why don't you go fuck your mother since you love her so much more than me!" She was always baiting me to punch her in the nose. She'd get right up in my face, screaming at me over God knows what—usually something about how I left the kitchen cupboard open.

So she was staying up, doing speed with other people while I was, like, passed out on the couch. I was just drinking, drinking, drinking, drinking—pouring alcohol into my face. I'm kind of mourning the relationship at this point because I knew it was going to be bad, I just didn't know when. I could see that she was starting to make ties with this new guy we were hanging out with. And I couldn't seem to do anything about it. She was getting her next boyfriend lined up.

I was over my mom's house, drunk as a skunk, and I told her, "You know, I don't like my girlfriend, but I'm not going to break up with her." My mom was like, "Well, that doesn't sound very smart. What do you plan on doing?" And I said, "I think I'll drink myself to death over the next six months." And my mom just looked at me, like, "You rat fuck." (*laughs*)

I was in a deep slump. I was doing over a bottle of vodka

every day. I drank enough to black out on a daily basis. I'd lose
entire weeks. I drove drunk, I drove blacked out. I'd developed
liver failure and jaundice. I'd actually turned yellow. And every
time I got sober, I'd start getting drunk again.

I know psychology. So I know that people have their own
velocity when they go through trauma, pain, guilt, all of that
stuff. And I know it's retarded, but I wasn't done with her. I
wasn't done with it yet. And I had nothing better to do.

One day, in between a double shift at the restaurant, I came
home and drank a pint of rum and went to take a nap before
going back. Chyna comes home while I'm passed out, turns off
the alarm clock, and goes back to work. At the restaurant, she
tells them I'm acting all fucked up and crazy, and I'm really
drunk. When I finally come in, I get fired. And the next morning, when I'm passed out again, Chyna throws me outside, calls
my mom and tells her she's calling the cops unless she comes to
get me.

Next thing I know I'm in Delaware. That's where my dad
lives. The minute I got there, I blacked out on his floor. When
I woke up, I knew I needed help. I went to my first AA meeting. I ended up doing probably four hundred meetings in the
next year.

They say that 3.5 percent of people who go to those meetings get helped. Well, I wasn't one of those 3.5. I started working again and started drinking again.

During the time I was struggling to get clean, I found out
from my mom that Chyna had become a manager at the restaurant she'd gotten me fired from. And that she already had
another boyfriend. Five months after moving to Delaware, I
finally wrote her a breakup note—which is hilarious, because

she had already dated two other guys by then. I was basically left
with nothing.

I was stuck with my dad in Delaware, because Chyna was
living in the same town as my mom. I just never wanted to see
her again.

You know, I'm an intimate guy. That's just the way I am. I'm
always kind. I'm very dedicated. When I'm with somebody,
there's nobody else in the world. And that's how I was with
Chyna. I was broken up bad for about a week, and then I was
like okay, this is how this was supposed to end.

But my body knows that it will always care for her and get a
little bit excited when I see her on Facebook. My body will
always wonder how she's doing. But that's just the body. It does
what it does. I don't get hung up on it. I mean, I've probably
shared more time and intimacy and knowledge with Chyna
than anybody else. If you count the nights we stayed up, we
basically spent the equivalent of seven years together. I've
known her since she was eighteen years old. And she's thirty
now. But the truth is, we broke up seven years ago.

I haven't had a real girlfriend since we were together. I
haven't lived with anybody except my parents. I'm on disability
now because of too much trauma and who the hell knows what
else. I still drink, but I switched to whiskey because it tastes bad
and so I only drink a pint or less. What I'm drinking right now
won't kill me—not until I'm fifty-five or something. Which is
fine. I thought I was going to be dead years ago, so everyone's
kind of happy about that.

I'm in Tucson now. I moved back as soon as I found out she
had gone. I think she's in Vegas. I haven't seen her. I know she's
alive and healthy. The last time I talked to her was around a year

ago. I was about to go to a Pixies concert. I called her to tell her, because she loves the Pixies. But she took offense and hung up on me. We talked for five minutes. I was drunk, and I could tell she was fucked up. I was trying to be friendly and she took it the wrong way. I never heard from her again until recently. I think she accidentally sent me a group e-mail.

KELLY CUMBERLAND, 30

ROANOKE, VIRGINIA

"I think back now and I'm like, 'Whoa, dumbass!'"

My first marriage, it was just circumstantial. We worked together. He was my boss. We had gone out for drinks one night and when he brought me home, my ex-boyfriend before him, who I didn't like very much, had broken into my apartment and destroyed everything that I had. I mean every piece of clothes, every piece of furniture. He busted holes in the wall. I left that night to stay with Brett and he said that I could stay there until I could replace my stuff and get new stuff.

I didn't want to get married—I didn't even really like him very much. (*laughs*) But his parents, being traditional people, decided that we should get married. Then he asked me, and I got caught up in the whole wedding thing and I just wanted to be married. He made good money and I knew I didn't have to worry about anything.

That was a bad, horrible, horrible marriage.

He wanted me to stay home and have babies and do nothing. He told me what time to go to bed, when I could and couldn't talk on the phone. I wasn't allowed to work, I couldn't have friends. He didn't like my hair color so I changed; he didn't like my weight so I gained weight or lost weight—whatever it was.

I was in the bathtub, and he said, "Bitch, I didn't tell you that you could take a bath." I said, "Okay, tomorrow I'm leaving." So that ends in divorce.

I had just gotten the divorce in April and this is June. I was at Macado's drinking a beer. It's a little restaurant, and I was in the bar area, drinking a Miller Lite draft. Daniel was sitting across the bar, drinking a rum and Coke.

I was with a friend and I was shouting for the Baltimore Orioles, and Daniel was like, "The Orioles fucking suck!" So we were shouting back and forth. He had this look. He has a bald head and blue eyes. Like, shaved bald, Nazi bald. He's short, but he has a military physique.

Drink by drink, he edged his way around. One drink at a time. And then he was beside me.

He was in the army then. Twenty-four years old. He had to go on some duty thing for two weeks. He was sloppy drunk, falling off the stool. He got thrown out after a while because he had consumed too much alcohol for one evening. But I found out later that he called his number from my phone while I was in the bathroom, so he got my number.

He called me. I got my friend Bre and we met him at Cornerstone. It's like a little teeny hole-in-the-wall. I just went for fun, to go out and get free drinks. (*laughs*)

We all hung out and I ended up going home with Daniel. It was my first one-night stand. I wanted to have just one in my life—I was twenty-seven and no one-night stands.

It was horrible. He had whiskey dick. He was so drunk that

he couldn't finish. It was six hours and I was like, "I'm over it! It's not fun anymore." He just kept on and on and on. I got up in the morning and said, "Whew, gotta go!"

When I got home I called Bre and we were laughing because I'm telling her about his hairy nipples. The hanging out was fun. But the sex? No. The kissing was wonderful, though.

So Daniel calls me the next weekend, "Hey! Let's go hang out!" This time, we didn't get drunk. He came back to my house, and now I finally got to have my one-night stand. It was fine. It wasn't great, but it was better than the first time.

And then he's coming over on the weekends. I still didn't know his last name. I didn't know anything about him except for "Dan." And I did like him. But I still didn't want a boyfriend.

Well, the anniversary of my marriage date was Labor Day, September 1. And I was sitting at home having a couple of drinks—a pity party. He called and said, "Hey, let's hang out. It's Labor Day. We'll cook out." I said, "No! No relationship, no boyfriend, no weekend lover—just one-night stands. That's enough!" You know, I had just gotten a divorce. I just needed some me time.

So the next night he calls me, "Hey, it's Daniel. I got arrested last night, can you come and get me?"

He had gone out and had a couple of drinks and got pulled over and put in jail. At the time I was working three jobs because I had to make ends meet. I was kind of at a crossroads. He was by himself. I knew that his family was not from here—I didn't know from where, but not from here. I would want somebody to come get me if I was in jail.

I get to the courthouse and I still didn't even know his last name. (*laughs*) I see this guy with a clipboard and I'm like, "Hey, I think that's my boyfriend, or the guy I'm going to pick up."

So I get him out, and I'm rushing like shit to go back to work. And he asks, "Can I take a shower at your apartment and I'll find out where my car and stuff is?" I said yeah, but later I realized, what I was thinking? He could have robbed me blind! (*laughs*) I think back now and I'm like, "Whoa, dumbass!"

It was just spur of the moment and I just . . . if I was in that situation, I would want someone to do that for me. He could have left that day and I would not be thinking about him today.

But I let him shower, and I got back to work, and I came back that evening, and he's there sleeping on the couch. The next day, I said, "I'm sorry, but you're going to have to go. You're going to have to call your mom and she's going to have to come get you. Or I'll take you to your car, or whatever."

Then I get a phone call—a woman is screaming at me. I thought maybe he's married or something. But it was his mom. She's like, "You will bring my son to me!" She called me a drunken whore. (*laughs*) I told Daniel that he could stay as long as he wanted to, 'cause I would never send him home to that bitch.

So he just stayed.

Around Christmas, I remember I had loose jewelry everywhere—in the medicine cabinet, under the kitchen sink. It was just random, in little dishes. And he went and bought me the most beautiful jewelry box and put a little note in it. I just noticed, he really took the time to think about who I was as a person and something that I needed. Not just some random shirt or something.

Well, then he had to go to jail to serve out his DUI. They gave him twenty-three days. I asked him before he went, "How do you feel? Because if you're going to jail for twenty-three days, I might go out and have fun, because we're not in a relationship." He said, "Well, I care about you and I love you."

We had been saying "I love you" since he had been staying there. It wasn't real. We were just saying it, I don't know why. (*laughs*) He just said it one day and I just said, "Okay, love you too." But I didn't mean like, "I love you."

Well, I couldn't help myself. I missed him by the first week. I went to see him in jail, and he was crying, "I'm so glad! It's so lonely in here!" He was in pieces, and so was I.

I'd told him you can love someone or you can be *in love* with someone or both, because there's a fine line. And he didn't get the difference because he'd never had a girlfriend before. So when he got out he said, "I now know the difference between being in love and just loving someone. And I promise to be in love with you the rest of my life."

And he's showed me every day since that he's in love with me.

Just little stuff—he just takes time to think about me. He built me a flower garden because all I wanted was a flower garden for my birthday. He built it himself.

We do something fun every single day. If it's just playing Scrabble at the coffee table, we take time every single day for each other. No matter how busy life is, how hard work was, we do something together.

We decided that every week we'd try something new. It's not always sexual, but that does happen quite a bit. (*laughs*) Sometimes we try different food—like we see something weird at the grocery store and we try it. That's how we started playing tennis. We just went one day and bought racquets and balls and said, "Let's try to play tennis."

My definition of love is just being with someone that makes you feel good about being who you are. And I think for the first time in my life I am my own person.

I was very suicidal at one point in my life. I always used to be so afraid of my dad. I went from that abusive bad relationship to another bad relationship to another bad relationship. I had a black boyfriend because I knew my dad wouldn't like it, and I was lesbian because I knew my dad wouldn't like it. I did a lot of rebellious things and it got me nowhere. It made me . . . not ashamed, but it just made me wonder who I was. I did a lot of soul-searching after I left my husband because I didn't know what I liked, what I didn't like. I just went along with whatever it was to go along with. So I've never been me.

Daniel reassures me that I am my own person. I do not depend on anyone. We have our own lives and we are separate, individual people, and we are just together to love each other. He helped me to just start working on me, and finding out who I was, and he's just been there, pushing me along.

We went hiking one time and it was a really tough mountain. I was heavier than I am now, and I was having a tough time. I wanted to give up about halfway up the mountain, and he said, "I can't carry you up. And I won't walk back down with you. If you want to quit you have to quit alone, because I won't quit anything with you." And I got to the top and I just started bawling my eyes out! (*laughs*) And he was like, "Okay, sop up your tears, it's just a hike."

And my feeling was that it was more than a hike; I got over a hump that I couldn't get over, not just on the mountain that day but in my life. I felt liberated. Literally. I felt like, wow, I can conquer the world now. And since then, I lost like sixty pounds, and I'm still going.

I used to be really, really obsessed with cleaning the house. If Daniel got one thing out of place, I would go and hurry to put it back. Or when he was done drinking his drink, I would get the cup and hurry up to wash it and put it back. I just did this because that's what I had to do for my husband—that's what I was ordered to do. Finally one day Daniel grabbed me by the wrist and said, "I'm not him! I'm a different person!"

And that was my big, big, wake-up call. To really just give myself to him. To trust that he is going to take care of my heart and take care of my feelings.

He was in the war in Afghanistan, and he has PTSD, post-traumatic stress disorder. And we've had some really dark moments with that. Like him spazzing out, getting in the closet to hide from enemies when it was just us at the apartment.

During the day he's usually okay. But at night he does some really weird crap—superweird. The other day he grabbed my boob and said, "Here's the remote control if you're looking for it." Stuff like that! He was dead asleep. But you know what, we get through it, and if he gets bothersome I just go get on the couch.

His PTSD is getting under control, though. It's better. He's on medication now. And we quit drinking. I drink wine but I don't drink liquor or beer, and he'll drink two beers, that's his limit. And that's changed a lot.

We have a great sex life now. I think it's better too, now that we are in love. I think that makes it a lot better. He is very quick and so we just kind of get around that. We have a lot of foreplay before he's allowed to be quick. So we've just kind of talked about it.

I'm still uncomfortable being 100 percent open as he is about it. He wants to talk about it like, after, when we're in the shower. Like, "Did you like this? Did you like that?"

That was a thing with him. It became a thing. If I didn't give him a high five after sex, he'd think that it was bad. Because that first time he finally came, I was like, "Yes! Woo-hoo! High five!" Finally, I was like, "I'm over the whole high-five stage." (*laughs*)

Daniel likes to have sex every single day. He's different than me. But that's okay. I have this shirt. It's the no-sex-tonight shirt. It is so disgusting. It is really big, like it comes all the way down past my elbows, almost to my knee and it probably has seven thousand holes in it. If I put this shirt on, he doesn't try. I get to wear it once a week.

He's just a different person from the person that I met. He used to not like people and he still doesn't like people, but he'll tolerate them for my sake. He doesn't like to go to cookouts and stuff, but he'll go because I like to go. He's changed a lot. I think we've both changed a lot.

We very rarely fight. And we have a promise that we will not hurt each other. If we want to be with someone else we will be up front and forward about it. Not cheat because it's not worth the pain that you have to go through.

His mom cheated on his dad the whole time they were together. They didn't separate until he was about nine and so he just kind of grew up with that. His dad never cheated; his dad was faithful. And I think his mom had a big impact on him—running around and sneaking, and she would have him lie for her and stuff. Then finally his dad got custody when he was ten, and when his mom fought back for custody he went back to live with his mom. His dad has never talked to him since. I think that impacts his life because he wants to be a good man in life and true to his word.

When I first met him he didn't work for a month. I kept thinking it's not right that I'm buying him food and beer or whatever. But for some reason, I did it anyway, and now I know: because last summer, I decided to go back to school full time. And I don't work now. We have eighty-seven cents in the checking account—that's it. (laughs) And his paycheck is my paycheck. He gives it to me every Thursday.

I think that . . . I now know—I'm going to try not to cry—I now know that you don't have to have money to love someone. You can be the most poor, broke person in the world, and love does make the world go 'round. People always say that money can buy you happiness. I don't agree with that anymore. I think the fact that we make money together and we do stuff together is what makes us work. I'm still waiting on my fifty bucks, though—I always tell him before he dies to please give me my fifty dollars back that I bailed him out of jail with. (laughs)

I gave up a lot of who I was for guys who didn't like certain things about me. Daniel, he just takes me 100 percent. On my fat days he loves me just as much on my skinny days. When I'm down he picks me up. He just makes me laugh, intentional or not. We're happy.

Daniel James Blondell. Have to take a deep breath. I love him.

SHAWN WHITWORTH, AGE 31

NEW YORK, NEW YORK

"I met my ex-wife, Jackie, when she was twelve years old and I
was seventeen. We kind of had this little thing."

I was born in Orlando, Florida. My name was S-H-O-N-E to
start out with, because my family was so country, that's what
they put on my birth certificate. Let's see. My dad was in the
military when I was born and my mother didn't bother to tell
him that she was pregnant so he didn't know until after I was
born. I saw him a couple of times between the ages of three and
five. But we moved to L.A., and then to Tennessee, and I never
saw him again.

I had a stepfather. He wasn't like the most loving father, but
he did provide for us and, you know, I love him. I call him Dad.
But my first stepdad was really abusive. I was burned and
slapped and punched and beat. He smoked weed with me and
drank, and I was only two or three years old. I can remember
actually being burned with a bottle—he lit it, so it was black,
and then stuck it around my nipple. And it just seared into me.
My mother was an alcoholic and she didn't really fight. But she

got at him by being really stubborn. There was a lot of friction, a lot of argumentation. It was very dramatic.

Like, once I went fishing with my mother and a guy came down to the river where we were and she started talking to him and they ended up drinking some beers together. And this is a small town where everybody knows everybody, and he had his hand on her leg the whole time and she'd been married to my stepdad for like fifteen years, or ten or twelve or something like that at the time. They did it right there in front of me. And then a couple of days later, the guy pulls up in our driveway, and I'm standing outside, and I'm like, "Oh, shit." I walk up to the car very calmly and he's like, "Is your mom here?" I'm like, "That's my dad over there. I think it's best that you leave." So he backs out of the driveway and my dad comes over and he goes, "Who was that?" I'm like, "He got the wrong address." That's tough to do when you're twelve. So my mother pretty much ruined me as far as trust goes with women. I don't think that I could trust a woman. It's just not something that I would immediately do.

Being raised in Tennessee from around seven to fourteen, they have a lot of mixed ideas there, a lot of backwoods, backward ways. I remember my grandmother slicing her wrists. I saw the blood trails. When I was six or seven, this kid named Kevin molested me. He was like, "Don't tell anybody." I was like, "Well, fine. I'm not gonna tell anybody." He was thirteen. And when I was four, I had two girls in my neighborhood that used to fool around with me. They were sisters. They were seven or eight. They'd be like, "Do this to me. Do that to me." I basically went down on them, and I mean they definitely didn't have hair down there, anything like that.

I pulled a gun on my brother when I was eleven years old. It was a .410 shotgun, single shot. I pointed it at him because he was being rambunctious and I was like, "You're gonna calm down, you're gonna listen to me." So I got sent to a mental hospital. And then the day I got back from the mental hospital, my mother was in jail for DUI.

When I was like thirteen, fourteen, fifteen, my mother would be out drinking and driving almost every night. I would sit and wait by the window or outside on the porch waiting for her. Like a dog waiting for its master to come home. I didn't know what to expect. Was my mother dead? Was she in jail again?

I met my ex-wife, Jackie, when she was twelve years old and I was seventeen. We kind of had this little thing. We did drugs together, smoked weed, basically. I really didn't get involved too much in the heavier drugs. But she made it known that she liked me and I was like, "You're twelve." At that point in my life, I had girls flocking all over me so it was more, like, we'll be friends.

And we were friends. She was really mature. I think it's because maybe that she was molested when she was a kid and it made her grow up really fast. She never told me who it was. She was afraid I might do something about it.

I never tried anything with her. Maybe I kissed her a couple of times or something, but I never tried to get down her pants 'cause she was so young—I think she was like thirteen or fourteen around that time. And she told me she had been molested, but she hadn't been raped, so she was a virgin. And basically she told me that she was ready for me to take her virginity. At the time, she stayed with her sister in Georgia. And she called me and was like, "Hey, we want to meet you in Chattanooga." She's like, "I'm ready." And I was like, "Oh, my God, man. I don't know what to do." But I wanted to see her. I took my brother with me, and I told her, you know, "You don't have to do this if you're not ready." She was like, "This is what I want." I'm like, "Okay." So later on that night I took her virginity.

And then immediately the next day I felt bad about it. And also, her sister, Carrie, was older. I thought she was more my type. I just kind of stayed away from Jackie, which made her feel really bad, like basically, you know, he doesn't have feelings for me anymore and he took my virginity. But you have to remember I lived in a different state. I called her from time to time but, like, I wasn't pursuing her for that.

So a few months went by and I went to visit her in Florida, and when I was going there, my car broke down, and her parents had the great idea to have her sister in Georgia pick me up. So she met me halfway, took me back home to her place, and was like, "Yeah, I'm tired. I'll take you home tomorrow." And then another day went by and she's like, "Oh, I'm tired. I'll take you home tomorrow." And every day she did something else to try and lure my attention. And every day it got more and more difficult and I was trying—not that I had any commitment with Jackie, I just didn't want her feelings to be hurt. I knew it was probably the wrong thing to do. So a week goes by and like Carrie's coming out of the shower in her robe and she's like, "Do you want a massage?" And with the hot oil and all this. So I broke down and ended up spending about a month there. And then finally, I was like, "Look, I can't do this."

So I made her take me back home. And then Jackie comes to Georgia to stay with her sister and . . . things are really fuzzy. All I know is that I went back to Georgia and Carrie didn't

want to tell Jackie I was sleeping with her because she thought
her sister would hate her. Which she did when she found out.
But when Jackie got there she wanted to sleep with me too, so
I was at a loss what to do. I ended up sleeping with both of
them at different times of the day. While one was at work I
would do it with one, and while the other was at work . . . it
was a very confusing, exhausting time for me, and they both
were subconsciously aware of the fact, though I don't think they
admitted it to themselves at that time.

Then Jackie started hanging around with all her friends
doing heroin and coke and roofies and all these different drugs.
She was fooling around with this kid that was fifteen, and she
ended up getting pregnant. She told me about it, and she was
like, "You know I don't believe in abortion." And she was going
to have the baby. Well, I felt guilty. Because I'm the one who
took her virginity. I fucked around with her sister. I felt like she
had done this stuff to find a way to try to get me off of her mind
or to forget the situation. I felt like, you know, I had to marry
her and get her away from these people.

So when I was twenty-one and she was sixteen, we got married. I mean, I loved her, but I didn't love her like "in love," you
know, like a fairy-tale love story. Basically, before we got married, I had sex with another woman, because I felt like once I
got married I wasn't gonna do that stuff.

I adopted her kid by the other guy, Robbie. It wasn't a legal
adoption. It was basically like a mental adoption. But immediately we had problems. Her memories as a kid, she blocked a lot
of them out, but they were still with her constantly. Like her
father was abusive toward her mother and shattered her knee in
a domestic argument. Every time I would raise my voice, it

would scare the hell out of her. And I'm a very passionate person. I tended at that time to get in people's faces.

So she would leave me. I trusted her, but because I cheated on her before we got married, I always had it in the back of my mind that she's gonna try to get me back. I really thought she was gonna try to really hurt me. So, you know, I was really jealous and really afraid, and every now and then when she was pissed off she would tell me some shit, like, just to enrage. And this went on in Florida—you know, every time the police are called somebody's got to go to jail. So one time she went to jail, and three times I went to jail.

But she loved me. I mean, she still puts it this way today, she "worshipped the ground I walked on." And I didn't appreciate that at all. I was very self-centered, very selfish, you know, was like, "Okay, I'm gonna go to work, you stay here with the kids, you cook, you clean, and like, the money that I make is my money." At the time I had not a great job, you know. I was a nurse's assistant. I was working sixteen-hour shifts five days a week so I was bringing home fifteen hundred dollars every couple of weeks. It was horrible. I look back and think what a ridiculous person I was—I mean it was so bad that she'd be like, "Can you buy me a water?" And I'd be like, "I'm not buying water. What's wrong with you?" When she would cry I would be like, "Shut up. Be strong." I would run her in the ground for crying. Because I never cried as a kid, really. I remember being slapped so hard that my ears rang—and I didn't cry. And when my grandma died I didn't cry.

We stayed married for four years. However, we only lived together in that time maybe a year. Three or four months after we got married, Jackie got pregnant with Bethany. And then after that came Jason and Amber.

After we were divorced, I moved back to Tennessee, and we still maintained contact. I was living with my brother in a duplex. And my stepdad's father had died, and my stepdad gave us each four grand. So I'm talking to Jackie and I'm like, "I'm gonna come down and see you. Can we stay at your place?" We wanted to go have a good time with the money. "Can you hook my brother up with Andrea?" She had a friend living with her named Andrea. I've known Andrea since she was like twelve years old. And now she's like twenty or something like that. So I talked to Andrea and Andrea said, "Sure." Okay, so we get there, everything works out. My brother gets with Andrea. I get with Jackie.

And then Jackie and I get in a dispute, so I have to leave. The money was running low by the time the dispute happened. So I went to a dock and tried to get on a shrimp boat 'cause I heard you don't need any sort of documentation whatsoever, it's under the table, you just jump on the boat and go long days, whatever. So I'm on the boat, and my brother's been at Jackie's for, I guess, three weeks, something like that, and I'm like, "Yo, don't you think it's time you go back home?"

And he's like, "Yeah. I just need some money."

I'm like, "Well, get a job."

So three weeks turns into three years and Andrea has moved out and, you know, I get to Key West, and then my captain was on heroin, and I couldn't take it, and a friend offered me a place in New York, so I moved to New York.

And every time I'm talking to my kids and Jackie, I'm like,

"Yo, he's gotta leave. This isn't right." My kids are there, you know. It doesn't seem right. And at some time, about a year into it, they're like, "We're together." So I completely freak out. I think I had a nervous breakdown. And I talk to my brother and I'm like, "Look, man, if you had sex with her that's okay. I can forgive you. Just please, just move out." And he's like, "No, we're together." And at that point I start screaming like a madman. I'm like, "I'll fucking kill you!" Like, "Don't even turn your back for a minute. If you see a shadow out of the corner of your eye it's gonna be me. I'm coming to kill you. You better believe it. You're dead. You're dead."

The thing is that he's my brother and coming from a trailer-trash background the last thing I felt my kids needed is to have some sort of shit like that go on in their life to affirm to them that they are redneck trailer-trash hillbilly fucking hicks and that that's all they're ever gonna be. You know? And now he's not their uncle anymore, he's Trevor. They're married now, and they have a kid of their own, so now my kids' sister is also their cousin. And it pisses me off. They didn't have any kids at the time and I felt like they should have walked away from it.

I don't talk to him. When he answers the phone, I say, "Where's my kid?" But . . . there's a joke I didn't get for a long time, but now I get it. This guy who's in prison for ten years comes home and he knocks on the trailer door and his wife answers the door. She invites him inside and he looks over and there's a guy sleepin' on the couch. And he says, "Who the fuck is this guy sleepin' on my couch?" She says, "That's the man that's been payin' the bills for the last ten years." And the guy says, "Well, shit. Give him a blanket! He looks kinda cold." My brother's paying the bills, you know. He takes care of my kids.

He gets 'em private tutors if they want. I'm like, "Well, shit!" That man is doing better than I could've done. I think they're really in love and I'm happy for 'em. My kids are happy and I don't pry too much.

You know, I felt bad when I left. She begged me not to go. And I'm like, I can't live like this. I can't. My youngest son was like a month old. I didn't know what my responsibilities were. I was really selfish and it was to my own detriment, and now it's to my children's detriment as well because their father's not there to be with them.

If you were to see me ten years ago you wouldn't believe I was the same person. I had a mullet. For like five years. When I was a kid you probably couldn't understand me when I spoke. I was like—I'll spell it out for you. I'd say "an-kur" for "I don't care." That's what I used to say to my teachers in school. I was such a disgruntled kid.

When I first moved to New York I had not the slightest idea of what prosperity was. This was only five years ago. In Tennessee, it was always just a hundred junked cars parked on the property, you know, the front porch falling in, everybody living in trailers, nobody wanting to do better for themselves. It was like knowledge was evil and the more you learned or the more diverse you are, they think you're a pussy or you're . . . I don't wanna say liberal, because they don't use that word. Like, "nigger lover."

So in New York, I saw people that not only had jobs, but they were in school at the same time and they still had a social life. That to me was so awe inspiring. How do people do this? And I sort of had this moment of epiphany, like, to try to be a better person. I think that there was just some ingrained desire to be a better person. You know, I want to learn. And the fact that I'm uneducated is balanced by the fact that I'm smart, witty, and I search for knowledge. I'm self-centered, but I'm loving and I'm caring and I'm helpful. I've learned a lot of restraint. I think a person gets older, you kind of calm down a little and you start to learn that this type of behavior is unacceptable. And that nobody is going to be comfortable until you learn to deal with your anger a little better.

I don't think I've ever been in love or trusted a woman— except Jackie. I learned more from her than I've ever learned from any other woman in my life. And also, she dealt with more than any woman could ever be expected to deal with. And when I look back I know at the time she truly loved me, and I took complete advantage of that.

If I met her today and she was the same person she used to be, and I was the person that I am now, I think things would be a lot different. I think, yeah, I could love her, that I would be lucky. I don't think that I'll ever find that kind of love again. I think I really screwed up.

I admire her and respect her because my children are in safe hands. And I'm so lucky that she is the person that she is. You know, she dropped out of school in the seventh grade, but she doesn't drink, she doesn't do drugs. My children are safe. They go to school, do their homework, she's there for them— emotionally, physically. She loves them. She doesn't talk bad about me. I mean she could say a million bad things about me and totally ruin my children's thoughts about me, but she doesn't do that. As far as I know.

I just recently met someone. She initiated the whole girl-friend boyfriend type thing and I found it rather odd. She's seventeen, which is legal in the state of New York. I was waiting for lineup for my stripper job. I do go-go at a gay bar. I went outside for a smoke break and she was outside, and I said hi to her and she ended up giving me her number and I called her up. This was like a month ago.

I'm really skeptical. You know, the age factor. The fact that she has a lot of guy friends that she's possibly had relations with in the past. I don't want to talk too much about this relationship.

My views on love are conflicted in my head so much that I may be an old man before I figure it out. I think that some form of companionship and "love" is necessary for human beings. Maybe not every single human being, but for most human beings, having a companion and someone that you love definitely helps heal the hurt, the stress of life, even if sometimes it makes life more stressful. But love is very elusive, and if there were a precise definition I would like to know it.

I'm sure that I've felt something like love plenty of times in my life. I know it exists because I love my children. But have I loved anyone unconditionally? I mean even with my children, there's conditions. I think that maybe things are what you perceive them to be. That if you think that you love, then you love. I would like to choose to believe that I have loved or that I can and am capable of love. I'm almost sure that it exists. But if it slapped me in the face, I couldn't tell you what it was.

THOMAS OUK, AGE 58

EAGAN, MINNESOTA

"We don't know each other. But if we don't live together, they gonna *kill* us."

I was born in South Vietnam. I am Cambodian nationality living in Vietnam. They didn't allow Cambodian schools in our village, so anyone want to learn the Cambodian language must go to the Buddhist temple. I became a monk when I was sixteen years old, in 1967. Daytime, I went to the Vietnamese school to learn Vietnamese. At the nighttime, I went to temple and study Cambodian and Pali, which is the Buddhist language. After I became a monk, my parents sent me to Phnom Penh, in Cambodia, to learn Cambodian culture.

The monks have to be strict with the rule and study hard. We only have one meal a day, like some breakfast. Monk have no women, no girlfriend. No dancing, no movie.

I aware that in the Buddha teaching, love is the foundation for the human beings. For any religion. They teach you about without love, we cannot survive. Love for nature, for god—so many different love. But for Buddhism, love for all kind of being, living beings. Not to kill is first in the Buddha teaching.

It means love. Not to kill, not to steal, this means love. That is the first. Not to kill, try to do good, control yourself, to love yourself. All the things around us is useful. Even small things, it's useful for us. You have to care and share. To help the community first. That's the Buddha teaching.

The Khmer Rouge take over Cambodia in 1975.*

First, they killed the high rank, the officials. Second, they killed the rich person. Third, they killed the monk who is against them. Fourth, they looking for who wear glasses. This is high-educated people. Even you don't have high education, but you wear glasses, they will kill you anyway.

Then the Khmer Rouge told the monk still alive must take off the robe. They get rid of everything. No monk. No currency. No school. No market.

They forced all the monks to go to work. They send me to countryside. They don't allow to eat much. The rice they sent to somewhere, we don't know. So they make people get weaker and weaker. No strength to fight back. And we worked so hard—from six in the morning to six in the evening.

Many people eat whatever they can find. I eat grass, I ate live—I eat *anything*. Anything! Insects (*laughs*), gecko, lizard, you eat everything. And sometimes people cannot walk, and die, and nobody bury anybody. Like that. So, so skinny, like a skeleton.

It's very hard time for me. Khmer Rouge soldier, we call

*The Khmer Rouge was a Communist party that ruled Cambodia from 1975 to 1979 with the aim of creating a classless agrarian utopia. Systematically dismantling society, they exterminated intellectuals, professionals, and former government employees, outlawed religion, closed all schools and hospitals, evacuated the cities, separated children from parents, and relocated the entire population to collective farm and labor camps. During the regime, an estimated 1.7 million people, approximately one-quarter of the country's population, died from execution, torture, exhaustion, disease, and starvation.

them detective. They wear black uniform. They are very, very young kids, fourteen, fifteen, sixteen, seventeen. Very short. They cannot kill you if you stand up, so they told you to kneel down, kneel down before they hit you, they beat you or kill you.

When I was living South Vietnam, they did not accept me as a Vietnamese. Even I came to Cambodia, the Cambodian government didn't accept me as a Cambodian people. I don't have the Cambodian green card or passport or certificate, I have none. I was born in South Vietnam but I am a Cambodian.

They said, Are you Vietnamese? I said no. Do you speak Vietnamese? I said yes. Do you read Vietnamese? I said yes. Do you read Cambodian? I said yes. Why you read Vietnamese? Why you know how to read Vietnamese? I said I live in South Vietnam, so I have to learn something over there to protect myself. I don't know why we have Cambodian live over there. Cambodian right now eight million live in South Vietnam!

Two time, they made me dig my grave, my own grave. Before they kill me, they want the information. Finally, they spare my life.

One day they called all the name from the boy side, from men side, everybody who single. And women side, who is single. They just call it meeting.

They come, stand in the middle, and marry sixty couples in one time. Just call the name and push our bodies to hold hands. "Okay! You are wife and husband!" Look like priest, says, "Here, you can kiss!" Pick man and woman (*laughs*) together, we don't know each other, no any ceremony (*laughs*), no any nothing. Just hold hands and say, "Wife and husband. Done!"

We do not expect do like that, because Cambodia used to have good culture, good tradition. Marriage, we have celebration three day and three nights. Okay? And engaged at least one year. You have to engage one year before you get married. They look over the groom for many months before they allow to marry. If your behavior changing, they gonna end the engage. If the groom behave good, then they are allowed to get married.

So my wife, me, we don't know each other. Almost twenty-six years old I never have any woman. But if we don't live together, they gonna *kill* us.

At night they went around the village. The detectives go to spy family to family: Who do what? What are you talking about? What are you eating? They don't allow any pan, any dish, any fork, or any cookware, nothing. Okay? If they find we are cooking something, they gonna kill, they don't allow to eat in house.

At that time, we don't think much about pretty or good person. I don't feel she is my wife, she don't feel I am her husband. We feel we escape from be killed. We want to survive only. We don't kiss. We just talking. The country used to have currency, we have school, the foreigners help us, the embassy. We have now no nothing, no foreigner, no embassy, no school. We just talk to each other, someday, somebody gonna come to rescue us. We kinda say like that. We pretend to be wife and husband. But we don't fall in love, no, nothing.

Unfortunately, man and woman, when we are awake, we feel different. But when we sleep together, we felt different. We started like we help each other and understand each other. One month later, we sleep together.

How do I know how to kiss? And how to have sex? You know about the animals. The animals, you see? That is the way of life. The natural way. Love is like that. Automatically, it connect. You don't have to teach kids how to have sex. Okay?

Here in United States, you looking for love. *Love.* Over there, we don't thinking about have fun, have love. Not during the Khmer Rouge control; you are like a prisoner. Okay? Even prisoner in this country you have TV, you have food, you have playground, whatever. But during Khmer Rouge, we compare to hell. Hell, okay?

I mean, if you don't have fun, no school, no currency, no market, no food, no nothing, how do you feel? If you have nothing for food, you thinking about hungry, you don't want to talk to other people, right? We just live the life, we cannot say much. Really, we scared to death, every day.

We don't know what day we gonna die, because every day we saw the bone, the skeleton, see the people that cannot walk. We saw they take the people go to kill. At nighttime, we heard the noise outside the house, we are shaking (*makes hand tremble*) like that.

We thinking about how can we survive. If we not stay together, they gonna take us and kill. We don't have much strength. We don't have much thinking about the future. But nature law, man and woman stay together for a period of time, we have feelings a little bit, okay? Every day, little more close.

I think: I am alone in Cambodia. I was so lonely, because all my parents, all my relatives live in South Vietnam. When I have my wife, yes, I feel a little bit better, because I have people to talk. Over there, that time, you cannot let the third person know anything. The third person tell others, you gonna be killed. Something like that. The secret can talk only with family, okay? Only wife and husband know. Cannot be loud. Very quiet.

So I am a little bit comfortable and happy, because I have people to talk to. So yes, I little confident, can say happy. But we don't have happy that time. We scared to death. Until today I have nightmares, big problems, until today. Nightmare looking for me, I dig my own grave. Everything comes to haunt me.

I get married in 1976, one year after the Khmer Rouge took over, and I have two kids. One born in 1978 and one in 1979. One boy, one girl.

In 1979, the Vietnamese invade Cambodia. We heard the guns fighting, not too far from us. The Khmer Rouge collapse. The Vietnamese took over.

I cannot stay in Cambodia. In 1968, I fight against South Vietnam for Cambodian people in Vietnam to be independent. So they know who am I. I hide my background. I changed my family name, and changed everything. Said I was born in Cambodia. But I scared. Soon or later, they are going to find out. They know I am from Vietnam, they looking for me, so I run.

I have to leave my kids, my wife. My wife couldn't come because her parents very, very old. We talked at least four months before I left. I waited for her delivery my baby. The day I left, my daughter was four and half months.

Hard to leave her, but I had no choice. One: you want me to live in jail? Two: you want to see me die? Three: you want me alive, but far away a little bit, but see me in the future? Which one? We don't know what will happen. If I am lucky, I still alive, come back. If I not come back, I die. Fifty-fifty.

So I went to Thailand. The frontier in Thailand and Cambodia that time, bombing and fighting to each other. People—
we went across the mountain, we stepped on the mine, killed so
many people again. And who is go back, they gonna shoot us.
So. Very, very hard.

I escape to Thailand, I volunteer to be the monk in the
refugee camp. Finally, I get help from Catholic Charities. I
think they understand Buddhism, they send me to build first
Buddhist temple in Washington, D.C. And later, I was sent to
Minnesota, to build another temple in Farmington.

I came to United States, work hard. It's very hard time for
me. I am so lucky than other people: they were killed in Vietnam or Cambodia, when they come to this country they have
cancer, they already die. I am still lucky. But often, I don't have
much fun for my life.

For five years, we don't have any relationship. Cambodia
don't allow anything. After five years, we have telephone, post
office, embassy there. My wife and I started to write letters. We
started to call.

At that time, they want me to go back. But Farmington no
have any monk. I am alone over there to build the temple. So I
build the temple. I cannot go and leave the society empty. So
I have to stay. I said cannot go now. Maybe later.

The problem is for the security. Here, the law, control,
stronger than over there. There, we don't know who is who.
We still don't know who is who gonna kill you.

My son was kidnapped six years ago. And right now, I have
only my daughter still living in Cambodia. I live far away from
them, so I do the best I can.

My wife, you can say, she become wealthy. Compare to this country, she is just okay. But for there, wealthy. She has another guy can help her, drive her to where she wants to go, like chauffeur for her. That she can live a good life now. She has one guy. He helps her, but they not married. She never wants to get married again.

But all my life, I devote to my kids. And especially you have kids, and they kidnap your kids, you can do nothing. That is so painful, so hurt. That is sometimes I . . . I get mad. Sometimes I get angry. I don't know what I angry with whom? I don't know. Sometimes I am angry with myself: Why I am come to this country? My family over there, my parents over there. Come here for what? Just working for buy food to eat, etc. Just have a broken car—see, like that? Sometimes I get confused too.

I can go back. But it look like too late to go back. I have a American citizen, so I can go. But if I live over there, I have nothing, empty hands. You know, I never take any money from the society. I've been the monk. The money offered to me, I put back. I bought that land, build the temple. So I have nothing.

I've been in the hospital for three times. I never told anybody. I don't want to bother anybody. I get to hospital the third time, before they surgery me, they need somebody to sign. I have nobody to sign. Finally, I said, "Yes, I call one friend. She working here at the hospital."

"Oh, you have friend working here?"

"Yes."

"What is the name?"

Okay, I said, "Channy." I know her family for many, many

years. Twenty-five years. Her mom and her support to build the temple in Minnesota, so we know each other quite well.

So they called Channy. Channy came. I said I been in hospital, they want to surgery me, they want someone to sign. She say okay. I ask, "Can I sign a check for five thousand dollars for you to keep? If I die, you make my funeral." I signed the check for five thousand dollars, and this and that, and she left.

I came to see her on the Thanksgiving Day. She invited me to have dinner. After dinner, we went to movie. My whole life, first time I see movie. (*laughs*) But I don't know. I don't pay my attention to the movie.

Channy already divorced. So look like we can trust each other, can help each other. We get involved. So even I learn about Buddhism, but I am human being, I am not a Buddha. I do the best I can. I said yes. We get involve from that Thanksgiving Day. We can go back and forth, back and forth until today. Every day, four years.

With Channy, she is good. Because she supports me and I support her. We know each other quite well. We live together. Channy introduce me like "my husband." It's okay, because usually in United States, live together they can be wife and husband. But in my culture is different.

You see, when you have kids, you cut half for your kids: your time, your pleasure, whatever you get. So for me, I cannot forget my daughter and son. My feeling is for my kids. It's strong in my kids. Even my wife. I still have feelings because she is the first woman I have in my life.

My wife she do whatever she wants. She even helps me and Channy. When I went there with Channy, she welcome us very well. She spent a lot of money for us over there. We have two cars, then we went to anywhere. Stayed in her house. They spend everything.

Channy like my best friend, okay? We tell everything, we don't hide anything. I don't want anything problem for her, and she don't want problem for me. But doesn't mean responsibility for everything. She has her own kids. They are grow up. If I have kids with her it's different. Yes, we are love each other. But we are not responsible, like wife and husband.

The difference is the circumstances. Different time now. Different. For me, here like the port. The ship go to the port. Okay? My first wife, she keeps my kids; she's my home port. And now, the port is different. Just borrow the port to park. For temporary.

I still have feelings because the first time of my life I know a woman. And the bad situation and the poor time, we had no pleasure, no fun. We work for to survive. I still feelings for that.

I thinking about the safety for my first wife. But for the love with her? No. Not much. I thinking about the security for her. I don't want to jeopardize her life over there. The guy there helps her. So I let her free, whatever, I let my mind free too. So we understand each other.

We are still friends. She really wants me to go there. But I don't want to go over there. Channy here. Make Channy unhappy. So no, no useful. I gonna live how many years in this world? I don't want to make trouble for people. Real love means share and care.

The love connects people together, they don't say much, they connect each other. That's true love. If people understand the world of love, that bring more happiness, bring more peaceful, bring more joyful.

But in one thousand and one million, not easy to find. Like heaven. Everybody hopes to go to heaven. But really, heaven is hard to go. Even from here to Washington, D.C., very difficult! Two hundred dollars to get Washington, D.C. Very hard. So imagine how hard to go to heaven!

Five Years to Ten Years

*"We have this sweet, cuddly, amazing, understanding love.
But it's not hot."*

I saw Adam briefly before we met. He was doing his PhD at Cambridge and was on a break from one of his classes. I said hello to somebody that was sitting with him. Adam was wearing these jean culottes, like jean shorts, and this thing flashed through my head: I really couldn't fuck that guy. I could not have sex with a guy who wore jean culottes.

I was working at the time for a company in London doing British college test prep for high school kids applying to U.S. colleges. I was the boss lady, the executive director. It was a lot of responsibility—kind of a lonely job. I never got asked out; the staff would party and I wouldn't be included. Or people would bullshit me with their PhD, trying to chat me up. It was just kind of a bummer.

So later we're in this staff meeting, and we've got overall two hundred–plus people on staff, and the owner of the company, Jim, was presenting. I was vaguely aware that Adam was there. The boss guy was talking about grade sheets, and I made an announcement. I said, "This year we're gonna get the grade sheets done a week before the kids leave for the summer, which has always been Jim's biggest fantasy." (*laughs*) And I said, "It's my job to fulfill Jim's fantasy."

And Adam says, "Yeahhh? That's what we hear about you!" The whole room fucking fell down laughing. I was shocked. Like, "Who is this guy?!" He had kind of a devilish thing going on. He seemed really brave and direct and very sexy.

So we went to the drinks reception afterward and he was circling me like a shark. We were having this conversation and he wouldn't let anyone get to me. We went to the pub, and as we're all walking home, Adam and I kind of coupled off and then we purposefully fell behind. We sort of ducked into this alleyway and Adam said, "Do you want to get another drink?" We were really drunk. I was like, "Yeah! Sure!" It felt so straightforward, so sexy, like pulling me by my hair through the streets of Cambridge. He felt very much to me like kind of a caveman: You. Me. Man. Woman.

We went to this bar and we talked and we talked. He's very magnetic in his personality and . . . the tractor beam—I was in the tractor beam! There was something so simple about being in a bar and being appreciated and admired by a cute guy. It was like 1952. We could have been sipping a malted through two straws. That's how it felt. Except we were wasted.

I remember him sort of going in for it—it was a soft, slow kiss. This energy just shot through my body. I remember it so clearly. It was probably the best first kiss I ever had. He walked me back to the college and we kissed again.

On our second date, we went to an Indian restaurant with a deck that went out over the river. We ordered champagne and

we were watching the water and the swans. This friend of his
was in town, Weylin, from Maine. Adam said to me, "Do you
mind if we go and see him?" So we went out and Wey ran
across the street toward Adam, beaming this huge smile, and
they hugged each other in the middle of this busy street, and I
remember Wey being like, "Oh, my God, it's so good to see
you, man. I missed you so much." And I had this overwhelming
feeling of like, "This guy is special, the way people react to him.
He really touches people." That was the second date. I knew I
was falling in love with him.

We slept together on the third date. He literally walked to my
bedroom and he took his clothes off and was like, "Let's do this
thing. Get your clothes off and get in bed." You know, like, "I
am going to fuck you now and then we're going to go to dinner."
It was like a checklist. It was weird but it was neat. Again, it was
all part and parcel of this very straightforward caveman thing.

I was way more experienced than him. It's just something I
think you can feel. I was like doing cartwheels and handstands
and somersaults and showing him all my tricks and he was just
laying there in awe as I was performing. Like I was a sex god-
dess, and he knew he was lucky. Not to be crude: I'm not the
best-looking woman. But I will give you the best blow job
you've ever had.

By date five, I rented a hotel room. We had crazy sex, with
me dancing around, screaming, and riding him like the electric
bull. And then a day or two after that, I left. He was in England.
I was in Chicago. We had a year where we saw each other like
five times. He came out in September. I went out in November.
He came for Christmas for two weeks. He came for Easter for a
few weeks. And we talked on the phone. God, we talked every

single day. Most of the times, we talked like two or three hours a night. It was always really fun.

He was very present, from the first moment. He was like, "You and me." He fed me emotionally. He said all the right things. He did all the right things. He was very loving, very appreciative, very into me, very nurturing. He was so gutsy and treated me so differently from anyone I'd ever met. In my previous relationships, I had all these guys that waffled or sat on the fence. So many men in Chicago, they talk in the abstract: "I will be in love someday" or "I understand the idea of love," but it's implied you're just not it.

I got married young and divorced young to a guy who was very sexually adventurous. And then I had a bunch of terrible misses where I dated guys, and the sex was great, but nothing else was going on. I had a lot of adventures and multiple partners and experimented a lot.

A friend of mine refers to all these guys I've dated as "the meats of the world," because I've always dated all these guys from really different parts of the world—like I dated a Sri Lankan guy and a Filipino guy and a Chinese guy and an Italian guy. I was always into this exotic thing. Typically, I was attracted to guys with dark skin, dark hair. Although the guy I went out with right before Adam was like whitey-white. He was muscular and six feet, very blond and built, very chiseled and pretty, like a cold Greek statue.

I think that I was just really ready for Adam. I mean, a lot of people fixate on the physical—"he has to be tall" or "he has to be this or that." Physically, Adam's not anyone's description of good-looking. Like five seven, my height. Stocky, like a barrel with legs. He's one of those guys you look at and think, "He will be fat when he's older. And have thinning hair." I know that's terrible to say, but he will.

But as a person, he just fit me so well. Even from the first date or second date, it was very much like, "This is a guy I could marry. This is a guy I could build a long life with. This is a guy who's like stable and sure and smart and dynamic and so into me."

The thing is, I wanted it to work with Adam. He felt the same way about me. It was that instant feeling that somebody recognizes who you are and how great you are. It was that reciprocal feeling of you're just sure that that person is the one. They fit in your life. We had that same vibe. It just clicked.

He's an academic. He has a blue-chip PhD from Cambridge. He's really, really brilliant. He got the perfect job in Chicago. It took him, like, two seconds. His intelligence is sexy, for sure. He's very proud of his brain and very proud of what he's accomplished, but he has a lot of humility about it. And I think that's a really lovable quality. And yet he's not the least bit insecure, which is interesting.

But his lack of athleticism—he never exercises—it shows in bed. He's kind of a lazy lover, just lay there and ride me, that kind of thing. It's interesting, because it's what I love about him—that very simple straightforwardness. But he has it in bed as well. Like missionary is good enough, interesting enough.

When I talk about him not being the greatest in bed, Adam has no idea, like no concept. He thinks he's a fucking stud. Do you know what I mean? He thinks he's just the greatest thing ever. And that's neat. I love that and I would never take that away, like I would never ever. It's so great for him to not have self-awareness about that. It's really refreshing.

But for me, it just doesn't work. You cannot be a lazy lover for five years. After feeling like I was doing all the work, it kind of just got boring. It's not like a huge crisis in your face, like somebody's crying about not getting sex. I always knew the physical attraction wasn't the main thing. But we've just gotten into a routine of not doing it. And I think that's a bit of where we're at now.

Right before we got married, like two days before we got married, all these exes randomly got in touch with me, and it was really weird. I don't know what the hell was going on, but people I hadn't talked to in years were calling me. And not just one guy, three or four different guys, like this guy that I had this really hot sex with in Copenhagen.

It felt like this huge message from the universe that all these guys that I had hot sex with were suddenly calling me, and I was about to marry a guy that I wasn't having hot sex with. This one guy said something that just set me off. He was talking about how he had been dating this girl for about a year, and he's like, "Every time I see her, I just want to rip her clothes off. I just want to fuck her." And I was just like, "Holy shit. I do not feel that way about Adam." And at that moment, I was like, "Shit, am I okay with that?" I called my girlfriend and had a nervous breakdown. And she said, "You do not have to marry him. It's okay not to go through with it."

And my instant reaction was, "What the fuck are you talking about? Of course I'm going to marry him! He's the greatest thing ever!" And it put into focus what I love about him. He's engaged. There's that feeling of being loved and being taken care of. When he's listening to me, he's really listening with his whole being. It's really genuine. We have this sweet, cuddly, amazing, understanding love. But it's not hot. It's not burning hot. And it was the understanding that in marrying him, I was giving that up. Do you know what I mean? It will not be hot.

The fact of our sex life not being hot isn't actually all Adam. Part of it is me. Part of it is I've had a lot of adventures that no one could match up to. Unfortunately, I think when you have a lot of sex and you have a lot of different and dirty and experimental and wild experiences and all that stuff, it's a bit of a slippery slope. It's like when guys watch a lot of porn, and then they want every girl to be like a porn star in bed. When there's a lot of sex with so many people, I think your brain gets formed in a different way about what's sexy. And in marriage and in life, you just can't have like swinging-from-the-chandelier sex every day.

So what keeps us together basically is this feeling that even if he's not like this athletic dynamo, there is an overwhelming feeling of "I will never find anyone like this." I feel that no matter what happens in our relationship, physically or whatever the challenges are, I will not let go of how special he is. I think I'm smart enough to know or had enough experience to know that he is just like a rare bird. It's just so hard to find that person.

When I reflect on what's great about the relationship, it really is in the details, the small bits. Like when I go up to his study, which is sacred ground—we call it the clubhouse—when I walk in, even now, today, five or six years after we've met, everything for him stops. You know what I mean? I'm not talking about a party, where I'm wearing a dress, but when we're at home and I walk into a room. Because we both work at the

house, so we're together every single day of our lives. And when
I walk upstairs into his study—even though his work is everything to him—he stops and turns his chair and looks at me, and
I'm the only thing that exists in that moment. He takes me in
and he just like stops dead, with that beaming smile. I can see it
in my mind so well. And he'll be like, "Peachy, how are you?"

He's very much a morning person. And I'm not. He always
wakes up before me. And when I open my eyes, there's this
beaming face looking at me. Adam has these very pretty baby
blues, very crinkly and sparkly. He looks like he's Chinese or
something. And when I open my eyes, he always says, "I want
you. I can't wait for you to wake up so I can play with you."
He's so excited that we're having a day together. He just can't
wait for me to wake up and be with him.

BRAD KELLUM, AGE 36

CLAYMONT, DELAWARE

"My feeling is: God created the orgasm. How cool is that?"

In high school, I was dating a girl who I found really pretty. We became sexually active—not having sex, just doing the things that high school students do.

The relationship was primarily based on a physical connection with very little emotional depth to it. I sort of maybe talked myself into the fact that I thought she was more interesting than maybe I really did at that time. I know I fought back and forth: "We don't really connect. I'm attracted to her physically, but the inner part of her is not so interesting to me."

I grew up in a home where premarital sex, in any form, was frowned upon. So there were times when I thought, "This isn't fair to her." What we were doing was going beyond my convictions. And yet I was a red-blooded guy, and part of me wanted what I wanted, and screw the convictions, you know?

I began to develop a guilty conscience. Like, one time we were messing around, and I suddenly just totally lost interest. I couldn't do it. And I knew why—it's because while I was enjoying these wonderful feelings, I was suffering from this terrible guilt.

I wanted to be better than that, I guess. When we split up, I decided that I would at least *try* (*laughs*) to live to my highest ideals and not treat women as sex objects.

I went to college at Liberty University, which is the brainchild of Jerry Falwell, with a fundamental, evangelical type of environment. My commitment to love at that time became very idealistic. With my girlfriends, I would pretty much stick with just kissing. There was a sense of nobility about not groping a woman, the idea that chivalry is still alive. I looked at it as a sort of knighthood.

It's a lofty standard and, some would say, unrealistic or repressed, but there was something attractive about it that was almost as powerful as the attraction I had in the other direction.

If you're being realistic and practical about love, love begins as a very primal desire. And I believe that that's God's idea. So, sex is good. My feeling is: God created the orgasm. How cool is that? (*laughs*) I think we're created to be naturally promiscuous. You know, I am made to find attractive every pretty woman I see.

But sex is not just a physical experience. It's a spiritual experience. People think of sex as just nerve endings and body parts, and it's so much more than that. It's a connection between two human beings on a heart level.

I believe it's what God intended for us, this pleasurable experience that people share, that connects us and entwines us, you know, as we penetrate, as we go down deep, you know. I open myself up to you and I go into you, and you go into me and we become one. *We become one.* So literally, every time you sleep with someone, you give them a little piece of yourself. Every bed you have occupied, you have left yourself in it. And you cannot recover that part of you once you get out.

So for this reason—so that we can be whole—sex is reserved for marriage. That's the Christian ideal. And part of maturity, and part of love, is learning to show self-restraint and direct these desires toward whoever we're married to.

In high school, I never felt necessarily that the desires were wrong so much as the context in which I wanted to fulfill them. Because of my value system as a follower of Christ, I had to wait for marriage to make a physical, sexual connection with a woman. So for me, marriage was very much a practical release. You know, I needed that marital commitment to be able to fulfill my sexual fantasies, to be honest with you.

Of course, I was also raised to believe that relationships have to transcend the simple goal of me just meeting my needs. So that sexual aspect of love is just one facet that had to come along with the other sides—like sacrifice and platonic servanthood.

When I first met my wife, Nicole, we had just been hired by an organization called World Help, a nonprofit agency that does everything from distributing food to the poor to helping create work. My friends who also worked there said, "Brad, you're going to love this girl," because somehow, they saw this connection.

When we met, my first thought was, "Wow, she's really pretty." Her beauty did something inside of me, and that was erotic. It was sexual. I thought she was attractive, but I also thought she seemed shallow and a little immature for me.

I was not totally impressed and neither was she. (*laughs*) I was wearing a long-sleeve flannel shirt and gold corduroy pants, and she basically summed me up as, "What a nerd." You know, the way I handled myself was too serious.

Yet through working with her, something clicked with us, and I started feeling different feelings for her. As a matter of fact, I came to a place where I wanted to see if she was the kind of person I could give my love to in marriage.

By now, I guess, I knew enough about love to realize the unsustainability of just *feeling* love, or *feeling* attraction. You've got to *think* about it as well. Because it takes more than love to keep a relationship sustained. There are practical concerns when you join your life to another person, like money, children, job responsibilities. It takes a balance to navigate things, and that doesn't really have to do with love as much as it has to do with that person's character and life management skills.

With Nicole, my very first feeling for her was physical attraction. You know, when I first saw her, my first thought was not, "Wow, you know, look at her sense of responsibility!" (*laughs*) I felt that I needed to try to be objective about my feelings. And this was definitely something I'd had a lot of trouble with in the past.

When I was in college, I was diagnosed with this thing called OCD, obsessive-compulsive disorder. It's like, people who wash their hands one hundred times a day because they never can quite get the feeling that they're clean enough. It's a biochemical imbalance; the person's brain is not processing serotonin correctly. You have these repetitious behaviors that drive a guy or a gal nuts.

I didn't have the hand-washing thing, but I did have troubling, erratic thoughts, and problems with focusing and settling down. It had definitely wreaked havoc in my relationships and my ability to love. So what I was really looking for were ways to kind of be systematic about my feelings and overcome my own internal, unsteady gauges.

A friend of mine at that time, he said, "Brad, you're interested in this girl. You know that you're physically attracted to her. Why don't you try this experiment? Watch her for six months and see what her character is like."

So I did that. For about six months, I watched her. I watched things like her work habits. I saw the best of Nicole and the worst of Nicole. I saw her in contexts where she was hot, she was tired, she was stressed. And I began to see her as not shallow and immature, but actually a lot more mature in many areas than I was. She was a leader. She was very capable.

And then, after I'd known her for about a year, we took a trip to India with this nonprofit organization. She and I were working on the same team. One day, four or five of us were sitting around a small table, trying to cool off on our break. We were playing a card game, and we were sitting next to each other.

All of a sudden, she moved her leg under the table and touched mine and looked at me and started rubbing my leg. We'd never had this kind of interaction before, and I liked it a lot. But I didn't know how to react.

There had never really been that kind of flirtatiousness, and then all of a sudden it was there. And so I started following that feeling.

I believe that love is the collision of your sexual attraction to another person, which brings you toward them, and your experience of them, which causes you to choose to bind yourself to them. So beginning with that sexual attraction, and then augmented by our experiences together, and my reflections on them, love had grown like a line around my heart and entwined it.

While I had been watching her, asking myself, "Can I live with these traits or can't I?" at a certain point it had suddenly become, "I can't live without her."

On the plane home from India, I tried to kiss her, and she wouldn't let me. You know how planes are at night. It's sleepy, the lights are down, and so I moved from my seat to sit beside her. And at some point my arm was touching her arm, and I was having this mental debate: "Do I hold her hand? Or don't I? This feels nice . . . Brad, what the heck are you doing?! Once you start, then it's going to trip the domino!"

But once I held her hand, I began to get those butterfly feelings. I couldn't put it into words. All I could say is it's a feeling I'd never felt before: It's strong, it's mysterious, but it's real and it's there. It was like being lovestruck, and after I was lovestruck, it never left me.

Later, she had fallen asleep, and her head was angled toward me, and I went for the lips and she didn't go for it. And she was kind of like, "Why did you do that?" It wasn't a rejection; it felt like she was saying, "I'm going to crack the door open, but I'm not going to let you in quite yet."

From then on, I was like a lion pursuing his prey. I couldn't get her out of my mind.

I knew at that point that she was interested and attracted and all that. But the problem was I was more into her than she was into me. She wasn't sure that she wanted to commit to me. She was also attracted to other guys we were working with. For her, there had to be a dance about it, you know. It was my role as a man to pursue her, and it was a chase. That was an important aspect of the guy she'd end up choosing.

Now, it's not my belief that love is either there or it isn't. I think love is something that can be developed and cultivated. And this goes to what I call being cognitive about emotions. There's a science to love. (*laughs*) So I went out and got a book called *Get Anyone to Do Anything*. And I figured out how to do it. It was systematic. It was strategic.

I read the section on attractiveness, and I started doing things like working out with her. Very casually, I would say, "Hey, let's go work out," you know. We would jog together. The theory is that exercising together releases endorphins.

One of the main things I learned was that I needed to hold back. Because to tell the other person how you feel too early on is dangerous. Suffocating them with these wonderful feelings you have about them, and pouring it out on them and drowning them—they feel like, "Whoa, whoa, back up. This is too early, too fast." If I'd laid it all out there, it would have peaked too early. So I learned a little bit about the wisdom of hiding love and knowing when the right time is.

Another suggestion in the book was to strategically make yourself unavailable to increase desire. So there were times when I felt like, you do love her, but you got to be cool here, and you have to project confidence. I'm not this groveling guy, and you're not the center of my emotional world. I can have fun when we're not together. I'm a stable, solid person, and I have goals and dreams and ambitions and that's where I'm headed. If you would like to go there with me, I'd love it, but if not, then

I'm still going to go where I want to go. And that purposeful-
ness I think attracted her, and I think she wanted that.

The truth was, though, that I wasn't an entirely stable, solid
person, because of my OCD. I would be with her, but then I
would think of someone else. I didn't know what that meant.
Was it just OCD? Or was there some deeper meaning? The
OCD made everything a lot worse. There were points where I
had doubts.

I was trying to sort through these very intense emotions. I
was twenty-six or twenty-seven when we really started dating,
and I was really ready in a big way for our physical relationship,
and for me, it was like, okay are you just enjoying this? Or do
you love this woman?

Most people don't delve this deeply into love. They really
have not formed clear ideas about love, what love is, what will
love mean to them or for them, what will love require of them
in a relationship. They just sort of do what feels right. They
move in the moment.

But I've always been very interested in what makes love sus-
tainable. I'm very interested in the permanency of love. You
know the saying, "It's better to have loved and lost than never to
have loved at all." My feeling is, "It's better to have loved and
lost than to have loved and have that love break apart." Because
what do you give someone when you love them? You give
them you. There's this intermingling and interweaving of two
hearts, and when you take a knife and slice that in the middle,
you get to a point where it's going to do irreparable damage.

So I wanted to be very sure of our love.

But Nicole and I had a very up-and-down relationship—we
broke up and got back together about six times. You know,

you're going with someone, you're not going with someone, we were a thing, we weren't a thing.

I think her uncertainty was in response to my uncertainty. I think she needed me to be more emotionally stable. (*laughs*) I'd put all this effort into trying to be cognitive and to use logic, but the emotion and the feeling were really ruling the situation for me.

And at one point, I just gave up. I finally felt . . . you know, I'm giving all of this emotional energy, and it's just not going anywhere and so I just decided enough is enough. This is crazy. I was finished. I was truly done with the relationship. I'd written it off.

And it was Nicole who took the step that finally led us toward being in a committed relationship. Like I said, she's a leader! And more mature than I was. (*laughs*) She opened her heart, and she risked rejection and told me how she felt. She said, "I thought things through and I really care about you and I want us to be together. I think this could be wonderful."

I felt her sincerity. And the moment we began to date with the understanding that this was heading toward marriage, it worked.

We just celebrated our sixth anniversary last June. We think that Nicole got pregnant with Ethan on our honeymoon. I think she would have preferred a little longer, but when you're hittin' it two or three times a day, you know what I'm saying? You just can't help it.

Our family is growing fairly fast. We have three children. I pastor now at the Bible Baptist Church, in Wilmington. I've been pastoring here for about five years.

Are we going to make it? I do ask myself that question

sometimes. And yes, we're going to make it. We both have the same vision of marriage. We're both looking at the same map. It's something that is not perfect but is permanent.

And sometimes, there's a tremendous rush of love and warm feelings for one another. She's a wife, she's a mother, she's a finance secretary, she's a pastor's wife, she's a worship leader, and I watch her in these roles and my respect for her keeps growing, and that makes me love her more and that's pretty cool, so it's a good place to be.

Now, I'm not saying that I have written the last word on how to love, how to court a person, and how to get married. No, no, not at all. But because I'm a pastor, I listen to couples sharing their frustrations as well as their good experiences, and I've realized how fragile love is. You've got to protect love. Just feeling love is unsustainable. You've got to think about love as well. Because it's more than a feeling. It's also a choice.

JENNY GATLIN, AGE 20

FORT LAUDERDALE, FLORIDA

"I'd be up for doing things like climbing and biking and skydiving. And he'd be more like, 'Hell, no! I don't want to do that!' "

I live in Fort Lauderdale, born and raised. My mom and dad came down from Indiana when they were eighteen, and they had me quite a few years later. My dad died when I was eight, in a motorcycle accident, so that left just me and my mom, the two of us, together. It was a big deal, but it wasn't a horrible, traumatic thing that affected me for the rest of my life. Not life changing. I'm not emotional about it now when I think about it.

Ricky asked me out officially at a school dance. I was in seventh grade and he was in eighth grade. He was something new compared to the boys I had hung out with previously. He went to church and his mom was very into the church life—going to church outside of school and on the weekends.

When we were younger, it was more about the fun toys to play with—the four-wheelers and the airboats and the buggies. We had a lot of fun together. Now it's become more of a life partner kind of thing. We know that we could easily spend the rest of our life together. I definitely feel like we're already married. Family, friends—everybody always jokes about us as the married couple.

Ricky's twenty-one and I'm twenty now. I go to our local community college. It's the same college that Ricky went to for an emergency medical technician degree. That was his first step in becoming a firefighter. I'm going for elementary education. I would have preferred to go away to college and sleep with a bunch of guys, party, drink, all that crazy stuff you shouldn't do but you do anyways because you're a college student.

I skipped a lot of things in life. I did cheerleading and gymnastics in middle school, which were major loves of mine. But I gave them up because I wanted to spend time with him. I had always pictured my high school years as head cheerleader, prom queen, and getting asked out to prom in some special way. Prom was a really big letdown. I went without him. He didn't want to go.

I'm the wild girl. I'm the one that wasn't tamed. He's really hardheaded. I guess he holds me down a little bit. We balance each other out. I liven up his life, he calms mine down a little bit. I mean, we make each other better people

If it wasn't for him, I wouldn't have a lot of the goals and morals that I have today. I'd be this insane, crazy person that would be arrested all the time and caught on *Girls Gone Wild*. And he would be this homebody that worked on his airboat all the time, and as far as going out and having fun, oh, no way. He'd rather be around his little select group of friends and never meet a new person in the world.

I'm more up for rolling with the wind. Like, if we go to the beach, I'm the one who's going to do something crazy like get into a conversation with another couple at the bar. Afterward, he's glad. And there's occasional nights where he does come out and, you know, we have fun together. He enjoys it once he's out. But he's not open-minded to doing new things. Like, I'd be up for doing things like climbing and biking and skydiving. And he'd be more like, "Hell, no! I don't want to do that!"

After high school, it was kind of assumed that I would go live with Ricky at his parents' house because I was there every other night anyways, and we'd been dating for years by then. They own an automotive supply company, and I was working full time for them. Forty hours a week during the day and I was going to school full time at night. So I moved my stuff to his parents' house.

We're still living there, which has been causing a lot of hard feelings between us. I hate living in his parents' house and feeling that I owe them something. I never feel at home. And I feel like I'm obligated, you know, if there's a dish in the sink, that I should be doing it, and if the house is dirty, I feel like I should probably be cleaning. So there has been bickering and tedious arguments.

When I started college, I wanted me and Ricky to move, and he absolutely, positively was not having it. He could live at home for free. Why would he pay money? He's spoiled rotten. His mom would bend over backward to do anything for him, total like baby forever. So why would he want to move away from that?

He thinks the woman should do all the womanly duties. If I could change him, I would make him more appreciative of the things that I do for him—the dishes, the laundry, putting his checks in the bank every week, and cleaning his truck. I would like him to acknowledge it as "thank you" as opposed to "that's your job." I don't know if I want to be his mom and be that Southern woman who does all the chores.

I work all day, and if he works all day, what makes it so different that I should have to come home and do his laundry and his dinner and clean his house and, you know, he gets to go play with his airboat? I tell him, "This is a man duty. Take out your trash."

After fighting with him for fifteen minutes, he'll say, "Okay, well, I'll take out the trash, but you have to put a bag in."

"Well, when I do laundry, do you fold it? Do you put it away? No. So just do it."

Ricky's a manly man. He stands for everything redneck and Southern. He doesn't like holding hands and hugging and kissing in public at all. He doesn't like to talk about things that make him upset. He keeps his composure. I like to think that I can read him completely and know why he does what he does. As far as him understanding me, absolutely not. He doesn't get that when I'm mean to him, it's because I'm upset and I want him to come talk to me. I'm more of the needy one. I need attention. I guess that's sad. I don't know.

He has this tough-guy status and has always pushed like he didn't want kids. I've always had a life plan to have kids by the time I'm twenty-five. I want to be young enough that when my kids are gone, I'd still be able to enjoy my life. It really upsets me because that's really the only thing in my whole life that I've ever dreamed about

I grew up with my mom, and my mom worked all of the time to take care of me and her, so I never had that family thing.

He has had, his whole life, a big family and so it doesn't mean as much to him as it does for me. We've had quite a few nights with me crying myself to sleep. We have come to an understanding not to full-out talk about it. But I throw little comments here and there. I want a boy, and so he has said, "Well, if I knew it was going to be a boy, then I would definitely have kids."

When he does something that upsets me and he knows that I'm upset—I don't know how to describe to you about getting feelings out of this boy. It's not an easy task to get any emotion or feeling out of him. But he'll write me letters. And they're normally really, really corny and he's got awful handwriting and he draws awful little hearts and uses nicknames for us, and he'll draw a picture of our "one day" family at the bottom of the letter. There's always a little house and little stick figures of me and him and dogs and a kid and his airboat is in every picture. I think it's hysterical that he has to add his airboat into this family picture. (*laughs*) I absolutely adore it. I love it. That's his way of letting me know that he does think about it; he just doesn't want to talk about it or he feels uncomfortable or whatever.

We both say, "I love you," every day, all day. When we hang up the phone, we make a conscious effort to say, "I love you." If we forget to say it at night, if he falls asleep and doesn't get to say, "I love you," I'll kiss him on his back and whisper in his ear, "I love you." It just gives you peace of mind that you told him, because God forbid you didn't wake up in the morning.

The actual meaningful "I love you's"—you know, looking deep into each other's eyes, "I really love you and I care about you"—normally happen after a fight. You're working it out and crying and holding each other, and those are normally when the true, sincere "I love you's" come out. The other ones are just the reminders.

I still find him attractive. As long as we're good, I see him as loving and caring, which makes him physically and emotionally attractive as well. He's good about the whole back-rub thing— definitely. If I need a massage or I'm tired or grumpy, he's all about tickling my back, which he hates to do but he knows I love. He's very open about sex. He's into definitely doing what- ever that I need. We're both equally giving and more so at other times. Our sex life, I'd say, is definitely the best part of us—sad but true.

We have never, like, been on a vacation just the two of us. I don't know what we would do if we did. He's still into hanging out with his friends, and we don't go and do things by ourself. I've kind of always had this feeling like we might get bored of each other, like we've never really spent time just the two of us together.

I'm hoping with everything inside me that he will eventually mature into being able to meet my needs and do what it takes to make me happy. I hope that with time, I can fully understand what he wants and expects out of me. I think there's got to be something more out there, but that's with everything in life: I could have the best of the best, and in the back of my head, I'd still think there might be something better.

I have thought about leaving him, about moving out, trying out a new lifestyle. But do I think that it would last? If we broke up, it could cause a whole bunch of problems, putting his cousin and his aunts in a position to choose sides. I'd maybe even lose my job over it. It would not be good. And of course, we would have the whole jealousy thing, seeing each other in public with another guy or another girl. Whether I broke up with him or he broke up with me, we would be completely, insanely jealous. No. I've had a ton of options to leave Ricky. Since I feel like he's not willing to give me the attention I deserve, I'm willing to get it from other people. I've had relationships with other people—not sexual but just talking, meeting other people, getting to know other people. I've gone out for dinner a couple of times. Nothing too serious, but serious enough where I wonder if it might turn into something more.

There has been a couple of times where I thought I might have found somebody. It's great for a couple of months and I love it. But none of them have ever stuck. I guess that's got to mean something. With other people, things eventually just stop, the fun stops. You know, you figure everything out about each other. Eventually you just say, "Okay, I know everything about you. Now what?" I don't know if the fun stops or I get tired of the secret thing or if I feel like I'm betraying Ricky in some way, but I know if he was talking with some other girl that I would be devastated.

The only reason that I know that I still love him is just that there's this feeling. It's not something that you can describe, but it's just this feeling that I don't have for anybody else. I'm assuming that that feeling is love. I mean, with Ricky, it doesn't go away and it hasn't gone away and I can be the maddest of mad at him and say that I want to leave him forever and there's still always . . . I can't think of what kind of awful thing that he could do to make that feeling go away.

Our biggest struggle right now, we're currently arguing because . . . it's just a mixture of a lot of things, but like I said,

I've talked to other people and thought, "Oh, this might go further. If I weren't dating someone, I'd like to hook up with this person."

I think about it all of the time. (*laughs*) My conscience is killing me, because my brain is going crazy about this stuff probably 90 percent of the time. (*laughs*) I think about it all day, every day. Maybe that's just recently. It hasn't always been that way. But my brain has been fried about it lately.

If I leave him, well, yeah, I can find boyfriends. Absolutely. But there's no guarantee of anything going further. And you don't get younger; you only get older. And then you think of, well, what's the common age that people get married? Or should get married? I don't know. I'm so scrambled about the whole thing that it's almost easier to be like, "Why the hell are you making such a big deal about it? Just let it be. It is what it is and that's it. If it works out, it does."

We go through these months where I'm stressed and he's stressed and we're just not getting along, but it always ends up working its way out. I'll threaten, "Maybe we shouldn't be together. Maybe we need time apart." And he looks at me like, "You're so stupid. You say this all the time, and it never happens, and we never want it."

Eventually it all mellows out and it goes back to happy-dandy. And where do I think it will land us in the future? Together, married, forever and ever. (*laughs*)

KATHY BARRETT, AGE 72

RUTLAND, VERMONT

"People say after your spouse dies, you will get angry at them.
I never got angry at Bob."

I was a very lively person. Very into a lot of things. Very much
into people. I had traveled a little bit—taught a year in Alaska
and two years in Germany. Third grade. Then I came back to
Vermont, 'cause I love skiing and my family lives here. I got
really serious about my teaching and went to the University of
Vermont to get my master's. At the same time, I was active in
our ski club and all the social events.

When I was in Europe I must have fallen in love at least
twenty times. But what it was, it was good-time love. When
you're younger you want a good-time guy who's just going to
be lots of laughs. And there's a lot to be said about that. But I
would not have thought of marrying them.

It was in 1970, I was thirty-four. I went to a party in Manchester, Connecticut. And at this party I met Bob Barrett. He
was working in Hartford. We hit it off. And then at the end of
the party, he invited himself to go skiing. He used to say that I
invited him, but whatever.

A couple weeks later, my friend invited me down to Connecticut, and Bob said he'd like to go out the next time I came down. We went out. This was the first time he had been with me alone, and he said, "What will we have to talk about?" Believe me, we did not have to worry there at all.

A couple weekends later, he finally ends up coming to Vermont to ski. He was a very natural athlete. Good golfer, tennis player, and all that, but this was a new sport to him. And I admired the way he went at it. He really went at it big-time.

If Bob and I would have met earlier, I don't think we would have clicked. He would have been too stable for me. Too solid. But as you get older, you're looking for different values. I could see in him what I would want for a future. I thought of him being somebody you would marry, somebody to have children with.

He really zeroed in on the person he was with. He wasn't worried about anyone else in the room. He was a really wonderful listener. He would listen for what wasn't said, not always for what was said. There was a kindness about him—not just a kindness for me, but a kindness for the people around him.

I think he was so in tune to people because he had been a priest. He went from high school to the seminary, the seminary to Rome, Rome to Africa, Africa to Washington.

Bob was very bright. In Rome he got two or three master's degrees. They sent him to Ghana, where he taught black missionaries that were going to become priests. He did that for three years, then came back to Washington. That's when he knew that it just wasn't for him. He left in good faith, and when I met him, he was already a civilian, on a leave of absence, getting his dispensation from Rome.

He had been very devoted to his calling. He loved it. But getting married and having children was important to him. That role—that celibacy role—was not for him.

Within about, oh, six to seven months, he proposed to me. And in June of '72, we got married.

We had a lovely home in Connecticut, a house we had built in Granby. I got a job as a reading consultant working with two different schools. And Bob was working for United Technology.

After a year and a half, I had Michelle. About a year later I had Eileen. If I was married younger I probably would have had ten kids. Maybe not ten, but (*laughs*) family was important on both sides of the aisle. He's from a family of four and I'm from a family of five. And he was very good to his little girls. Very good.

On most major issues, we thought alike, and if it was minor issues, we didn't bother arguing. We were both Roman Catholic, we believed in the tenets of our faith. I really think there's a spiritual side to love. I do.

Neither of us were extravagant spenders. We loved our home, our family, our extended family. We believed in being good to people. We loved to travel, go to the beach, to the ocean. To exercise. We both liked a good meal. (*laughs*)

Life was treating us well. The girls had a lot of little friends in the neighborhood, and Bob and I made quite a few friends too. We had one neighbor that was going through a very bad divorce. Bob would be down there to see what he could do to help. People would often come to him for advice. He was well liked and he was a very solid guy.

He was my best friend. By far. If something was bothering me, he wouldn't ask about it. He would wait for me to come up to him and say it. I thought that was wonderful. It's not that it

would go on for a year and a day, but if something was bothering you, he would want you to be able to speak about it. His
role as a priest played a big part in what I benefited from, what
my daughters benefited from, and what his friends and employ-
ers benefited from—that wonderful listening ability.

Between us there was always a loving, good evening at the
end of the day. I never had to worry about him looking for
somebody else. I knew it in my bones. Even in a social gathering, in a party, I could have been in another room from him, it
never would bother me.

I do remember this one time. I was at a party. Bob did not
drink, but I was (*laughs*) feeling no pain. One of the neighbors,
a real Irish guy, he was always putting the make on me kind of
thing. So I was kidding around with him, just having fun. That
was it. And we got home that night, Bob didn't speak to me for
about an hour. Not one freakin' word.

He was really royally ticked off. I said, "You have nothing to
worry about. I was just kidding with Murphy." But I tell you, I
never did that again. (*laughs*)

In May of 1980, things took a turn for the worse. I remember Bob waking up and he said he felt like his lung had
collapsed.

So I drove him into the hospital. They diagnosed it as lum-
bar pneumonia. He was out of work for three to four weeks.
And then one night he got a real coughing spell and was spitting
up blood, and we took him back to the hospital. After ten days
of testing, they found out he had cancer of the lungs.

They felt it was localized—it had not spread. He was going
to be operated on. And he went into that hospital with a 90
percent chance of survival. But I always remember the night

before the operation. I brought the girls in, and we all had a little visit. And I said that night to the girls that I didn't know what was going to happen, but I told them, "I don't think Dad will ever be fully better."

At that point they didn't make you come into the hospital ahead of time if someone's going to be operated on. You came after. He was supposed to be operated on at eight in the morning. But that morning, during the time he was being operated on, I got the weirdest feeling. I just got these funny vibes. I can't explain it. I called my friend who was going to watch the girls and said, "Come right over." Other friends drove me to the hospital. The minute we got there, they were paging my name. And I thought, "Oh, no."

He had died of cardiac arrest.

My main concern was telling those two little girls. How was I ever going to explain it? Actually, that was the easiest part. I don't know. It's like God gives you the wisdom how you can do it. And for them how to take it. That's all I can think. They had their days. But they had seen him in the hospital. They had seen him sick. And I had said he might not get better.

My faith helped me through this, I'll tell you that. It definitely did. But once I got the prognosis and knew that that cancer had spread into his heart, then you would never want a person dying that way. So that part definitely helped me.

We ended up staying in Connecticut for three years. That was our home, our neighborhood, our friends. I felt that's what I had to do. You know, you just keep busy—you keep busy for your kids. With your job, with the house.

But my family was in Vermont. My mother was still alive. I had two sisters and a brother up here. So I came back.

At the time, we're into the school year and there weren't any teaching jobs, so I worked in a deli. It was probably the smartest move I ever made, because it made me get out and meet people, see people I had known.

Within a couple of months I got a teaching job. And the girls: One thing you learn about your kids, they adjust very well. They got into school, they made friends. And of course we had a strong family support.

People say after your spouse dies, you will get angry at them. I never got angry at Bob because I knew he was sick. But Bob handled all our finances, and I got angry at the fact that I had to do them—which I didn't understand for shit. (*laughs*) I also gained a lawn to mow. I gained a lot of things to do.

I'm not a heavy drinker, but I did for a period. My neighbor was going through a very, very bad divorce. So we'd be at her house, with five kids running around, and the two of us with a gallon of wine. We were solving all the problems in the world. (*laughs*) That probably went on for maybe six months or so.

Some people say, "Why me?" That never happened to me. I never did turn on God because of this. I never did.

There's such a strong bond of friendship with your spouse if it's really good. That's hard to replace. I have two sisters and a couple girlfriends I can pretty much share with. They share quite a bit with me. But I've never had that type of friendship that I did from him.

I did date a little. There was a man, and his wife had died, and he had five kids, and I did see him several times. But I think he was in overload, and maybe it was too much for him. And I really wasn't interested.

After Bob died, some of the girls invited me to these singles things, where you go to different houses and have drinks and all. Where I lived in Connecticut, they had a lot of them. It'd be maybe fifty people at this house. A few of us were widows or widowers. Most of them were by divorce. I found in most cases it wasn't one divorce—people were there after two or three divorces. I thought, "Ugh. This isn't for me."

I have a very active circuit of friends. I do a lot of volunteer work. I go to Florida in the winter. The things I do don't have to have a male included. Now, if a male popped in on the scene we would all enjoy him. (*laughs*) In Florida, you'll meet a couple guys by the pool and just shoot the breeze. But that's where it stays. That's just the way it is. It's friendly and that's as far as I'd want it to go.

I know what I had for the time I had it. And I don't know if I'll ever have that again. I don't think it's in the cards. But I'm satisfied with my life the way it is. It's perfectly enough.

I feel Bob is watching out for me all the time. I do. He's watching out for me and the girls. I think, "Oh, God, I know he's in heaven."

I'll tell you a cute story. Every Friday, Bob and me and my girls, we would go up to a golf driving range, and Bob would drive a bucket of golf balls. That was his thing.

So a couple weeks after Bob died, I said to the girls, "Let's go play miniature golf."

They didn't know how to hold their clubs, and I wasn't much better. And this was a difficult miniature golf too. When we got to the last hole, if you got a hole in one, you got a free game. And when that happened a little ring goes off, you know.

Okay. I cannot believe this—all three of us got a hole in one! And you don't think that wasn't Bob putting those balls in there? (*laughs*) I do. I said, "Oh, my God." I said, "I know it's not our golfing."

I had something very special for the time I had it. And I feel fortunate to be here. Right now it's absolutely beautiful out. I'm watching the birds. I look out my window, through the icicles at the trees, and we've got these gorgeous evergreens all covered with snow. Big blue sky. I love nature. I think nature's God's doing. I don't have any curtains on my living room windows. I've got big oversized windows. And it's just like bringing all of outdoors, all the nature, into your living room. It's just beautiful.

Ten Years to Twenty Years

REBECCA DANIER, AGE 47

NEW YORK, NEW YORK

"We've managed to keep things sensual. To a fault."

I was thirty-six, thirty-seven, maybe. About ten years ago. I was working in a little English restaurant. I worked eighteen shifts per week, so I spent most of my time there. And it was mostly South American guys in the kitchen; American customers, businessmen, mainly; and English waitresses like me.

The man I was with at the time wanted children. He was an Italian count. I knew I wanted children, but it really stressed me to think of having them with him. Because he was always like lying in a hammock, having a cigarette. He was very charming, but you know . . . I had three jobs and he had no jobs. And I always thought to myself, if I have a child with him, he's going to be the child.

And then we had this new busboy. I remember seeing him one day when he was leaving. I was talking to my friend Carol and I said, "Cool! Who's that?" and she said, "It's the new busboy."

He was Brazilian. He didn't speak a word of English. He was

picked up at the airport by another Brazilian guy, and the next day he started working in our restaurant. He didn't know anything. He had a family in Brazil. Kind of left his wife, really. They kind of split up. He had gone straight from her to working here and sending money back—that was the aim.

We worked together for a long time. He had a really nice aura. Full of kindness, and he was hardworking. I suppose I really fancied him. The first time I saw him, I said to Carol, "I want to have his children." (*laughs*) But I meant it. I had this feeling, "That's the man I'm going to have children with." I wanted to have children with someone I fancied and really liked. And I was in a relationship with someone that I didn't really have a sexual sort of connection with.

He was two years younger than me. We would talk. He would ask me, "Can I have Coke, please?" and I'd say, "Who do you think you are that you can ask for drinks? Get back to work, you dog." (*laughs*) He'd go really red. And I'd say, "I'm kidding. I'm joking."

Most of our conversations were conducted between the Mexican busboy. Hector couldn't speak English, so he would talk to the busboy in Portuguese, which is somewhat similar to Spanish, and the busboy would speak to me in English. Or he'd write me little notes in broken English. And then we arranged to go on a date. We met at the Telephone Bar in the East Village. He was all dressed up for it. He brought flowers.

I remember saying to him, "Do you want some wine?" And he didn't understand that. I was like, "Vino! Vino!" He had this little dictionary, and he took it out and I remember thinking, "How can he not understand 'vino'? My God! He's good-looking, but he's an idiot!" And then we had sex and everything and . . . I really did like him a lot!

And then I went back to France to visit my mom, and so it kind of stopped. I still had the boyfriend. But it was all right, because I'd found out that whenever he went back to Italy, to Rome, he would have little flings. Which I had never done. So I thought, "Okay, I understand now." I understood why it hadn't been right between us. And when I came back from France, Hector and I had another date. Next thing, we were sort of going out. We didn't tell anybody. They caught us kissing in the corner, and then it all kind of came out.

When I said I wanted to have children, he gave me this little lecture about money and drinking and responsibility and not having money and how having children is a big responsibility. I ended up getting pregnant the next month.

We wouldn't have bothered to get married, but we needed to, for him to get legal, to get his papers. So I had to get my citizenship, because I'd never bothered with that yet, then we got married after my daughter was born—Dominique. We got married twice, actually. He found out he hadn't gotten divorced properly in Brazil, so we had to get that annulled, and then we got married again.

My brothers laugh at me. Because the count, just before I left him, he'd always be talking about his big estate. The big estate that he was going to get. Which he did. So my brothers always joke, "Ah, yes, she left a distinguished Italian count for an illegal alien . . . who doesn't speak English and is retarded." (*laughs*) But now they really like him.

I love him. But I sometimes hate him. We fight a lot. Sometimes it's money, because I spend more. I'm really bad with money. And he's more organized. He's a plumber's helper. The money's pretty bad, and he works long hours. Sometimes we argue about me going out with other guys. I have a lot of male friends. They were friends I met before him. And it's like this very Latin thing—who you can see and can't see. He won't speak to me for a few days.

Oh, and we argue sometimes because he says I don't let him finish what he's saying. I finish his sentences with not the right ending. We argue like that for lack of communication. On the phone, I don't know what the hell he's talking about. He doesn't speak English properly. I don't speak Portuguese. So sometimes he says something, and I say, (screams) "I don't understand you!" In the office the other week, I found a plumber's job for him on Craigslist. And I called him and told him, and he said, "What? What do you mean?" And I said, "I'm fucking helping you!" It drives me to distraction.

I think it's a lot to do with not having a formal education. He doesn't read . . . he didn't even go to school. He went back to school a bit when he was about eighteen or nineteen. I mean, he's intelligent. But he was working when he was eight. He has made an effort. But he's crap at it. I thought he'd learn . . . and he didn't! (laughs) But I'm not great at it either.

A friend of mine says you have to have three things in common: intellectual, emotional, and sexual compatibility. So we don't have intellectual. But that's the thing: I have friends who have very intellectual relationships with people. That's really important to them. So sometimes I think, "Am I missing out on all that?" But that's the choice I made.

A lot of people don't have much sex because of their

lifestyles, but they're still into each other. But a lot of people who have been in a relationship for quite a while don't seem to really talk about those intellectual things anymore. You talk to people about how did you meet, and the way they describe it, it's so clear that the memory has to keep them going. They argue a lot. The way they speak about their partners, the way they speak to each other, the way they . . . everything. It turns my stomach.

I'll give you an example. I had a friend that I thought had a really wonderful relationship. She'd been with her partner for ten years. They were both very intellectually in tune and very successful in the media and everything. They discussed everything and they seemed like close, close friends. And then she met another guy and she just fell in love with him. And of course, you know, problems had been happening, but nothing they ever talked about, or they were problems that other people wouldn't think were necessarily problems.

And she fell completely in love with this other guy who was completely the opposite of her partner. She broke off her relationship and her children and everything for this other relationship. When I thought back and I realized there's so many times when there was a kind of contempt. He wasn't very good at doing practical things. And I think a lightbulb or something had gone off, or maybe it wasn't a lightbulb, it was something a bit more demanding, maybe the fuse or something, and he was slightly unsure of what to do. And she said, "Just put that in there," and she starts looking at him with absolute contempt and hatred.

I think being physically tied to somebody maybe makes you kinder than that. I think if you have a good sex life with somebody, there's a fundamental respect for that person. There's a boundary that you can't cross, in terms of behavior between you.

When your lover becomes your best friend, you tell him everything, and you share everything, and you work together, and you do everything together. Maybe in the end, it becomes boring. Like you can no longer smell the person, and it affects the sex. And ultimately, if you don't have that physical connection, you will leave, or you'll have an affair, or you'll find someone else, because that's what really you're hungry for. I think sex is the only intuitive thing that you do. It's not verbal. I think it demands a certain amount of mystery or independence to keep it good.

I have a lot of friends who, when they're talking about sex with their partner, they go, "Oh, I can't bear it." They pretend to be asleep. You know, this isn't just one of my friends, it's *most* friends, like 97 percent. They say that they have sex maybe every month or two months. And I'm thinking, "Why have I ended up different from my friends?" And I think it's because we can relate sexually.

When kids come along, the relationship isn't, "I love you. Oh, my God, I love you, I love your mind." It's all about the kids and about work and the division of work. It becomes incredibly unsensuous. I know this because I'm around our kids all the time. We have three of them now. But we've managed to keep things sensual. To a fault. (*laughs*) It's lovely. It's still good.

It's better, even. But our relationship's gotten better as well. I am connected with him. I look forward to having sex and I look forward to seeing him and kissing him and those things, you know. I like the way he smells and lots of things like that. Kind of simple things. That man-woman stuff has lingered since the day we first met. He's very strong about who he is. He always wants sex every night, so it's just sexy, you know? It just feels natural: have sex and then sleep. It connects you to something. To life, you know, to something important.

But it's more than just being turned on by hot, foreign dark guys. (*laughs*) It's a certain emotional sensibility he has. His emotional instincts are right—about people, about things. He's much quieter than I am. He's quite shy. And I notice this so much in New York. So many people never consider other people, how they have to struggle to get by. They pass them on the street, lying down on the ground, and they never stop and consider what it's like, what it means that they don't have proper food or a place to stay. These people go around all the time saying, "Oh, I deserve this or I deserve that." Hector's of the other kind. He's had a hard life. He understands people. He stops and gives money to people. He's not judgmental. It's a goodness. He has a goodness in him.

I followed my instincts. I've never regretted that. I thought, I can never stay with someone who I don't have that intimate connection with, that chemistry. It wasn't like, Oh, I want to have good sex with someone and then marry them. I'm not that naïve here. With Hector, it's the feeling of his being independent, capable, and hardworking, the very opposite from my last boyfriend. And the thought of having someone who could look after you—it's kind of an instinctive thing. Someone who's responsible—to me it's a turn-on.

I'm one of those people who things always happened to. I

never chose a career. And with this relationship, I wanted it. I created it. It doesn't matter if it was a good idea or a stupid idea. I wanted to live with this person, have a baby with this person. I'd never dreamed it would last this long. But I hope I grow old with him. Why not let it happen? I thought, "What's the worst?" The worst is that we don't stay together.

I'd been with my girlfriend since I was eighteen. If someone
had asked me, "Do you love this person?" I would have said,
"Oh, yeah. Absolutely. Absolutely."

When I was twenty-two, I decided to start researching graduate schools. And I discovered that you have to *pay* for graduate
school. (*laughs*) I started researching scholarships and fellow-
ships, and I discovered a program at a university in Michigan
that's funded by a foundation—they'll basically fund a certain
amount of your graduate education if you get a master's degree
in public policy.

I applied to it and got accepted. The program was seven
weeks.

During orientation, one of the teacher's assistants invited us
one night to a little kick-back, so we all went. And we ended
up playing some sort of stupid truth-telling game where people
have to tell the truth. And of course, we were drinking.

I remember this one fellow, Miguel, had a dare. He had to

kiss somebody or . . . I think it was a lap dance, actually, that he had to do to the TA. I remember laughing and enjoying that or whatever. And then we walked back. It was a group of us.

One of the girls and I ended up making out in a cemetery. But the thing is, in the Midwest it's extremely humid and hot during the summertime. This was in July. Also there's a lot of mosquitoes. They're really vicious. And they come out at night. So I'm making out with this girl, and we're rolling around in the cemetery, and I'm getting eaten alive by these mosquitoes, and I'm really hot, so I'd taken off my shirt, so they're eating my back, and I'm not paying attention, 'cause I'm drunk and making out.

We finish, and we say good night, and then it's time to go to bed. So I go to the bathroom and I start to brush my teeth, and Miguel comes in as well. It turned out that he had taken another one of the girls back to her room, and I guess they had sex. Basically, we were exchanging stories of what had just happened. And we were kind of laughing and recounting the evening.

And then all of a sudden, my back started to burn. So I took off my shirt and I asked, "What's going on with my back?" It was basically like tons of mosquito bites that I had gotten in the cemetery.

My back was to him. And then the next thing I knew, he had grabbed me and pretty much thrown me against the wall and started making out with me. And I . . . at first was pissed, like angry, because I'm not accustomed to people throwing me against walls and making out with me, and me not making the first move, and me not knowing what's going on.

I was actually going to push him away. I was going to push him off and kind of get pissed. But then I was like, "Wait. I like this!" (*laughs*)

We ended up in the shower, naked, and just going at it. It must have been three in the morning. It was really a hot incident. Very, very random and very not planned.

So we went to our separate dorm rooms. And then the next day we had to do everything together, so you know, we had breakfast, we went to class, and we sat on opposite sides of the room. I remember we were just looking at each other with a lot . . . well, I had a lot of questions. I didn't know if it was just going to be one thing or if it was going to be like . . . We really didn't know.

I mean, imagine: You're stuck with all these other people for the whole day, all the time. It was awkward. I didn't really know what he wanted and I didn't really know what I wanted. I remember I said something like, "We should talk," or something like that.

I had had sex with men, I would say like twenty times, but I never really thought about a relationship or intimacy or feelings. I thought it was kind of just a sexual thing. They were all very quick and brief and never with the same person more than once. My girlfriend and I had sex often. At that time I thought it was satisfying, because I really didn't know any different. I wasn't even out to myself, you know.

Miguel and I ended up going to an arboretum that was right next to the dormitory. A river ran through it. It was actually a beautiful place. There was a field near the river, and we sat down. And we talked and he sort of explained his story and his experiences with men, and I pretty much gave him an update on where I was and that I had a girlfriend and we just basically, you know, spilled the beans.

And then we ended up making out again.

So from that point on we ended up pretty much getting together, I would say, every night if not every other night. We found a dorm that was empty where we would get together.

We came at it from two very different places. Miguel had had sexual experiences with men, but he'd had girlfriends, primarily. I remember him feeling shame around his few encounters with men. And I remember he said he felt differently about this because he said he didn't feel that. He was enjoying himself, and because he *wasn't* feeling that shame, he was worried. He didn't want to enjoy it. I think in some ways he was more aware than I was. He wasn't out, and I think he just didn't want to feel those things. I remember him trying to break it off a few times. He said he didn't want to get together again. But inevitably he would.

And I was in a space where I was like, "Oh, it's just fun and, you know, it's just sex, and it's not really that serious." I was clueless. I didn't really think there was anything possible more than just a physical act. I remember thinking, "Why are you trying to stop this? We're having a good time and nothing's going to come of it, so what's the big deal?"

Well, so we continued for seven weeks.

He was very physically attractive. I mean his presence, his skin color, lips, and yeah, just a very attractive person. He's Colombian, he's darker-skinned than I am. He had a very deep, sexy voice. And also just a very deep person. He shared the spirit that sort of embodied the people in this program—the passion, the commitment, the intellect, the curiosity.

I had never really met anybody like him who was gay. But in all fairness, I wasn't out on the scene, so I really didn't have anything to compare him to.

It's funny because at that time . . . I've obviously had many more sexual experiences since, but in comparison now, I would say that he's really not that good in bed. (*laughs*) I really enjoyed being with him and the sex was very passionate, but compared to what I've had since, he's a little bit passive in bed. Which I don't like. As it turns out.

We used to make fun of his ass. He didn't really have an ass. But he was very, very sexy. *Very.* I mean pretty much everybody wanted him. His attitude, the way that he talked, the way that he carried himself—he's just a very sexy person.

I received a call from my father that my grandmother was very sick. She was in the hospital and she was probably going to die, so I needed to come home to L.A. two or three days early.

And you know how in the Midwest you get those summer storms? They're really crazy and dramatic, and there's tons of lightning, and sometimes they might even turn into a tornado. Well, actually there was a tornado warning, and I remember the sky turned this gross orange-pink color. They wanted us to get in the basement. I'm like, "Fuck the basement. I'm going outside. I've never seen anything like this in my life."

And it was awesome. I loved it. The sky turned orange, and it was raining and hailing and lightning, and everything that possibly could come out of the sky came out of the sky. I was totally entranced. I thought it was the coolest thing I'd ever seen. Everyone thought I was crazy, but I didn't care 'cause I was like, "I'm never gonna see this again."

So we were having this crazy storm, and I was telling him that my grandmother was going to die and I had to go home, and the dorm had windows looking out onto the arboretum. Then suddenly this big animal passed, like a raccoon or a possum or something. And it was at that moment that we both started to cry.

I'm not really sure why we were crying. It was multiple emotions—sad because we weren't gonna be seeing each other, be in close proximity; sad because, you know, I had to leave; sad because I think at that moment I started to actually feel something. It took me seven weeks. It wasn't a lightbulb. It was a buildup.

I was feeling something I never felt before, maybe mixed with uncertainty about whether it would continue or what would happen.

The next day, I was all packed up. It was raining, and I was looking out my window. My friends were going to class and waving goodbye. And he was in the group, and he didn't even look at me. I think he didn't want everyone to see him—he didn't want to reveal what we'd been doing for the past seven weeks. He didn't even wave.

It's a very dramatic scene, you know. Everyone waving goodbye and saying, "Good luck! Bye!" It's raining, and he's just face down looking at the ground, hands in pockets, walking away fast. It really kind of revealed everything.

I told my girlfriend that I had met somebody. A guy. She was pretty open-minded about it. I think like myself she didn't take it very seriously. We were definitely still together. But I really,

really missed Miguel a lot. Oh, it was awful. My heart hurt. Like physically, my heart hurt. I remember.

I remember hearing songs that I had grown up with and understanding like, "Oh, *that's* what they're talking about." Even something as cheesy as Stevie Wonder's "Sunshine of My Life," you know? And songs in Spanish. Any number of songs—like, you know, the whole fucking canon, American soul and pop. All of a sudden it came to life, and I understood the words for the first time, even though I knew the song like the back of my hand.

I dreamed about him. I would have these frustrating dreams—they were always in New York, and we would see each other, but we wouldn't be able to get physically close to each other. Maybe in like a social setting or something like that. Then I would wake up and it was kind of scandalous 'cause my girlfriend would be next to me. That was a little disturbing.

I mean, it was a series of events. The tears on the last night that we were together, and the fact that I had never cried over missing somebody. Ever.

What I took away from it was that I never felt that way before. It hurt, but it also felt really good to feel love and to feel truly alive and awake and having access to the broadest scope of self and also feeling sadness and longing, you know. To have that heightened sense of consciousness.

But it really threw me for a whole new direction that I wasn't prepared for. Was I gonna be bisexual? Was I gonna be gay? How are people gonna take it? I had had my eye set on one pathway. I always wanted a family. And the realization of being in love totally switched my life course. It forced me to realize my homosexuality. And so I was like, "Oh, shit!"

I had never seen a gay relationship, so I had thought that love was not possible between two men. The idea wasn't repulsive to me. It's just that the idea wasn't there.

At that time, growing up in the eighties, there was this pretty monolithic presentation of gay life. And it didn't look like me. It was primarily white, older, and I don't know why, gay people would always drive black Jeep Wranglers with the hood off. And they would be wearing tank tops and short, like, jean cut-off shorts, and always like fairly muscular. And I wasn't any of those things.

I just had a lot of questions and I didn't feel like I had any resources or anybody to help guide me through these questions. On one hand, being very much in love and loving that feeling, and being awake and alive, and on the other hand, just feeling very overwhelmed.

It felt lonely. It felt even more lonely because I felt so good and I couldn't share it with anybody. I couldn't, obviously, share it with my girlfriend, because that would be very insulting and hurtful, and I couldn't share it with anybody around me, because that would demand that I first come out to them before I start telling them—it was just too much.

I asked myself, like, "Do you think it would be possible to love a woman—any woman—in the way that you love Miguel?" And I answered no. I didn't think it would be possible. Like, the way that I felt about my girlfriend just couldn't compare. The level of intensity and connection just didn't compare. The intimacy was much stronger with Miguel. And even the sex: Technically, I had physically, mechanically better sex with my girlfriend. She actually had a great body. But you know, he was the object of my affection. I really did love him. That was love.

A level of closeness and a certain level of understanding, like an ability to understand each other's weaknesses as well as strengths. Being able to recognize and provide the things that the other person most either implicitly or explicitly wants. An unspoken language that you can communicate with, not just because they're a man, but because they're gay *and* because they're also a man.

I guess the analogy would be to think of the moon and how you only get to see part of it because of the way the sun shines onto it. It's analogous with a person in the sense that a whole side of them doesn't get to be lit up, basically. It includes all aspects of the self: intellect, emotion, spirit—even the way you talk and think, and perceive yourself, the way you perceive the world. It's a whole side of you that basically the sun is not shining on. I felt like a whole new side of me was alive. That's how I knew.

ADJOA AKINYELE, AGE 38

"I guess everything that my husband doesn't do,
he was doing."

Last January, on January the first, I received a text message from my high school boyfriend, Rick. He was a basketball star back then. I hadn't seen him in literally twenty years.

He would text every holiday. But that day, he texted from a new number, and I didn't know who it was, and I think I called him instead of replying back by text. We talked for a while and began texting throughout the day.

It started out very clean. He sent pictures of his wife and children, and I sent pictures of my husband and the kids. Then the text messages started getting later and later at night.

My husband was gone and I sometimes have a very filthy mouth. "How are you doing?" turned into "What are you wearing?" And that turned into, like, other stuff.

It was wonderful. It was exciting, it was different, and very much needed.

My husband's very cut-and-dry. He's stable. Doesn't drink. He's good with my kids. He's gentle. He's a hard worker. I love him. But he's not very affectionate. And there's no romantic side to him. There's no lovey-dovey hugging. When he's traveling, he doesn't call me to tell me he's arrived, or to tell me good night. He doesn't give me a kiss when he leaves or comes back home. When we got married, I wanted to take dance lessons. He didn't want to do it. So we have never danced together. That's the type of person that he is.

He's a software consultant, and he's gone most of the time. He goes everywhere—abroad and here in the U.S. He comes home on Friday and then leaves again on Sunday.

When Rick texted, we'd been married nine years, almost ten. I think that I just started getting bored. The idea of someone else more attentive became appealing to me. My husband is very passive and so Rick was exciting. My husband doesn't like to talk on the telephone, and Rick would call and we would talk—about old stuff, about new stuff. I guess everything that my husband doesn't do, he was doing.

By February 25 I had a plane ticket to California, where he lived. I was born and raised in California, so I had lots of friends there. I told my husband I needed a break. My oldest daughter at the time was eighteen, so she cooked dinner and got the baby off to school and she got my oldest son from the bus stop.

I showed up on Thursday night, I remember. I met Rick at his niece's house, and OMG, it was like a movie. We met at the car, and we were in the street just hugging and kissing forever. We drove to Vegas for the weekend, drove back to L.A., and I saw him almost every day after work for two weeks. It was really good. I enjoyed it. I enjoyed alllll the moments. (laughs)

· · ·

I felt like it was supposed to happen the way it happened. But then it became bothersome for me. The distance. I didn't know when I was going to see him again. His wife—I don't know if she could tell that he was different, but she started being around too much. "Where you going? When you coming back?"

It just got to a point where it was like, "Okay, I can't do this." So we ended it. I guess I did. I have no regrets, though, even when it ended. And I didn't feel guilty. Because my husband didn't know, so therefore he wasn't hurt.

It's hard to explain. You know, it's all the little things that he doesn't do. I've been telling him for almost twelve years to call me when he's gone! He doesn't listen. I told him the other day. I said, "I am done telling you to call me. I'm done." He's been gone for three weeks now, and I've talked to him once or twice.

He says, "I'll do better." Every time, he says, "I'll do better." I'll say, "Yeah. Whatever."

I try to understand that he is the way he is. I do wish that I could change him, but . . . I don't know.

He's very square. And I'm loud and playful. Before we were married, I was the party girl, you know. I wanted to go out, drink, have fun all the time. But then when I moved back to Georgia, in '97, I was living with my mother and I was like, "Okay, I gotta get the heck up outta here! Figure something out!" Yeah, I was living at home with Mom and my kids, and I had Mama on my back. I was new in the area, no prospects. I wanted to get married and he was the perfect type.

I'd never been married before. And I knew I needed security—financial security and emotional security. I needed to know that I wasn't going to have to worry about him cheating on me. I wasn't going to have to worry about him keeping a job.

When we started dating, he was all the things that none of the others were. I had two kids before I met him, and he was good with the children. He suggested things to do with all of us together. He never tried to keep me separate from them, to keep me all to himself. He participated in my son's soccer. A lot of the times with the kids, he helped them with their home-work better than I did. He's good at math and science. He's very smart. It was just several qualities about him that I knew I needed in my life.

He never tried anything, though. (*laughs*) I was the aggressor, and so it was always in the back of my mind, I was thinking, okay, he probably has a small penis. (*laughs*) Then one day we were going on a date and I had gone over to his apartment and he had just gotten off work and had to take a shower. I went into the bathroom for something and I peeked in the shower and so, seeing everything is what made me say, "Okay. We have something to work with! I can train him!" (*laughs*)

But it turned out he has the equipment but not necessarily the talent to use it. He was very passive. I think he was just very shy, not wanting to do the wrong thing, maybe? While we were dating, the joke was that I would go to his apartment and rape him. (*laughs*) I didn't want to hurt his feelings, so I would let him do whatever he was doing, and afterward I would bring it up in conversation. You know, "This is what I like." Or, "Can you do this next time?" As opposed to saying, "Hold up! You ain't doin' this right!" And we got it working. Sorta. You know, he just does not like the journey. He doesn't want to stop and smell the roses. He just wants to get to the destination.

So there's no spark, you know? It's a really good home life. It's a good situation—with no spark.

I can't even count up all the differences between us. Like, I'm really into reading and literature. If I have a book to read, I take it with me everywhere. And I write poetry, things like that. Well, my husband is not a reader. If he has a two-thousand-page manual from work, he'll read that. It drives me crazy. He won't pick up a book. So that kind of leads into this next story.

So, okay, I get on Tagged. It's like MySpace or Facebook. At first, I got on there and I was friends with all my cousins and things like that. When I started getting the hang of it, I deleted all of them, everyone else except for, like, guys. (*laughs*) And oh, my goodness! You can almost say anything to a stranger! So I began putting my erotic poetry on my page.

And there was three guys from Tagged that I met, like actually met up with in person. At Starbucks. We chitchatted. Then one day, back on Tagged, someone tells me hello. I said hello back. He said, "You know, I really liked your poetry. What do you think about mine?" And he wrote something and it was really good. So that's how it began—we started writing to each other poetry and things like that. We did this for maybe a couple of months. I called him "the Country Poet."

We text messaged a lot. He would send things, you know, "Whenever you are feeling bad just know that I am there with you." Things like that. Then we spoke on the phone. He was a barber. He was thirty, divorced, lived alone. He lived about eighty-five miles away. I would drive there two or three times a week. We would watch a movie, we would talk. And his thinking was not normal—in a good way. I felt like I was at home. It just seemed like everything was wonderful when I was there.

This guy, he was like . . . he looked okay. He was just average. But he was so poetic it was almost weird. We were really in tune. I could text him and he would text me; we would get our text messages at the same time and it would be saying the same thing, you know?

I never thought I was much of a kisser, but I became one with him. The way he kissed, you felt it not just physically but emotionally. It was more than kissing. I've tried to explain it to my husband, like, "Can you kiss me like this?" (*laughs*) I don't know how to explain it. I felt it *inside*.

I mean, of all my years I had never felt like that. We thought alike, we were interested in the same things. When he touched me, when I thought about him—I mean everything, it was just magic. Everything. It was fate. It was divinely ordered that I experience him. With him, I felt like I could get on the bus and take a job at a Wal-Mart and be happy. As long as I was going home to him.

But then after three weeks, he said, "I don't think we should do this." He's very into church. Every morning he got up, and him and his neighbor would have their daily devotions. They would read from their Bible. I suppose that had something to do with it. I think, looking back now, he had a lot of childhood issues, and you know, this is the Bible Belt. I think he was just trying to do the right thing.

He said, "I can't do it anymore. You're married." I thought that I was going to lose my mind. I yelled and screamed and cried, and I'm *so* not a crier. I was ready to leave my husband. But it didn't matter. His mind was all set up.

So I was like . . . I don't know. It wasn't up until recently that I got totally and completely over the barber. In the back of my mind he was still there.

And then I had one I call "the Toddler." That's my name for

him. He's twenty-two. He was just something to do. I don't know. He was close, about forty minutes away. And it was cool. He was hot. Oh, he was. He was. But the emotional part wasn't there. I wasn't getting it mentally. He was just a kid, going to a community college, lived at home with both parents, almost wanted to be a gangster type. He was average and wanted to be a little harder than he was, I think.

I think that he saw me as an older woman that he could get things from. Like, he'd say, "Oh, when are you going to let me drive your car?" and I said, "Oh, uh, never?"

Things like that. So, yeah, that's gone.

I realize now that I was searching for something that doesn't exist—or at least not in the real world. What I want is not out there. It's almost like the movie, you know, this is *As Good as It Gets*. (*laughs*) I'm only going to get 80 percent of what I need from whoever I'm with, and I need to learn to live with that.

I don't think I'll be finding any more Tagged friends. I can't see it being exciting and fun anymore.

I think I just got off track for a minute. I've been at home with the children for many years. I've been the perfect mom for all of these years. I was always on PTA, soccer, track practices. Then I did a complete one eighty. Totally. It's like the alter ego finally picked the lock to the closet and now she's out.

I thought that's what I needed. And actually, I did need it to keep me going, to stay in my marriage. It was almost like a recharge. In the end I'm better off, I think. Because you almost have to have something to know that you don't really want it.

An affair is like living in la-la land. It's a temporary fix, and nine times out of ten, it's not real. Everything that I already had with my husband is the total opposite of la-la land: It's real, it's honest—I guess, not on my part—but everything that I have already with him are the things that are most important to me: the commitment, the trust, and the stability.

I guess I don't know what love is. I don't know. I would say that to me, love is just a word. It's not a feeling or an emotion or any of those things. It's just a word. You know? We still go on living and doing and being, whether we think we have it or we don't. In the end, it doesn't change your actions.

Maybe I just need to slow down. I get away with too much. You know? Like if I do this every few years then that shouldn't be too big of a problem. (*laughs*) Like every twelve years? (*laughs*) The last thing that I would ever want to do is to hurt him. But I don't know. I want to be happy too.

BRIGITTE AITON, AGE 44

NEW YORK, NEW YORK

"How do you deal with the fact that the person
you're with might hate you?"

It was the first summer we were together. We were twenty-three years old. I felt like I met the most amazing person and the path of my life was completely changing, going in some completely uncharted direction. Everything was this amazing adventure. Everything became creative and fun. We could go off and do things in a way that would defy convention and defy the things that make life tedious and difficult.

Once we started dating, we were inseparable. We probably spent every night together. It felt really comfortable to be with each other—incredibly comfortable. We were like two peas in a pod. From the beginning. Very calm, very comfortable. It was really nice.

You know that sense of being invincible and insular? I remember walking through the East Village, holding hands, and we'd stop at every corner where we hit a light and kiss. The rest of the world didn't matter; there was this new life that I was stepping into.

We had the same childish sense of fun. We really enjoyed the same kind of silly things. Like, "Oh, let's go drop acid and go to Coney Island and go on the roller coaster over and over and over." (*laughs*) It was just that kind of really silly feeling—totally lost in the moment, totally protected by your own bubble of happiness.

I don't think I was ever that happy with anybody else.

He was so talented. It was a given that he would be successful. I really admired that he seemed so willing to be different from other people, to take the contrary point of view, to be very confrontational with the world, and yet be incredibly sweet and kind to me. He was able to talk baby talk in this sort of shamelessly unadulterated way.

And really, what sort of happened was that at a certain point (*laughs*) I didn't want to keep dropping acid and going on roller coasters. The good times and the things that were interesting in the beginning . . . I grew up a little. And he continued using drugs continuously and constantly. The bong was the first thing to hit his lips in the morning and the last thing at night. Quite a few times during the day, he would duck outside to get stoned. He was high continuously.

Sex was a problem from the beginning. Because he was a pothead, his interest was much lower than mine. If I didn't push the issue, he could easily have gone a month without sex. When we did it, it was great, but in general, he wasn't that interested. Also, looking back, he definitely had a porn addiction that got worse over time. Me being naked wasn't necessarily a turn-on for him. There was a lot of aesthetics that had to accompany it.

I think that he had this kind of adolescent vision of himself in the world. I've never met anyone who wanted to be famous as much as him. He had this idea of himself, sort of, "I am somehow this person of enormous insight that will inform the world of something." If you have no desire to become famous, it's a weird thing to be around.

He had this band that he rehearsed with four nights a week and Fridays and Saturdays. And it meant that we didn't have that much time together. When we did, it was really fun. But he just wasn't around.

Rehearsing so much would have been fine if the band had improved. But they were a shitty band. Basically they centered on smoking pot and thinking they were sort of brilliant. You know, when you smoke a lot of pot, you're like, "Oh, this ninety-minute jam is really interesting!" (*laughs*) It's just not!

It was excruciating at times to watch him do things that were completely misguided, to watch somebody just slowly messing up. And there's nothing you can say to them—because they know better.

I was always very encouraging when I thought things were good and had promise. But when things weren't, I would be honest, which he couldn't take. He felt that as his partner, my support should be unconditional. I mean, children get unconditional love and unconditional support. I don't think adults in their thirties still get that.

In large part, I didn't agree with his aesthetic. He was very aggressive toward the audience in ways that just weren't productive. It's hard being with someone who's performing and what they're doing is so antagonistic and confrontational and unpleasant. His band would start out with a room of thirty people, then end up with three. "Didn't you notice that people were, like, leaving?" I said this as tactfully as I could, and his interpretation was that I was mocking his entire artistic career.

It goes back to being a heavy drug user from his teens and having parents who just adored him and let him do anything he wanted and were always like, "You're brilliant and wonderful." I found it very annoying because he had such a childhood of privilege. His grandparents were self-made millionaires.

The worst thing that ever happened to him was when his father had a job transfer and they moved to another city. And meanwhile, I was like, you know, my father was killed violently when I was a kid, and our whole family was disrupted. My mother struggled raising four kids by herself and I had all these orthopedic devices. So I wasn't that sympathetic to him on some levels. He had all the resources to do so much more in the world, for other people, for himself.

The world got really small, like in terms of things that we could do. He wasn't one of those people who would make small talk—he would have absolutely no interest and was completely unapologetic about never asking anybody how they were. And I can't tell you the number of plays we went to that we left during the intermission because he didn't like them. He had such contempt at a certain point for so much stuff. And he was so unhappy about how unrealized he was in his life.

I was trying to be loving and accepting. When I met him, I thought he was an exceptional person, and even in the later stages, I felt the essence of somebody who had exceptional promise and capability, that I knew was really kind and really fragile and really insecure. And so, you know, there was part of me that was very protective because . . . I loved him.

I resigned myself to the idea that if I left, he would be in terrible, terrible shape. I resigned myself to the fact that life was
getting smaller and smaller, because everything was governed by
his depression and complete disdain of things.

I think a couple of factors allowed me to remain in a situation
that was progressively getting worse. The household where I
grew up was pretty erratic and volatile, and you just get used to
constantly figuring out how you can adapt and fix things. I
think I spent a long time with Andrew just trying to fix things,
not necessarily noticing how badly things were going.

I remember, a friend of ours, he was like, "Brigitte, the guy's
jealous of you." I was like, "What are you talking about? That's
not possible." I couldn't accept it. And I started to run through
these memories of me talking and him looking at me with, like,
total contempt, and I could clearly see him thinking, "Shut the
fuck up," you know, and realized, "Oh, my God. It's true." I
think he really did resent me on a lot of levels.

At one point, this guy I was designing an album cover with,
he got a crush on me. He told me I was just wonderful, the sun,
the moon, the earth. All these things that I hadn't heard for a
really long time. It made me realize how unhappy and how
lonely I had been. I'd felt like a pair of old shoes. Your classic
starving person who suddenly finds an oasis. I told him, "I can't
do this. I'm married. I'm trying to figure this out." I didn't even
like him that much. But it was so amazing to have somebody be
like, "You're interesting and sexy and you're beautiful."

I moved out, to my sister's apartment. I told Andrew that we had to get to couples counseling. And I made Andrew pick the counselor. We went for about two months. You know, it seemed wrong to have the relationship end without trying. But our therapist was really annoying. And I think that that sort of brought Andrew and I together against her.

We got back together.

I was still completely committed. But I think some of us are just loyal in a way that's sick. You know? How do you deal with the fact that the person you're with might hate you? (*laughs*) It's really hard to look at. You start qualifying it in these ways, like, "Yes, I'm kind of annoying."

I thought, "This is what I accepted. This is the situation, and I'm in this for the long haul." I was very happy with my work and my friends and so I think it was more of this resignation: This is what it is and I will keep working to try and make things better. I think it's really cliché, the whole living a life of quiet desperation thing, but I think that's really true for a lot of people. But what are you going to do? You just keep moving forward.

I think it's also an aspect beyond love: You've shared this history with them that they alone know. You don't want to just get rid of it, if that makes sense. Also, I just didn't want to be seen as the bad guy with his family.

The fall of 2000, that's when things started to get really bad. We went on a trip to Las Vegas for my thirty-sixth birthday. I had arranged it. And within thirty minutes of our arrival, I got super sick and was, like, throwing up every thirty minutes for twenty-four hours. He got the same thing, twelve hours after me, so obviously we got something on the airplane. The weekend was terrible. We had tickets to see Penn & Teller and we didn't go. It was basically three days of continuous vomiting and diarrhea.

Months later I was watching Bravo and they had one of these *Cribs*-like shows on about this house of Penn's that he designed called the Slammer that's built to look like a penitentiary. So I said to Andrew, "Why don't you come watch it?" And he was like, "I can't. I'm really upset. I really needed that vacation." It was all about what an incredible loss he suffered, you know, from not having this relaxing trip.

He wasn't blaming it on me, but it was just like he had suffered this incredible loss—worse than I had. He just saw himself so deeply as the center of things.

And this is where life gets really complicated, because you can be like, "This person is completely self-involved—oh, but they make me a cup of coffee every morning even though they don't drink it." Probably up until, like, a week before we broke up, he did this. No one is just so completely bad all of the time. If they were, then you'd be an absolute idiot to stay with them, right?

He was coming home from work really late. I had a feeling he was having an affair with his assistant, Courtney. I asked him about it and he said no.

Once I found them sitting on a park bench near the house. She had just found her natural father and I remember thinking, "I'm sure the newness of her natural father is so much more interesting than twelve years of hearing about my dead father." I just knew that something was happening between them.

It was October 11, a month after September 11. He confessed that he'd been going to therapy for the last several months and hadn't told me about it.

And then he said he was unclear whether or not he should have ever been married to me.

I felt like I had just been hit by a bus. I was like, what just happened? (*laughs*)

The next day he was so hostile that I had to leave. I walked out to Ground Zero. I had to go somewhere that was worse than my own house. I had to go experience somewhere else's badness. (*laughs*)

When I came home he had taken down all the pictures of us. The walls were full of empty picture hooks. I said, "Do you not love me anymore?" And he said, "I don't think that I ever loved you enough to do any of this."

He told me he decided in therapy that he should end the marriage.

And I was like, "Your therapist feels it's okay to end a twelve-year relationship without having any kind of deeper conversation?

And he said, "Yes."

I said, "Does your therapist know how much pot you smoke?"

And he said, "No, we haven't gotten to that yet."

So I realized he had been lying to his therapist completely. And he still insisted that there wasn't anybody else, even though two years later, one of his assistant's friends confirmed for me that he'd left me for her.

He refused to see me in person. He said he felt too badly to see me. He sent me some really, really mean e-mails about how he never should have married me, and how this was the reason why he wasn't artistic, and he had sacrificed his dreams.

I never saw him again.

We got divorced entirely through e-mail.

There's all this space in your brain that's filled with information about this other person. You know, like what they like to eat, and just their little habits. And then all that information is totally useless.

I remember the first time I went to the drugstore and didn't have to pick up his products. I'm in the Rite Aid, crying because I'm not picking up Tucks Medicated Pads for Andrew's hemorrhoids. And I'm like, "I'm crying over *this*?" (*laughs*)

HENRY HAMILTON, AGE 47

NEW YORK, NEW YORK

"You can forgive the person but you don't forgive what
they did to you. I guess I'm in that boat."

I don't know if everybody has one great love of their life. Definitely Shauna would constitute that for me. She may not agree but . . . yes, definitely.

We met in college in New Mexico, in 1986. She used to save my ass all the time. She was very, very sweet in the mathematics tutorial. I would be flubbing it and Shauna would come to my rescue. She was very talented as far as mathematics went. She acted on kindness, and I responded to it. And though we're dissimilar intellectually, I think the dissimilarity was a big part of our romantic attraction toward each other. I tend to be more intuitive and much more of a visual thinker, and she's very, very analytic and logical.

That was the foundation of our relationship. That's how we became friends and then it developed from that. We started spending more time together and then I just sort of fell in love with her.

She has a great Irish sense of humor. There's a little bit of morbidity in it, just great, sarcastic, and that was a big thing in New Mexico because a lot of the students there came from California, so there was no sarcasm whatsoever. Set to float in a sea of sporty earnestness.

So we were the only two people that . . . we'd like sort of roll our eyes at each other. Being native New Englanders, we shared a lot of common regional traits. Shauna didn't know how to ski and so I started teaching her, and then I got her to go rock climbing and like that, so our friendship became more extracurricular.

And then it became really extracurricular. I invited Shauna to come over for Christmas Eve at my mother's house in Santa Fe. By the end of the night, fueled by tons of champagne, we ended up running off together to this apartment that she was house-sitting. It was just lust at that point—and then the next morning, we kind of woke up and, yes, I was definitely smitten.

So we had this love affair that turned into a pretty long, lasting love.

I think that things that we didn't have in our childhood we were really good at bringing and giving to each other. I come from an old Yankee family and she comes from an Irish Catholic, New England mill town family. I guess we always lived with that which-side-of-the-track-did-we-grow-up-on consciousness. Shauna's family was very dour, and there wasn't a lot of adventure. In fact, adventure should be avoided because it's dangerous. And I had the classic preppy upbringing—you learned how to ski and play tennis, you learned how to drive fast cars and drink gallons of liquor and still be charming and serviceable.

She was attracted to that. It was something that she admired
and wanted, and she grew up without money, so money is a
good thing, whereas I grew up with a lot of money and never
thought money was any good for anything because it just creates
dysfunctionality.

My family could move about the world wherever they
wanted to and none of them worked. But it's an old family and
after, I don't know how many, six generations, the trust fund
began to give out. (*laughs*) You know, I could probably get a
membership at the New York Yacht Club if I needed to
(*laughs*), but I doubt I would have the money for the initiation.

So I kind of grew up disgusted, because it was outrageous in
a lot of respects, and it was definitely a dynasty in decline.
Drunkards, drug addicts, the whole gamut. I didn't really want
any part of that. My mother's preoccupation was class and all the
entitlements that brings you. You know, for her generation,
WASPs dominated the world. I wanted to escape that, and I
guess I saw in Shauna, well, this is the way out. She used to
chide me every once in a while, "You should have married the
blonde English relative with the pearls and the sweaters." And I
said, "I didn't want that kind of person."

Her father, he's very Irish. He had potential; he wanted to be
a chemical engineer but his girlfriend got pregnant and he did
the noble thing and married her. He gave up his notions of finishing his degree. He was a machinist in Vermont. I think he has
regrets about it, and that while his choices were honorable, they
weren't particularly ones that he wanted to make.

Shauna was the eldest daughter. She was supposed to be a
son, and as the eldest, she was the child that got to go to col-

lege. None of her brothers did. So he invested a lot in her education even though he would have preferred it to be one of his sons.

I admired her work ethic and her practicality. Nobody in my immediate family is tremendously practical, because they grew up with great privilege and a sense of entitlement. And so I think both of us wanted aspects of each of the classes that we grew up in.

But class was always a hurdle in our relationship. My mother behaved really badly with Shauna. She didn't see how Shauna could possibly fit in. When Shauna was definitely going to be my fiancée, my mother sort of ran up the class attack, with a good mixture of, you know, Freudian Oedipal complex mixed in with it. Let's get the Tennessee Williams collection out. (*laughs*)

When it was time to plan the wedding, negotiating with the families was an issue. It was more the older generations, really. You know, making catty comments about "wops" and "micks." It all got really ugly, so we sort of wrested it away from them, burned all the invitations, and started from scratch. And we ended up doing it on our own so that we could have control over it.

After we graduated, we continued to live in New Mexico. In New Mexico, none of that stuff really mattered because nobody made any money anyway. We could kind of make it up anew and that's what we did.

We had this idyllic period. We'd left Santa Fe and moved up

to this small ranching community in northern New Mexico.
We lived in an old prairie-style adobe house and it was a very
beautiful spot in the world. The guy we were renting from was
somebody that I worked with in Santa Fe. He was a gay perfectionist and had created this little farm setting with peacocks
roaming around the lawns and gardens everywhere, surrounded
by lavender fields.

We had our first daughter and I was very happy. Having a
child really bonded us together, so we were very intimate and
we actually got to spend time with each other and it was very
quiet. Everything was centered on, you know, you, me, and
baby and, for me, it was the first time that I had a sense of
unconditional love for somebody. There's no asking, there's no
questions between a child and its parents. It's just there. We'd
created this perfect little being. Nothing really had to be said,
and nothing had to be worked out. It was very sweet. It didn't
last, but it was there and it was kind of unspoken.

Then we got a little restless. New Mexico is a very enchant-
ing place. It's beautiful and you normally don't have to work
that hard and you don't really have to aspire to anything. And I
think both of us were fairly ambitious people, so we needed to
leave or else we knew we would just be there forever. We
decided to come back to New York.

We kind of did it in reverse order—we should have come to
New York and done our suffering and then had a baby somewhere else, but we did it the other way around! We had our second daughter. The city doesn't make it easy to have children. So
the focus that was so enjoyable in New Mexico became like a
job in New York.

Shauna ended up going into banking. And that created a whole new set of problems about money and aspirations and so forth. It was a kick for her because she started getting recognition for her innate talent and ability, and that was a good thing. I was glad to see it happening, but at the same time I think that's when the snake started crawling into the garden.

I was Mr. Mom, and I took care of our eldest daughter. On the side, I took on freelance projects, art fabrications and graphics work for publishing. We both started working long hours and not seeing each other, and, slowly, that started chipping away at the marriage. The preoccupation was like, "Well, if I get a better job, then I'll be working in certain circles and we'll get the recommendations so the kids can go to a better school." There's no differentiation between your life and your career. It's just one big mosh.

I think especially for Shauna, starting to see the gobs of money that were being made on Wall Street created a certain tension. People in their twenties with multimillion-dollar properties. Keeping up with the Joneses became a real stress because nothing is normal on Wall Street, you know. There's never enough cash in New York.

The thrill of living in New York is that you get that buzz when everything is going well. And I think people get addicted to the rush and you don't really focus on essentials. You know, it probably happens in Paris and London. You have these big megalopolises—everybody has high aspirations and you don't really have to face up to each other, so that changes the rules in a lot of ways.

We had something that was really grounded and very intimate that started in a very small place. And it just didn't translate when we got to New York. Our marriage couldn't survive against New York.

I started running into friends that I'd had before I left to go out west. When I brought Shauna into that fold, I became like a little Emily Post about all the social obligations—treating people like zoological exhibits. This old friend of mine, from one of those old New York families, blah blah blah—his ninety-year-old grandmother was having a party at the Knickerbocker Club and we were both invited. And I gave her a primer about how to respond. I said, "Don't really ever mean anything that you say, keep it light and social. So that you don't ever dig yourself a hole that people can judge you for. It's like playing *Upstairs Downstairs* or *Gosford Park* or something like that."

Even though I've always rebelled against it, it's definitely part of my makeup, so the fact that I could flip the switch and operate that way made her cringe. I mean, she was just like, "I don't understand why you have any interest in this." When I was growing up, there was a lot invested in me. It was like (a) you're going to save the family from oblivion or (b) since you're the only male left on your side of the family, you're going to be the head of the family.

The fact is that I did it—being an heir apparent—really poorly, so a lot of people did, you know, point fingers at me. I mean, I wasn't doing it very well because I wasn't really interested in doing it. I've always felt this obligation, and with Shauna, I didn't really have to feel that obligation; we could be like thoroughly postmodern and make our own reality together. But when the two worlds collided, I would fall into my old role as being dutiful scion or whatever, and I think she kind of regurged on that one. *(laughs)*

Similarly, we would visit her family in Vermont and I could see her role as the quiet, taciturn sort of daughter. Everyone cowered to her father's authority. I mean, he's a real chauvinist, Republican, gun-loving, salt-of-the-earth Vermonter, and it was always a very quiet sort of visit because nobody would say anything to each other. There were all these unspoken resentments, and we would literally become constipated. It was like this really intense situation where people were not saying anything. And then we'd leave, and like half an hour later we'd have to stop and go to the bathroom.

It was a difficult two-step. The two worlds never really conjoined. There were two distinct realms that we sort of migrated back and forth between.

If you work in banking, and are doing it because you're talented, you want to be compensated with millions of dollars. And working for nonprofits, like me, it's more the integrity of your project and money is not a preoccupation because it's assumed that you're not going to make any. *(laughs)* So we started traveling in different circles. She was heading in a very corporate sort of direction and I've always been sort of a bohemian, creative personality, and slowly over the years, that evolved into a sort of estrangement.

It got to a point where friends would wonder about her absence, and I'd say, "Well, she works really long hours. We don't really have any time together any longer, and when she is at home, she's kind of not there." And they would say, "It just seems like she's having an affair, Henry. Why are you being so obtuse about it?" And I guess it was denial, and so I was like,

"Oh, no, no, no, that's not possible—she doesn't have time for that."

And I guess I'll be frank about this one: Sex between us became . . . it wasn't terribly intimate, and there was something pornographic about it after a while. This role-playing weirdness started creeping into our sex lives. I wouldn't say I'm particularly missionary in my sex life, but she started to want a lot more games, she wanted to be ravished, quasi raped, and it was so weird. This had never been part of our sexual vocabulary. You know: Where is this coming from?

I started feeling like a sex toy. "Do it this way!" I wasn't doing it well enough, whatever this role-playing shit was. So I just started dreading the whole fucking process. Eventually we just stopped having intimacy, so that was odd. Once that goes out the door, conversation becomes impossible. If you don't have the physical connection, then it becomes really difficult to have a mental connection because one is foreplay to the other. So we just stopped talking.

There was a weird unspoken tension between the two of us. I could never figure out exactly what had gone wrong and why we weren't getting along as well. If she had come to me and said, "I'm having an affair," I would have been able to deal with it. But in fact, I just didn't know what the fuck was going on.

To protect a secret, you have to lie, and that's what really destroyed the marriage: the lying. And it was cataclysmic because we had this long history of telling each other our deepest, darkest secrets. And because she had guilty feelings, they popped up in another way, which was to be a bitch. (*laughs*) Her way of dealing with it was to get angry because she didn't have the gumption to come clean.

When the marriage deteriorated to the point where I finally asked her for a divorce, because I didn't want to be responsible for making her miserable, she told me that she'd been having an affair. It had gone on for several years. It wasn't really a love affair; it was a sexual thing. My impression is that she never really liked the guy other than in a friends-with-benefits kind of way.

We've been separated now, let's see, it'll be three years coming up. The divorce will be final in a couple of months.

The first year and a half was horrible, of course. Both of us were acting out terribly. I kind of went the Charles Bukowski route, "Woe is me." There's no better place for cheap sympathy than dive bars. (*laughs*) And Shauna just sort of threw herself into dating.

But once that passed, we started to confront what has happened. We kind of brokered a friendship.

I guess we didn't want to make the mistake of sticking with each other just for the sake of the marriage or the kids. Shauna's parents, they don't really like each other and they're still married, and I think that was not the paradigm Shauna wanted.

But I didn't want the kids to come from a bitter, divorced family and Shauna doesn't either. I guess both of us realized that we had to cut the shit out and try to find some common ground as far as raising the kids with the least amount of disruption. We can make it be healthy and nurturing, or it can be nasty and crippling.

One of our daughters is twelve and the other one is five.

The second child was an attempt to rescue the . . . a pull-the-marriage-out-of-its-nosedive baby. Unfortunately, that didn't happen, but we've worked really hard to make sure that they have at least some sort of semblance of family. We wanted them to have access to both of us whenever they wanted. I had moved out and rented an apartment but only like a block away. (*laughs*) Then, since I was only living a block away, it sort of became absurd; I might as well move back into the building. And that's why we still occupy the same house. I live in the basement and she occupies the top two floors. It's a peculiar postdivorce state. (*laughs*)

I forgive her—well, you can forgive the person but you don't forgive what they did to you. I guess I'm in that boat.

I did fall in love with her and was in love with her, and so what part, what aspect of her is it that I fell in love with? I guess I focus on that and that allows me to forgive her. In a lot of ways I've settled down into it being a fact of life. Time is a great healer. I think it just burned itself out. It doesn't make me irate any longer. It's personal history.

I don't really see myself getting married. Women I meet—it's pretty much all about sex for me. I don't really want to be intimate with them. I just don't. I just want to have a good time. Shauna is very into her work, so for her, not having a really committed relationship is great. I know that she sees somebody every once in a while, but it's really informal and it's recreation. Maybe I'll be like Pablo Picasso, you know, he was devoted to his first wife and everyone after that sort of had to pay a price for that, especially the last one. If I was in a plural marriage, Shauna would definitely be wife number one and the rest would be lower on the totem pole. And Shauna kind of recognizes that.

I mean, we used to say earlier, when we first started seeing each other and before we got married, that we were soul mates, and I still agree with that. She understands me far better than anybody else in the world and I understand her far better than anybody else in the world.

She also knows that when we get older, we'll always, like, look after each other, even though we're not married. She once said, "I know that there is going to come a time when I'm probably going to have to be around, when you're on your way out," and then I kind of looked at her and I said, "Well, vice versa, if you beat me to it."

So I don't know. As far as the love goes, we still have it. It's just a different form of love, without the romance. There is a lot of affection between the two of us. We still have a lot of the same sentiments toward each other that we've always had. And since we do have such a history we can delve way back into each of our lives. It's perhaps a little bittersweet.

It's a little confusing at times. It's only recently that we started talking again. When we start conversing and sharing ideas, every once in a while we freak ourselves out because we start getting emotionally intimate. Suddenly it's like, "Oh, there you are again." And every once in a while we find ourselves in situations where we're acting like husband and wife—and then both of us tend to pull back and run out the door.

I don't know if I trust her enough to get reattached. Sometimes I fantasize that maybe we'll have the single lives that we never really had because we were college sweethearts, and that maybe, when we're sixty, we'll get remarried. Like when we are well into our sixties and seventies, where sex isn't a priority or something. (*laughs*)

More likely, she'll be able to move on. Me, on the other hand, I don't know. I don't think anybody could replace her. I think part of me is still very much in love with my ex-wife.

FRITZ BAECKER, AGE 51

ORLANDO, FLORIDA

"I'm like, wow, wow, wow."

My ex and I broke up about four months ago. We were together fifteen years. And then it just fell apart.

We met back in 1984. I was twenty-six. She was three years younger than me. We were working in a Sprint call center. She sat across the way from me. I'd never seen anyone like her 'cause she was half Cuban and half Hawaiian. Right away when I saw her I felt like she was the one for me. Like, "I found her."

I'd once seen a movie called *Coming to America*, from the eighties. In the movie, Eddie Murphy says, "I want a woman who can arouse my loins as well as my intellect." Malia just had the things that I was looking for. She was beautiful looking, and she had the personality behind it. I was attracted to her mind, body, and soul. She was a Christian, she loved God, I love God, and she was very good-looking. It was the perfect package. She dressed like a businessperson—like a CEO—with the beauty of a model.

I said to a friend of mine, I said, "You know what?" I said,

"At some point I'm gonna have her." I made a prediction: "I'm gonna get her. I'm gonna get her." I never really said that before in the past.

She didn't intentionally want to get into a relationship. She was married, but her marriage was already going down the toilet. And I kind of sensed it. I said to her, "I know you have a lot of emotions in your heart." I said, "I'm going to take you out of your problems." I was very forward with her. I basically gave her the leverage to break into another relationship.

We became friends pretty fast. Probably six months, seven months, and then we started hanging out a lot. I was already in love with her.

She introduced me to her three children. We went to the park. The youngest one was a year and a half, the middle one was five, the oldest one was six and a half. And she goes, "Do you have any problem with this?" I said, "No. I accept you, I accept them. They're part of the package."

I helped her to get an apartment and to buy furniture. I up-fronted all the money. Everything. Basically, my intention was to move in with her. So I kind of made it very convenient for her.

I was her guardian angel. I came down from heaven and I rescued her and I saved her. I feel like I saved her soul from turmoil. Sometimes in the Bible, angels come and they help people, they rescue them. I told her, "I'm your guardian angel. If you ever have a problem, if anyone ever hurts you, I'll get revenge on them. I'll crush them." So I've been her protector. Like her bodyguard. That was my commitment level.

We all pretty much got along for the first year. She believed in me and I believed in her. She would call me at work, say, "I love you." And I felt like, "Wow, I've got someone else. I'm not doing this on my own. It's a two-way street. We're helping each other."

It felt like I was alive again. Because for years, I didn't have anyone. I finally felt happy. I loved to wake up in the morning. I felt like someone turned a light on in my head and there was hope out there.

I got fired from Sprint a few months after moving in with Malia. She ended up leaving the company too. I was crazy about her, so I put my entire life on the line for her. I didn't care what it cost me. I was living off some money that my father had given me, and that only lasted a few months. I had to borrow money from friends and family to try to stay above hot water.

We were broke for the first two years. It caused us a lot of problems because we were always worried about finances. I had to declare bankruptcy. It got to the point where we were almost living in the street.

In '97, I got a job at an insurance company. We started to do better. We were able to make money and sustain ourselves.

But the thing with the kids was a big deal. If it was just her, we might have still been together. I wasn't always good to her kids.

It was probably about two to three years before that started to surface. They started getting older and they started talking back. Sometimes I would spank them and be verbally abusive to them, and sometimes when our relationship was falling apart, I took it out on them. It wasn't really fair to them.

Any time you get into a relationship with someone with children you have to treat them the best. You mistreat them and then you pretty much lose everything. And that's what happened. She lost respect for me. I just kept falling over myself and doing the same things over and over again that she asked me not to do. I ruined a good thing.

When I said, "Okay, I accept the whole package," I wasn't really thinking straight. I meant it in my heart. But mentally I wasn't ready for the challenge. I was looking at it short term. I didn't really want to be father figure to them. I was more interested in hooking up with her.

Things were only good for about six years. After that it went down the toilet. She put her career as a priority over me because things weren't working out. She would basically go to sleep, get up, and go to work again. There was really no interaction. The last five years, we'd have sex every once in a while, but it was more like just to sexually gratify ourselves. There was no intimacy. There would be times when she wanted to have sex with me and she didn't want the intimate part. I didn't want that. So I turned her away a few times.

I was more like the woman in the relationship; she was more like the man. Our roles were reversed. I was more the emotional one, she was more the one who paid all the bills. She always had a problem with showing her emotion. I had to put forward affection for her to show affection to me.

She was a lot more mature and ready to make bigger decisions. She'd decided to make a mark for herself. While I was in the same position for the last ten years, within ten years she ran the office. I was still kind of like a little kid. I wasn't moving in the same direction she was. She would work really late hours and that became frustrating because I was left to manage the kids while she was gone working sixteen hours a day.

I told her many times, "I'd like to get married." She kept saying, "No, no, no, no, no." I wanted my own children. But she didn't want those things. I kept thinking to myself, you know, "Maybe she'll change her mind, maybe she'll change her mind."

Probably about three and a half years ago is when it really got bad. We were getting into arguments. And then four months ago, I found out she was with someone else. I couldn't allow that to continue. That's when I moved out.

I sensed that there may have been something going on, but I trusted her. I trusted her. I asked her several times throughout last year, "Are you seeing someone else?" And every time, the answer was no.

She had met this guy through work about ten years ago. For the first three years she worked under him. First as a salesperson, then as an assistant to him, and then eventually she became his boss. So in all that time, they spent a lot of time working to-gether, and they would hang out sometimes. And I really didn't like that. I said, "You need to get away from him. I don't like this."

There would always be rumors where we worked that they were having a relationship. She admitted she had kissed him probably eight years ago. I got kind of annoyed about it. I guess I was blinded because I was so in love with her. She was seeing this guy for over a year until I found out about it.

But you know, she never cheated. I mean, she wasn't, like, cheating, because . . . I felt like she betrayed me. She could have at least been honest, you know. It's not like she was lying to me. She was afraid to tell me. I just think she didn't want to hurt my feelings. Her heart . . . the way she did it was not in a bad way.

I forgave her because I had done other things to destroy the relationship. I let it go.

I loved her so much from the bottom of my soul. If she needs me, I'll come to her aid. That commitment level is still there. That will never die. I don't want to ever lose that with her. It would just destroy me inside if I could never talk to her. I could possibly have a heart attack or something. I could probably get sick and die.

I think she's maybe taking that for granted a little bit. I think there's going to be a point where she's going to fall out of love with this guy and she's going to want me back. But the time is expiring right now for her to take me back. Once that expiration date is—just like on a can of milk or whatever—it's going to be too late.

I think after a breakup the best thing to do is to heal a little bit. And maybe take a month or so to reevaluate who you are. But if you don't start getting out there and going out with friends and dating, you're going to be miserable. I'm miserable being by myself. When you're by yourself, you get scared. You get lonely.

I think Internet dating is good but you have to be very careful. It's happened to me a few times where I had people who tried to use me and stuff.

It's like this girl Shelly that I was talking to. She would play these stupid games with me. I'd ask her questions and she'd give me half an answer. I'd have to squeeze it out of her. She's like, "Oh, you're being so pushy, forward, and daa daa daa." I'm like, "Kiss my ass, motherfucker," you know. I don't care. She's just fucking . . . oh, God. These people. I don't know. I don't get it.

I got mad at Shelly. (*laughs*) I didn't want to talk to her again. I had this Christmas present waiting for her. I had this ten-dollar CD of Guns N' Roses' greatest hits and then I had a card for her with some cash in it. I ripped up the fucking greeting card, threw it in the garbage, took the sixty bucks and spent it. I opened up the damn CD and I started listening to it. I was like, "I don't need this bullshit! Fuck you," you know? Honestly, I don't owe you shit. She can shove it up her ass. I'm sorry!

This Puerto Rican girl, she seemed really nice. We e-mailed each other a few times. And then I meet her and she starts asking me for stuff. We went over to my place and she's like, "Oh, I like that purse. Can I have it?" And then she starts telling me all her sad stories. "Oh, you know, I don't have a lot of money." I think she's a user. I lent her some money and she only paid me back like a small portion of it. I think she was just trying to find someone to suck dry.

I met someone in the last few days. Too soon to say, but I've already told them I love them. I've known her four days. Maybe because of my desperation to meet someone, I've been very forward with her.

I saw her name on Facebook and her name was really long, and I'd never seen a name like that before. She was good-looking. She was attractive. Her name is Lucia. I don't remember what her whole name is. It's longer than my hand.

We started communicating through e-mail and then we started instant messaging. And then the next day, I said, "Look, I need to call you." We spoke on the phone for—well, within a twenty-four-hour period—for about fifteen hours. She just got out of a relationship. She actually said she's a lover, and she loves to hug. And as soon as she said that, I just lost it. In my head. As soon as she said, "I'm a lover and I love to hug and I'm a giver," that's it. I was sold. I was sold on the goods. She had me right there.

I think what concerns her is, "What if your ex comes crying and needs attention?" I said, "Look. If I'm with you, I'm with you. I'm not a cheater." I said, "A woman is like gold. You don't throw gold out the window. You wear it, you invest in it."

This girl, she just touched my heart in a way that's like, wow. I'm scared. I just can't figure it out. It seems like the more I talk to her, the more our lives are becoming one.

She works for Home Depot in New York City, and I live in Orlando. I could probably fly and see her. It'd cost me about $280 round-trip. I'm supposed to meet her in two weeks. She said she might be able to take a leave of absence for a few days, and I said, "You know what? Do it. Do it. Just take a chance." I said, "If you become my girlfriend, then I'll give you all of my resources. If you help me, I'll help you. Our money comes together. We become one."

Lucia is the kind of person that will help you till she's broke. She will give you her last dime and won't even think about it. I might be jumping the gun, but I feel that's how she is. She's the real thing. You know, I could see this turning into a possible marriage one day. She wants kids. She's from Colombia, so I said it would be nice to have a Colombian mess of kids.

When I look in the mirror I see her and it scares me because I see myself. The reflection of me. Who I am. What my beliefs are. I think she's got Christian values. She's a good girl. I feel like she's someone I've known for years.

I think I'm falling in love with this girl. And I haven't even met her yet. I'm going way too fast. My emotional immaturity is coming out again. That's my downfall—because of my lack of dating in the past, I don't want to be by myself. I want to cling to whoever.

I'm full of emotions. She's got tons of emotions too. I can feel it. And I love it. I need to love her, I need to hug her. I crave that. I miss that so much. I feel like when I see her I just wanna give her a kiss. I don't think I would wanna hold back. I'd just be like, "You know what? I'm sorry, but this is what I feel like doing. If you don't feel like doing it, that's fine." I told her a few times, I said, "You know what? I wish I could just give you a big hug and tell you it's okay." When I said that she's like, "Whoa." (*laughs*)

I've thought about moving to Miami, because my mother has a place in South Florida. And that place is available. Lucia's been asking me if there's a Home Depot in Miami and how far it would be from my mom's place. She could get a transfer. She doesn't want to stay in New York. No. I don't think so.

That's what I'm going to do. Maybe I shouldn't feel that way so soon, but I'm not getting any younger. I'm at the point in my life where I'm . . . honestly, I should fly her here to Orlando and she can just help me pack all this shit up into a U-Haul. I would do it. Honestly, I would. I'd get a U-Haul and drive it to fucking Miami.

In the meantime I just talk to her every day. I don't know. I don't know if I can wait. I just wanna start my car and drive up there. I'm like, wow, wow, wow.

MARÍA SIERRA, AGE 37

MINNEAPOLIS, MINNESOTA

"I made it very clear that this relationship was not
going to end when he wanted to end it.
It will end when I want to end it."

Translated from the Spanish by Sonia Bowe-Gutman

I was born in Mexico City, but when I was young, we moved to
a little village called Atencingo, in the state of Puebla. My father
owned a saloon, but when I was four or five years old, he abandoned us while my mother was pregnant. He came to the U.S.

My mother kept running the saloon. I wasn't exactly
ashamed of her, but it bothered me. I'd ask her why she didn't
find a different line of work. She doesn't know how to read or
write, and she had no other way of supporting us.

Mother didn't make much money there. We were very hungry a lot of the time and didn't have enough to eat. We sometimes slept there while my mother was waiting on people.

I could hear everything that was going on in the saloon. I
could see everything. She would disappear sometimes for several
days at a time. The relationships she had were with married
men. People on the street would taunt us for being children of a
saloon keeper. At school people made fun of me, and it was not
respectable. I would be left in charge of my siblings. At that

time I was eight to ten years old. I decided my children would
not go through this.

Father would send us money every once in a while, but one
day he let us know he would not be sending any more. He met
someone else. He started a new family.

I started to notice guys when I was thirteen. I was the nov-
elty in our little village because I was still somewhat new. I was
pretty. Lots of guys approached me.

My mother would not let me go out and do what I wanted.
I never liked it when anyone told me what to do, so I found this
guy, Roberto. I went with him when I was fourteen.

I became pregnant with our first child. Two months after we
started living together at his parents' house, he left to come to
California. I was still fourteen. It was very difficult for me at his
parents' house because their habits were very different. I didn't
know how to cook; I didn't know how to wash; I didn't know
how to throw tortillas, because at home we didn't do it. I tried
to return to my home, but my mom wouldn't have me back.

I stayed in this relationship with Roberto for eight years.
When he was gone, I had no support whatsoever. I was all
alone. I more or less ran away to join him in California in 1986,
leaving our oldest child behind. We had another kid in California.

He started to sell drugs and went to jail several times. The
last time he went to jail, I didn't know what to do.

Martin was the friend of a friend. I barely knew him at all. I
wasn't in good shape at the time. I needed affection. And I was
quite shy. He and I went for a drink. I got very drunk and lost
consciousness. When I woke up I had slept with him. He

wasn't all that drunk. I interpreted this as him taking advantage of the situation, and I still see it that way. That's how it began. We've been together for fifteen years.

He's not good- or bad-looking. He is short—just barely taller than I am—and when I first met him he was very skinny, unkempt, with long hair, and he wore clothes that were way too big for him. Sometimes he had a beard. He came to the U.S. from Hidalgo, and he worked in a factory. He drank a lot. He smoked a lot. I didn't like either one. I stayed with him simply because I was taught that if you slept with a man, you stayed with him. And because I was alone.

I told him that what existed between us was not serious, and that I would not marry him. He had a relationship in Mexico, a girlfriend he planned to marry. He had come to the U.S. to earn money and then return to marry her.

We slept together almost every night for a month. He wanted to move in with me. We agreed it was silly to pay rent for two apartments. I had two kids, a four-year-old and a six-year-old. I didn't know how to feed my children. He said he would help me. I told him it was okay if my children accepted him. If they didn't, I wouldn't let him move in.

He started to get to know them and they began to really like him. He was very indulgent with them. I liked very, very much how he was with my kids.

So he moved in. We had serious problems. We fought a lot. A lot. There were letters from Mexico and problems about money. He got me a job at the same place where he worked, but he never had any money. He was somehow partners with a man at the factory, and if the factory did well, he had money;

if not, he didn't. He helped, but only minimally. I had to pay for food, the rent, the bills. Whenever it was his turn to pay for something, he would leave. He would return when everything was paid for.

We are very different. I like traditional Mexican music, mariachi, and he likes rock. I like tortillas and very spicy food, and he likes bread and no spicy food, very simple, no chilies. I would cook and he would throw his plate on the floor: "I'm not eating this!" I was not about to cook something else. If you want something else, cook it yourself.

He would tell me often that he did not love me. That yes, he was with me, but he loved the one in Mexico, that I was interfering with that relationship. That woman had found out that he was living with me. It was very complicated. He told me that for several years, that I'd ruined his life.

It made me feel bad. But I didn't want my children to see me with one guy and then another.

I think he really enjoyed my children. He would hug my daughter. He would cuddle with her. He would take my children to the park, to school conferences, and other places. I was very strict with them, very authoritarian. Sometimes I would hit them. He would talk me out of it and tell me to talk with them. He was very gentle with them.

But he and I hit each other. Sometimes I let him beat me and wouldn't respond, but other times I did. It was after one of these fights that he left. We'd been living together for a year. And then after that, every time we would fight, he would leave.

I would go after him to look for him—to different factory parking lots, to parking lots of different shops, wherever I thought he might be. Finally, once, when he told me he was leaving, I told him, "Okay, go." I didn't go after him. After two days, he decided to come back.

Our relationship just seemed like a caprice, a whim. Not love. Even though I didn't feel like I loved him, I swore to myself, "One day I will make him love me." That's just the way I am.

In 1995 we moved from California to the Minneapolis area. And then two and a half years after we were together, in 1996, we had a girl. When I was pregnant, it became a closer relationship. Now we had someone that depended on both of us. At first, when he realized I was pregnant, he wasn't very happy, because he still intended to return to Mexico and marry the woman who was waiting for him there. But when he saw my growing belly and he felt the baby's movements, he became emotional. It touched him.

When my daughter was born, he suggested I stay home to take care of her. I don't like that kind of arrangement. I couldn't ask him, "Buy me underwear." So we work alternating schedules; he works at night and I during the day. And that is how the next ten years passed. We lived through ten very, very difficult years.

We continued fighting. Ever since we started having relations, I have never had an orgasm, never, never. I do respond to him, but he takes care of himself more than he tends to me. I told him how I felt and he got very, very upset. He told me I should try with somebody else. I told him I wanted to feel it with him. I didn't want to look for someone else. I went to therapy and accepted some things, and some things have improved. But the fighting always continued.

I was working in one hotel in Minneapolis, the Whitney,

and he was working at the Ramada. He could perfectly well have dropped me off at work but he didn't do it. I had to take the bus. And the car was mine! I had bought it and he was driving it. He was calling girls to give them rides here and there, to go shopping, pick up their kids, wherever, and when I would ask, "Will you take me to work?" he would answer, "There is no room." For me, this was too much. I fought with him. I broke the car windows. He would just bend over and duck!

One of the many times when Martin left me, he went back to Mexico, to his mother's house in Cuernavaca. (*laughs*) I went after him. When I got there, all I wanted to do was have a fight with him. I told him, "I don't accept the way you left." I made it very clear that this relationship was not going to end when he wanted to end it. It will end when I want to end it. And then I couldn't fight with him, because he agreed with me. And he told me something I will never forget: "You love me and you love me a lot because nobody has ever done anything like this for me."

I was afraid of going home without this relationship. I was determined, absolutely determined, that someday I was going to make him love me. I wanted to prove to him that if I wanted us to be together, I could do it. I did not want my children to go through what I had gone through, to see me changing from man to man. It goes back to my mother. When I was a child I saw her with several guys. I am not judging her. But it is very hard to see one's mother (*cries*) with someone who is not your father.

I brought him home.

After we returned to the United States, I found out he was

with someone else. When this happened, I did not get angry. I had told him he should be with someone else who would hug him and who would be good to him, because with us, the sex was not there. Not anymore. And he would say, 'No, I need to be with you." But then I found a motel bill in his car. And there was the two-hundred-dollar phone bill from him calling Mexico, talking over our maximum number of minutes.

I talked with the woman he had the affair with and learned that her husband and Martin were friends. At that moment, I lost all respect for Martin. It's one thing to cheat, but he was cheating with his friend's wife.

I also had a relationship outside of the one with Martin. It was not an important affair, nor did it last for a long time. Martin and I were getting along very badly. I had decided to break up with him. I got tired of hearing him say he was leaving. I got tired of running to get him all the time.

This other person I did not love. There was no affection, no nothing. I won't try to tell you I didn't like him physically. I did. I simply met him at a time when I was going through difficulties and he was the only person who approached me.

I can't understand why Martin and I are still together. It is hard for me to understand how you can be in a relationship and be with someone else. For me this had been very difficult.

Our financial troubles continue to this day. We bought a house, and I have been the main one to pay for it. Martin has helped with the mortgage, so that has changed. But I am the main breadwinner. I have always worked to provide for our children and for my mother. In 2001, my brother's son came from Mexico to live with us. I have adopted him, and he is like my son now. I'm very proud we have been able to give him a home.

I have never thought of myself as a dumb person. After doing housekeeping at the hotel, I decided to do something more. I took a job driving a city bus. I did that for five years. And then I finished my studies to become a phlebotomist. I did my GED at that time so I could go to college. I went to study English. There were times when I worked seven days a week at a job, plus driving the bus on weekends. Martin told me he was very proud of me and he noticed that I always got what I wanted. And yes, I do.

After we had been together for almost ten years, Martin told me he loved me very much. I think it was the first time he told me that he loved me. He said that he couldn't be without me.

When the day finally came and he said he loved me, I think I lost interest in him. As if, now I have what I wanted, I didn't want him. I was just tired of it. I told him I was going to find someone else.

He cut his vein. He fell on the bed, his arms bleeding and hanging down, and he started to sing! I don't remember the song. He fell down the stairs. He hurt himself against the wall and we called 911. The paramedics arrived and tried to help him and he was beating up on them.

He was locked up in the hospital for a while. When he came out, I was afraid that something would happen, so we began to live together again. He kept saying he would kill himself. We had life insurance. He would tell me this money is available to bring up my kids and that I would be okay. Twice he tried to drown himself in a big river near our house.

It isn't so much that I cared about him as a man; I cared what my children would say. I didn't want them to tell me, "Our father killed himself because of you. It is your fault." So I told him we should live together but lead separate lives. He could stay with me until he felt strong enough to be on his own. But that from now on, it was just all about the children. He said, "I don't want to leave. I want to go on with you."

On our tenth anniversary, he gave me some presents and this ring and asked me to marry him. I was moved. But it doesn't change anything. I didn't want to hurt him, but I didn't want to marry him.

He is the most important man in my life. And he will continue to be. There are many things I don't like about him, but I start to think, and I realize we all have our faults. He became a very good father. That is the most important part about our relationship. When we all go out to eat, and we are together, that, I think, is beautiful. I want my children to have everything I never did. It is a deep relationship.

That is what I most admire in him. It is the *only* thing I admire. (*laughs*) He has sometimes hurt me verbally. But he has changed a lot. He has tried to please me more. He no longer humiliates me and he has never again said, "I am leaving." He has become a good friend. He can be very affectionate. But I do not love him.

Sometimes we talk about the future: When both of us are old, what will we do? I see my future with somebody else. I want one relationship that is beautiful. I want to know what love is.

Maybe I am not *in love*, but I do like him. I have feelings of affection, and I am used to living with him. It is very difficult for me to imagine life without him. It is the family picture for me: father, mother, and children—together. I always saw this image when I was a child. That's how I imagined it would be. Now I feel I have it. I have one of my dreams. But there are so many other dreams that went by the wayside in order to have this one.

KATHERINE LANHAM, AGE 48

LITTLE ROCK, ARKANSAS

"As one man told me, 'You're the most married woman I know.
But your husband's dead.'"

The desire from the minute he died—whenever he'd even mention dying—was always the same: "I'm going too."

His service was on a Tuesday and I think by Friday I was starting to take pills. I had this Dilaudid stashed away. I would be conscious enough to answer the phone every now and then, but that was about it. I know the cleaning people came on Friday, so it was a week later that they found me. I have a vague recollection of that. I only knew that my husband had died.

Finally my sister came over and got me to her house, tried to get some consciousness into me. Then I tried it again. I tried oh, about two dozen times. At least. Between February 2008 and August 2008, I was either recovering from an overdose or planning the next one.

At one point I took sixty-four Restorils and fifty Ativans. That was quite an experience, because I came to and I was on the floor in my dining room—on the hardwood floor, paralyzed from the waist down from the medications.

I was in this drugged-out state, calling for him, and I couldn't figure out why he wasn't answering me. Bill used to sleepwalk. I'd call for him, and he'd come back into the room. I kept yelling for him to come get me because I couldn't stand up. I kept falling back down, bruising myself. Finally I was able to crawl to the bed. I don't know how many hours it had been. I realized that he was dead and that was the reason why he wasn't answering. He wasn't coming this time.

I have doctors in my family who couldn't believe that these attempts didn't do it, didn't kill me. It made perfect sense to me then, and still does, in a way that I know isn't sane. But it is what it is.

In my mind, we were in this together; all of a sudden now, the game is over. I'm here on my own and that's not right. There are different planes of existence. And this was not the plane that I needed to be on. This is a warped universe and I've got to find my way back.

Until that time I was rationalizing suicide because I am a Christian—believe it or not—and I believe that there is last-minute forgiveness even if you had died with a sin. Jesus would forgive me, God would forgive me. I read in Scripture that Jesus wanted to give us the desire of our hearts, and this was mine—to be reunited. Surely, I thought, He will give me this.

I started thinking about it, and I thought of the Scriptures that said there are many rooms in heaven. And I realized, maybe I could be forgiven, and I could be in heaven—but not necessarily be in the same room as my husband. Maybe I would live in eternal life and not be in hell—but it didn't mean that I would necessarily be with him. So I'm just forty-eight years old; do I risk thirty more years of misery, not living with this man?

Or do I risk dying and being without him for eternity? That sounds crazy, but that's how the mind works.

Then I thought maybe Bill's not answering me was a sign that suicide was not the way.

I settled down a little after that and stopped intentionally overdosing. But for a long time the goal then was to try and find some illness or be in a wreck or something. I'd drive without a seat belt or pull out in front of cars. Climb the ladder to the attic after a few scotches. Or pray to get sick.

As one man told me, "You're the most married woman I know. But your husband's dead."

I've met widows and different people that I've talked to. It seems very easy for them to reinvent their lives following the loss. I don't want to have to do that. That's where the anger comes in. I've tried to get into relationships again, but the desire of my heart is reunion. I don't know how that's going to change—or when or if.

I would like to find things on this plane of existence that can be of a little bit of interest. And I'm getting there. But it's really this desire for reunion that's keeping me going. I hate that.

Bill and I were together sixteen years, married for eight. Four of those eight were dealing with the cancer.

During that time, my mother died of pancreatic cancer. She had been my other touchstone. She died in February 2007. I'm realizing how much I had been relying on both of them to keep me sane. My insanity's running rampant right now! I'm trying to keep it in check. (*laughs*)

I guess he was my anchor, my . . . oh, God, I can think of all of these corny metaphors, like true north—just the person that you feel like, "I'm at home." There have only been a few people in my life that I've felt like that with, just so comfortable with and so authentic. Bill used to call me "SBC"—seething bundle of contradictions. And the other one was "frighteningly authentic." The people that you can be that way with are very rare. There have only been a handful, and he was one of them.

We started working at the same museum on the same day. He was the curator and I was an educator. The museum was putting up a show, and I wrote the exhibit panels. They were very wordy, and Bill, in his curatorial expertise, said, "You've written way too much copy. Nobody's ever going to read it." So basically saying, "You have wasted your time." And I thought, "Who are you but the world's biggest jerk?" He was married and I thought he was the most repellent person that I had ever met. I tried to avoid him.

Not love at first sight at all. We worked together for several years and then I got a job at an art center somewhere else.

Later I heard that his wife died very suddenly. A mutual friend started talking about him in a more positive light and I started thinking, "Are we talking about the same Bill?" I ran into him at the art center and he was there with his youngest child and he was very personable and nice and I was fascinated.

It's funny—well, he asked me out and we went out for breakfast. I felt relaxed and comfortable and connected and was kind of surprised that I did. This is . . . what the heck, I might as well say this too: I called him up a few weeks later because I hadn't had sex in a while and I figured he hadn't, because his wife had been dead. So I said, "It's been a long time for me and I'm sure it has for you. Do you want to get together on Friday night?" He said he literally hung up the phone and jumped up and down. (*laughs*)

So, anyway, he came over and we had sex and it was re-ally . . . it was much more intimate as far as talking and being relaxed and having fun in bed than I thought it would be. A much better lover than I expected and really good. Even after that I thought, "Oh, this was just a one-time fling."

But he was so cute. The next day he called and said, "More! More! More!" kind of laughing. We were very comfortable about it. It was sex and it was fine. He took me to dinner a few days later and, all of a sudden, I thought, "I love him." I was just shocked. I remember thinking, "I cannot love Bill Hammond."

But once I knew, that was it. It's the same as being a Christian; they call it a conversion experience. You can remember exactly where you were when it happens. For me, I was sitting on the kitchen floor in my sister's house in 1996. For Bill, it happened while he was reaching for a wrench he thought he had lost. I mean, you know when it happens. Suddenly, you just have this insight that you have accepted Christ. It's the closest thing I can think of to how it happened with Bill.

He loved feeding me. He loved taking care of me, cooking all our meals. He was a gourmet cook. We had a great time, just enjoyed doing things together, even boring things. We used to laugh and say we had fun cleaning out the refrigerator together. Give me someone I can be fascinated with when I'm cleaning the old lettuce out. I was just fascinated by him and totally attracted to him and just zeroed in, in love.

In the fall of 2004, he wasn't feeling well. He was a man who liked his gin and tonics at night and we ate a very rich dinner at seven o'clock every night. I thought it was his heart. But all the tests came back negative.

Then on his birthday we went out to eat. His sons were in

town. Well, Bill couldn't swallow his meal. The doctor thought it was allergies, because it was the spring and there's a lot of pollen in Arkansas. Finally they did an endoscopy. His doctor came in and he said, "He has a tumor the size of a rock totally blocking his esophagus. It's probably been there for years." Bill had a lung condition called sarcoidosis and he would get X-rayed every year and so I was like, "Why did we not know this?" He told me, "These don't show up on X-rays."

He was on a feeding tube for about a year, which is ironic because of his love for food. We gave up our seven o'clock dinners. He stopped cooking. I mean his favorite channel was Food TV. We grieved that he couldn't cook anymore. So what could we do to replace the meal?

I started reading to him at night. We went through at least a hundred books. It was a wonderful time. At nine thirty, it would be pie time. Bill got hooked on Key lime pie. He had lost a hundred pounds and that was the only way he could gain weight.

The weekend of Hurricane Katrina, we went to the oncologist. They said they wanted to try a new kind of chemo. They said there was a 30 percent chance it would work, and if it didn't, he should get his papers together because he wouldn't last a month. During that weekend we were watching all of the Katrina stuff, just in shock about it and in shock about him.

I went to the grocery store and came back through the backyard. And there was the biggest tortoise. We're not anywhere near water. I couldn't believe it. Bill came outside to see it, wheeling all his stuff, his feeding tube, and his IV. He said, "Katherine, turtles mean longevity."

The next day they called. "His tumor markers are good—

this is positive. This chemo is working." So the turtle, that just meant a lot to us after that.

In December of 2007, for Christmas, we went to a place in Georgia called Cumberland Island. There was an inn on the island called Greyfield and he drove us all the way down there in two days and we had a great time. When we got there, he couldn't breathe.

I drove us back to Little Rock and I tried to get Bill to go to the hospital, but it was, "No, no, not today, because my brother will be here," so we watched football. He couldn't even walk. It's ridiculous now that I didn't call an ambulance.

He was in ICU for a month. His official cause of death was that he could just never get his breathing back. So there's some guilt that I feel that I didn't . . . that we didn't deal with that sooner. He died of lung failure. It was exacerbated by chemo and his lung condition.

The way he died was very precious. I was alone with him, and we took him off of life support at noon. His breathing got more and more labored. I kept saying, "There's no goodness, there's nothing good in this." My sister came in with her husband and one of the chaplains. The chaplain said, "Can I pray for you about this?" In her prayer she said, "God, we ask that we might see your goodness in the end of this life." That struck me because that's exactly what I believed I hadn't seen.

Not very long after that, Bill all of a sudden opened his eyes. He hadn't had his eyes open for any length of time for over three weeks. (*crying*) He stared at me with such love. All I could do was cry and say, "I'm sorry, I'm sorry." I don't know where that came from, if it was sorry that I'm not saving you or whatever, but he kept just gazing at me with love. Then he kind

of looked away. He looked past me and I know he was . . .
wherever he was going that he could see it. My brother-in-law
said, "Bill, Jesus is waiting for you, go to Him," and Bill closed
his eyes and died.

We didn't get to travel very much. I wish we had, but in
some ways it was the day-to-day things that made it more precious. I don't have memories of trips with him, but I have great
memories of cleaning out the refrigerator! Whatever, I'm all for
that, that sustains me.

I had total respect for him and just fascination and trust. The
combination was great because you can take someone for
granted if all you feel is comfortable with them. You sort of get
lazy. He kept me on my toes—the way he worded things, the
way he thought, the things he would tell me about his life that
he hadn't ever shared before. I had known him for sixteen years,
I'm like, what? He was fascinating.

He was also very open. He couldn't tell me enough how
much he loved me. I heard it constantly. He'd yell it. We'd be
getting ready for work, I'd be in the bathroom, he'd be in the
kitchen: "I love you!" And to not hear that now is just horrible.

I don't let myself have any prescription sleeping pills anymore. I will go and get over-the-counter sleeping pills to help
me sleep, but I don't overdose. I have a job again, so I've got to
pull myself together and go to work.

It's like I'm finding my way. I feel like I'm three years old
and I'm trying to learn how to walk and talk at the same time. I
kind of go around apologizing to people all of the time and
I don't dress very appropriately these days. I share too much and
I say inappropriate things. I figure if I can get through the day
without doing any harm to anybody, I'm doing okay for myself.

C. S. Lewis wrote in *A Grief Observed*, after his wife died, "The act of living is different all through. Her absence is like the sky, spread over everything."

I can go to the same grocery store as I always did, and they've got the same stuff. The grocery store didn't change. It's just a different experience. The absence of Bill covers everything. The things under the sky haven't changed, but the sky has changed.

BILL VON HUNSDORF, AGE 74

DYERSVILLE, IOWA

"I thought to myself, 'Well, it's about time that I
perhaps take on some companionship.'"

I was madly in love with a girl in high school. I danced with her
once. She invited me to her wedding. I think I was about seventeen years old. I was still mooning about her. Well, I broke
down at the wedding. I should have stayed home. That was the
end of that.

I went off to college. I had a hard time figuring out just what
kind of a horse I wanted to ride. I started out in premedicine
and switched over to the ministry. I went back into medicine
and more or less did a disaster there. I acquired a teaching certificate and taught science in high school for two years. I was
not really enthused with teaching high school kids because
they've got a fairly nonchalant attitude about this stuff.

About that same time, my folks were getting up in age and
were needing somebody to, oh, like for instance cut grass and
take them here and there when they wanted to go someplace.
They were by no means handicapped, but it was just sort of
handy for them to have a houseboy around.

I was single and I sort of felt indebted to my folks because they had given me all this education, and so I just felt that I would stay home. And if they were satisfied with me staying home, well, that allowed me to pursue my own endeavors.

I liked to play the piano at that time. I memorized several Beethoven sonatas. I memorized a couple of Chopin études and that kind of thing. I studied mathematics, I acquired a familiarity with French, also a familiarity with German.

I like my own company quite well. I'm not a guy that needs to go out to the bar and, you know, drink beer with the buddies from dusk till dawn. I can spend an awful lot of time trying to perfect a passage either on the violin or on the piano. That is where I prefer to spend my time rather than bullshitting with somebody down the street.

Dyersville is a farming community of about four thousand people. A lot of people here drive off to Dubuque to work at some of the factories. John Deere has a great big industrial manufacturing plant there. Most of the people in town knew me because my dad ran a drugstore and I worked in that drugstore when I was in high school. The population of Dyersville doesn't turn over that fast, so even ten, twenty, thirty years later, I still knew most of the people in town and they knew me. I never had anybody question as to why I wasn't running around with a girl. I heard a lot of people remark that it was so grand that I stayed home and took care of my folks.

Well, as all things ultimately happen, my dad passed on and then my mother needed somebody around here to take care of things for her. My sisters Rita May and Jolene and my brother Julian were all three of them married and off to raising their

own family. My dad died in the year 1976. My mom finally
passed on in 1986.

I did some traveling around the countryside and thought to
myself, "Well, it's about time that I perhaps take on some companionship to help me enjoy some of the financial benefits and
all that I was able to acquire." I just thought it would be more
appropriate for me to be living with somebody than not living
with somebody.

I joined the Toastmasters. They're a group of people who get
together to learn how to do public speaking. One of the great
fears that I had when I was studying for the priesthood is getting
up in front of a crowd and giving a speech, so I figured that if
I . . . whenever I got back into the ministry, I certainly would
have to know how to give a sermon. The Toastmasters just hit
that particular problem to a T. I was in the Toastmasters for
maybe about two or three years.

I met one of these girls that was there. I conversed with her
and took her out a couple of times. And then I found out that
she had a little boy. She was a very nice girl, nice-looking girl,
and it was not because she had a kid that I didn't continue my
relationship with her. The reason why I didn't continue my relationship with her was because she was a divorcée. And if you
are a divorcée, if somebody from a third party comes in, that is
a wrench into the gear works that will never allow these two
people to reconcile.

I bowed out of the situation. I stopped calling her and
stopped seeing her and I guess she understood that. It was not a
comfortable situation; I had a little loneliness about it. But I'm a
practicing Catholic and it's my own morality besides. In order to
completely sever the relationship, I quit the Toastmasters.

I found out that there's a singles outlet that encouraged the encounter of unmarried people to meet one another. It was in Dubuque. There was a meeting of these singles at Marshall Park, and so one Sunday afternoon in 1992, I thought what the heck. This was on a sunny afternoon day in June, and there was a bench along this pathway that overlooked the Mississippi River. And son of a gun, I saw a nice little girl sitting there on the bench. I figured that she was fair game. I got into a conversation with her, and the next thing I knew, we made an arrangement.

She was a farm girl, and her family farm was on Placid Road, about four miles south of the town of Epworth. I asked her if she would like to go to this dance at Dickeyville, Wisconsin. And she says yes.

And that, let me tell you, was the beginning of the end.

I was almost fifty-nine and she was in her late thirties. But she apparently thought I was interesting enough, and I found her quite interesting, and so we started dating. I used to ride my bicycle from Dyersville over to see her every once in a while. I figured that I wasn't getting any younger and she wasn't getting any younger, either. In November of that year, when I was fifty-nine, we were married, and we've been together ever since.

Before Annie, I wasn't living out as a hermit. I was always with my mom or dad or both. If you are living with people like that, you already have an ability to be tolerant of other people's feelings and desires and wants. I don't know whether my wife would agree with how easy it was for her to live with me, but I certainly didn't find it difficult to start living with her. I enjoyed doing things with her, and it's a continuing thing.

I must admit that before she came to live with me, the place was empty. There was a wee bit of loneliness. In the latter days of my mother's life, we had a dog by the name of Karen. Karen was with me for several years after my mother died. Karen did keep me company, and what really broke my heart was the day she died. One day, she wanted to go out to do her job. It was a real cold day and she could hardly move around. Then she did her job and hopped up the last two steps behind our back door. And she was having a very difficult time getting up the third step, and so I lifted her up and she looked into my eyes and died.

You might like to find out why I called that dog Karen—this is just a little side line. I did my own personal banking business in Dubuque, with a bank that was called the American Trust & Savings. And there was one of these little tellers in that Dubuque bank that I got sort of interested in, and her name was Karen. I did my banking there to expand this interest, but it was a dead end all the way through. She was not interested in me. But that is why this dog I got, I named her Karen. She had these real droopy bedroom eyes, just like this gal at the bank had. It was not because I was insulting the girl, but because I wanted to remember the girl.

Anyway, Karen finally died—the dog, of course. I don't know whether the other girl is alive or not. But anyway, afterward I found that the house was quite empty. And so that's why I started looking around shortly thereafter. And then I finally found one that satisfied my requirements.

I guess a person marries the person that looks like their mother. I can see a lot of resemblance in Annie's face similar to my mother's face. The eyes and the nose and the mouth—very similar.

When I first met Annie, she was a factory girl. She was a supervisor down at the toy factory. She worked down there for the first couple of years of our marriage, and then, of course, it closed, and she went to work for fast food out at Hardee's. Later, they needed a cook out at the hospital. The hours were much more civilized, and so Annie took that job, and that's where she works now.

I was especially interested in finding a person younger than me who would be able to give me some children if that were possible. I lived under the illusion that old guys could sire kids just as well as young guys. Well, apparently that is not the case, because our marriage has never been blessed with an offspring. But that does not say that we didn't try.

I was a virgin before I got married, and as far as I know according to her reports to me, she also was a virgin. I'm glad that this was my first experience with this person and I'm glad it was the only experience that I've ever had like that. It just seems to glue me to her.

I have found out that it's like the frosting on a cake. You can only eat so much frosting and you actually want some cake. I would imagine that every single couple in the entire world has different needs with respect to that personal facet. I suppose if I were a much younger person I would want much more frosting than what I have now. You're talking to a guy that's now seventy-four years old. I think that when you're my age, the question of this particular facet is not as important as what it used to be for a younger person—but frosting is still good!

You've got to appreciate, I was interested in becoming a priest, which is a celibate life, and I think that I have my animal nature fairly well under control. I think I am fortunate in having been . . . having allowed myself to be trained to accept the responsibility before having to deal with the raw animal nature of the problem. Hollywood has done a great job of showing us all about the animal relationship of love, but they have done a very poor job of making certain that there is another facet of love which is more intellectual, that demands that I stay with this person until I die, whether I like it or not.

She's nice to be around. She likes a good laugh. She puts up with me (*laughs*), which would mean that she has to be very tolerant, I would think. If she were hearing this conversation, I think she would agree.

We like to travel and live together. Just for instance, we went to Dubuque this morning. Yesterday afternoon, I opened my mouth and this cap fell off of my tooth, and so when Annie came back from working at the hospital I showed her and she says, "Well, you've got to get that thing fixed—period!" Her dentist is in Dubuque, so she took me there this morning to get my tooth glued back on.

That's just a short drive and then we did some shopping. But every year during our vacation we take a fairly extensive trip. We go down to Florida. We went over to see the Devils Tower one time. Another time we went over to House on the Rock. And we went over to Rome, Italy, one time. A couple of years ago, she got involved in that bingo program at our church, and of course I have to help her with that once in a while. So we do some fun things like that. The longest separation that I can recall was about two weeks ago; she had to be at the Catholic Daughters of America convention in Dubuque, and so, from Thursday until Sunday, she was there continually.

I was lonely. We now have a dog whose name is Plato, and of

course Plato did keep me company. But it was not comfortable with her gone. Of course, she can go. She's free to go wherever she wants to go, and she usually stays around. When I expect her back from work, and she's late, I get kind of uncomfortable. I know she's going to be coming, but I like to have her around here. If she's not at work and she has gone someplace else, I'm not really comfortable with that. But I realize that she has her own interests and her own needs, and so when she does go off, I tolerate it. I don't really worry about her running around with some other guy. It's just that I like to have her around. It's a living body. (laughs)

You know, it's hard to express. I was very comfortable living here all by myself until she came in, and when she came in, then the machinery within me just seemed to have changed.

I suspect that I could have this loneliness satisfied with any number of different people, but the relationship with Annie is very unique, very comfortable. I don't know if I'm made for her, but she seems to be made for me. I think that I had a fairly clear head on my shoulders when I agreed to take up this relationship. Without a doubt, I had a checklist, and she most certainly had a checklist with respect to me.

I liked her laugh. I liked her. When we're dancing together, her body is very soft, and I like that. Annie is a little bit more fleshy than a lot of people. And Annie herself is somewhat concerned with her girth. But it's not a problem with me. I could imagine that there are girls that are much more physically attractive to the greater population of men. But I would imagine that in close encounters, they feel a little bit more bony, if you get my drift. Annie does not feel bony at all. When we are next to each other, she's nice and soft.

CATE CARVAJAL, AGE 58, AND
NICK SHEPARD, AGE 64

PORTLAND, OREGON

"If you ever see anybody else, I'll kill you."

Nick: The first thing you have to know is that early on in our relationship, Cate actually said, "If you ever see anybody else, I'll kill you."

Cate: Oh, yes, I was completely conventional. I'd never heard of polyamory. I certainly would not have believed that it was possible to love more than one person.

Nick: When I met Cate, we'd each been married and divorced. I was forty-eight, she was forty-two.

Cate: We had sex every single night we were together. For something like five years.

Nick: Yeah, but we weren't together every night.

Cate: (*laughs*) My kids lived with me four days a week, and Nick lived with his full time, and we traveled a lot, so we never had the chance to devolve into a domestic routine.

Nick: I mean, we were in love—

Cate: (*fake sobs*) You said "*were*"! (*laughs*)

Nick: We met each other in January. In April, we did Ecstasy together for the first time. We began to do it every few months. It always resulted in this very significant affirmation of how much we loved each other. It did all the good things Ecstasy is supposed to do. About seven years into our relationship, we started fantasizing about various sexual possibilities. You know, just for fun. Cate wanting to see me with a guy—

Cate: I mean, we were naked, in bed, so it was not a totally abstract conversation on our part.

Nick: This went on probably two or three times, and at a certain point I said to Cate, you know, we don't have to just fantasize about this stuff. We can actually do it.

Cate: I smacked him! (*laughs*)

Nick: My best friend from high school, he's sort of a closet homo, and he's always wanted to do sexual stuff with me. So we were out at his house one day, getting stoned, and Paul was delighted, you know, by the prospect of sucking each other off in front of Cate.

Cate: I was not interested in participating. Paul's quite beautiful physically, but he's way too annoying. But it was fun because it was different. I'm generally up for anything different as long as, you know, no puppies or minors are being hurt. (*laughs*) I'm glad we experienced it.

Nick: There was something unfun about it for me. I'm not particularly attracted to guys. But I was doing it primarily for Cate's delectation.

The next day, we had dinner with Cate's best friend, Elizabeth, and got stoned. And Elizabeth and I were totally clear that the three of us could be fucking. Then and there. And when we left, I said to Cate, "You know, we could have gone to bed with Elizabeth just now." And she said, "Really?"

Cate: I was oblivious as usual.

Nick: I set it up. We went to Vegas and rented a room.

Cate: Because where else do you go to be sinful? (*laughs*) I just figured that life was short. I really trusted Elizabeth and I really trusted Nick.

Nick: Cate had a justification, which I have always found incredibly romantic. Which is that she wanted somebody to reminisce with at my funeral about what a great fuck I was.

Cate: I imagined all your lovers gathered around the casket going, "Daaaamn!" (*laughs*)

I thought it was exciting because it was transgressive. I had never been in bed with a girl before. And it's a turn-on for a lot of couples to watch their partner have sex. It was sexy to see Nick in bed with someone.

Nick: And what Cate said, which I find interesting, is that on one hand, it was one of the most terrifying things she'd ever seen, but on the other hand, it was one of the most exciting things she'd ever seen.

Cate: Yep, that's true.

Nick: And what happened next was that Elizabeth and I really wanted to be together again. Cate agreed to another meeting. And it was pretty disastrous. It turned out that neither of us was sufficiently bi. Threesomes weren't going to work out for us.

Cate: I didn't want to be in bed with them. I didn't know how to be. I'm just not sufficiently bisexual, and unfortunately, that's not going to change. I remember being acutely aware that

that we had opened Pandora's box. We'd unlocked the genie from the bottle. Because what happened was that then Nick got involved with Elizabeth. Emotionally. So we decided we would have sex with other people. Separately. Separate relationships.

Nick: Cate was unbelievably brave about it.

Cate: Well, the reason I went along with it was simply that it seemed interesting. It seemed worth it to me to push my psychological limits, to just work through it. I wanted to get to a better self, because I knew—I hope that doesn't sound preachy—but I just feel like if you can be generous in that way, it's better.

Nick: Cate, I'm just . . . I'm a boy, you know. It's not unusual when a boy wants to do this sort of thing. What's unusual was Cate, like nobody I've ever seen, decided at some point that this was a good idea. And she sort of never looked back.

Cate: But it was hard. It was complicated. I was so jealous. Oh, my God. Nick would be with Elizabeth and I wouldn't be able to sleep. She lived in California and he was there a lot on business, so they would spend the night together. They spent a weekend in Paris and it almost killed me.

Nick and Elizabeth, to their credit, would always offer to stop. And I knew that if I had asked, they would have. Once he was with Elizabeth and they called and said I was really present in their thoughts. And I knew that was true. But I remember really struggling with it. I remember explaining to Nick: "You have my permission 100 percent. But I can't promise that I'll be happy."

Nick: I remember we had a very interesting conversation

that I've never forgotten. We were walking around in Montreal and discussing how in your average relationship, at some point, somebody strays. And then you spend an unbelievable amount of energy either breaking up or salvaging things.

Cate and I realized that we would rather figure out a way to have a rich, sexual, romantic life with expanded boundaries than to constantly be trying to repair a relationship that was falling apart because somebody's got the hots for somebody.

Cate: It just seemed like a more interesting way to live, to have an infinitely greater sense of sexual possibility, to have the possibility of romantic love with more than one person. I mean, it's rare in life to really fall in love, but—

Nick: I mean, there's love and there's love and there's love and there's love.

Cate: But just that there's that possibility, if you're having drinks with someone, or, say, see someone standing on the subway, for example, and you know even just in the abstract that you could have sex with them and that it wouldn't send the entire apple cart crashing, there is a sense of possibility that is lovely to live with—even if you never, ever exercise it.

Nick: We started out with quite a few rules, and we ended up with three: no sneaking around; safe sex; and we each have veto power. If one of us says no, that's it.

Cate: Anyone who comes into our life has to understand that our primary commitment to each other is the foundation for whatever takes place with anyone else. And that's not up for grabs: I'm not leaving Nick.

Nick: Still, I like to say this is not a game for amateurs, you know? This is a high-risk game. Because we're definitely talking about more than just being simply in lust. Really, if you're going to live a polyamorous life, you have to accept the fact that your partner might fall in love with somebody else.

Cate: When one of us has a crush on someone new, the other one can't replicate that. They cannot compete with the newness, and the new relationship energy takes over.

Nick: Somebody said to me, "Jealousy obviously isn't a problem for you and Cate." I said, "Don't be ridiculous. If we weren't jealous, we wouldn't care about each other." It's that we handle it differently than the average couple.

To make this work, we have to appreciate each other all of the time.

Cate: You cannot take each other for granted.

Nick: Being poly, if you're going to make it work, you've got to work as twice as hard on your relationship. To the extent that Cate can go out and fall in love with somebody, I have to work pretty hard to earn her respect and her love. It becomes very important to express our love for each other. When I get on an airplane, I always text Cate—part of it is habit and part of it is I need Cate to know I love her.

Cate: I think the impression that people have of these things is that the guy is the sexual adventurer, and he somehow talks his girlfriend into this and she goes along to keep him happy. That was not the case.

Nick: No. I'm very jealous of Cate's love affairs.

Cate: Wait, whoa, whoa. I have *one*. One love affair. With Daniel. And I did have this intense thing—this—

Nick: It isn't over yet, and it counts.

Cate: Yeah, it totally counts, but you fell "in love" with

Christine, or at least you were; you certainly fell "in love" with Sara; you were "in love" with Elizabeth. You're not exactly sitting on the shore here.

Nick: I don't think I was ever in love with Elizabeth.

Cate rolls her eyes and makes a face.

Nick: (*laughs*) We had a very dark period, which came about when Cate first deeply fell in love with someone else. It was just the classic case where, you know, the boys tend to be the ones that say to the girls, "This is going to be great! Let's do it, let's do it, let's do it."

And when the girl finally decides, "Okay, this non-monogamy thing is fantastic. Let's do it," that's when the boy tends to freak out: "Wait! Wait! It was okay when I was sleeping around, but if you're going to do it, and especially if you're actually going to start falling for someone, this is way too nerve-racking for me."

Cate had been so brave going through the pain of me and Elizabeth, when it became my turn to go through some pain, because Cate had really fallen for someone, the last thing I was going to do was pull the plug on it. But I didn't have all of the resources necessary to go with the flow. It was problematic.

Cate: But Nick also went through open-heart surgery. And—can I discuss the chemical aspect, Nick?

Nick: Yes.

Cate: Okay, this is about seven years into our relationship. Nick was fifty-five. He had open-heart surgery. And I was in a relationship with Daniel, who was thirty years younger than Nick. Nick was self-medicating with cocaine for part of that time.

Nick: We call it the Dark Period. I had to go through what

Cate went through when I was with Elizabeth. But listen, part of it is that Daniel is thirty years younger than I am. It had nothing to do with mortality issues. It has to do with *vitality* issues.

Cate: What's the difference?

Nick: I wasn't worried about dying.

Cate: Liar!! "I'm only having open-heart surgery—but who thinks about dying?" (*laughs*)

Nick: The big problem with the Daniel period—it drove me crazy that I couldn't excite Cate the way that Daniel could. To know that we couldn't have that new relationship energy, as Cate calls it, that fresh excitement of somebody new, that I wasn't able to provide that for Cate, and conversely, that she wasn't able to provide that for me—

Cate: I think Nick was having a life crisis.

Nick: No. The point is that I was afraid you'd want to leave me for him. And by now, we've each had a half a dozen relationships that have been of any significance. Some of them have gone on for five or six years. But for me, none of them could replace Cate. If Cate fell off the face of the earth, it's unlikely that I would have sought any of them to be my girlfriend.

Cate: That's a relief.

Nick: I mean, I had a deep, deep crush on Sara. You always pointed out that my eyes just glazed over at the thought of her, that she turned me to jelly. But Sara's fucking crazy. I mean, I would never in a million years want to be with Sara.

Cate: But when it happened with that woman Christine whom you saw very briefly, every fiber of my body went WHOOP! ZHOOP! ZHOOP! I mean, it wasn't a matter of personal animus—

Nick: She was a really good person.

Cate: But I was just terrified of her, terrified—as I have never been before or since—that I would lose Nick. Not because of her, but this was during the Dark Period, and we were not on solid ground. If you want to have a nonmonogamous relationship like we have, you have to be able to communicate, and we weren't communicating well.

Nick: It was a complicated moment. Cate was several months into this very serious, deep love affair with Daniel, and I met this woman who I think would never have tried to take me away from Cate.

Cate: I was not worried about her being the evil player in this at all; I was worried about Nick falling in love with her.

Nick: I *was* falling in love with her. And I think the really interesting thing that I've never understood how to parse is that Cate has fallen deeply in love with people without ever thinking about leaving me, whereas I have found it difficult to fall in love with people, precisely because of that fear.

Cate: That's because I'm good at boundaries and rules and you are not.

Nick: That's probably a good answer.

Cate: Anyway, there's terror in any direction. It was a good example of the judicious use of veto power.

Nick: Whereas with Colleen, with whom you invoked the veto at the beginning, it was because you don't trust her.

Cate: (*hisses*) (*stage whisper*) She's a viperrrrrr. (*laughs*)

There were a million—not a million, but many—painful challenges. Enormous, terrifying. But if you have relationships that have real emotional depth to them, which is what we aspire to, then it is never safe. You're terrified about losing the person. It's high risk.

But if we weren't polyamorous, who knows what would have happened?

Nick: I can't imagine that I could have stayed in a relationship for this long monogamously.

Cate: It seems like giving each other permission to have these other adventures is definitely the reason we're so happy.

I would say that I love Nick for nine million reasons. Most of which have to do with the same conventional reasons that cause other people to love each other. I love him for how he takes care of me, and how smart he is, and how principled he is and blah-di-blah-di-blah.

And the fact that he allows me this happiness that I have been able to find with other people is a tremendous and trust-filled gift. I suspect that he feels this way even more so, in that he is more of a browser. I'm not implying that Nick is some big rottweiler and I have to say, "No, down boy." He's actually not a total horn dog—

Nick: I'm not.

Cate: But his default is "yes." I mean, that's the essence of what I love about him. His catholic taste is enormously appealing. Nick is the most interesting person I've ever known.

Nick: Oh, darling, that's so sweet.

Cate: I'm always saying this, but it's what Virginia Woolf said about Leonard Woolf: that when he entered the room she never knew what he was going to say. And I never know what Nick is going to be thinking or reading or wondering about, and it's intoxicating.

I want to live a life that is full of experiences. And Nick is maddening like everyone is maddening, but I trust him completely. I trust him with my life and my heart and my security. Life with him is just so much more interesting than it could be with anyone else in the universe.

Nick: I feel the same way. There's nobody I'd rather go through life with than Cate. Except for that one bad patch, it's been one long honeymoon.

JORDAN PERL, AGE 36

"She had many people pursuing her. I was like sixth in line."

I was in my junior year of college at Yale. I was dating a lot of different girls. But I was picking weird, wrong people.

I was really kind of feeling out what it meant to be Jewish, I think. I'm from Denver, and there was something missing from my past that I was sort of filling in. My family was deeply assimilated. We were sort of country club Jews. There are pictures of my great-grandfather playing golf with Eisenhower, and they grew up with Christmas trees in their homes. So now I was at college, reading Philip Roth. And when you're twenty years old, twenty-one, reading *Portnoy's Complaint* for the first time—it was just a very important experience for me.

So somehow I kept ending up with these girls who not only were not Jewish, but were sort of wayward Christians, struggling with their past. Like, the father was a deacon in the church, and they still half believed or almost all of the way believed.

There was this Southern Baptist girl from Tennessee. I de-

cided that we'd rent *The Last Temptation of Christ*. It seemed like
it would be interesting. That was horrific. Then there was this
old WASP boarding school person I went on one date with. We
got into a debate about Jews and Christians. I was testing out a
lot of attitudes. So I said there's no way that I'm ever going to
have a Christmas tree in my house. We had what I found to be
an enjoyable back-and-forth. Her roommate approached me the
next day and said that she'd come home in tears.

Something was going on with me and these girls. Our communication was stupid. I was like Mr. Forthcoming. I would ask
them out to dinner, and then talk and talk and talk. I think
there was something off-putting about that: too much talk. Me
making speeches, me being an exhibitionist—that ultimately
might have been unpleasant for other people.

I should say that I had not lost my virginity.

Then I spotted Rebecca. There was something identifiably
urban and cool about her. Very New York. Also Jewish. She was
wearing a yellow raincoat. I felt a biological, lusty sort of inex-
plicable attraction.

Rebecca was living in the same building as me, with a roommate, Hannah. They were friends from high school. Between
boyfriends and high school friends, they hadn't made any real
social connections at Yale, and now they were really regretting
it. They had made a commitment to make some friends, and
there I was. So they decided that I was going to be their friend,
which was a huge problem, because it wasn't what I was looking for. I had a lot of friends. I wanted romance.

But it was exciting. Rebecca and I both took a lot of pleasure in talking. There was something that was compatible, that

was similar. She had a jokey forthcomingness that matched mine, the endlessly swift verbal details about everything I was thinking and feeling. And she was a match to my loquacious, sort of inappropriate streak. Taboo subjects were a little less taboo for her. You know, her birth control pills were out on the table.

Rebecca was not religious but was deeply identified as a Jew. And somehow those traits, because they were so different from other girls, I was like, "Oh, it's because she's Jewish. I'm with someone like me now." It was kind of about self-discovery too. My family didn't have that old-world immigrant sort of remnant that Rebecca had in her Jewish past, and I was interested in that. Her parents, her grandparents all spoke with thick European accents. Looking back, some of that seems a little naïve. And it had to do with reading Philip Roth and wanting some things to be true about what it meant to be Jewish that maybe aren't, but there it is.

Rebecca let me into a level of intimacy much more quickly than I was accustomed to. She told me private details about her family life, dirty jokes, stuff like that. I didn't know, is this a New York thing? A Jewish thing? Or more specific to the two of us? There was a real mutual interest in our conversation. She was listening and participating and she was so *funny*.

She had many people pursuing her. I was like sixth in line. She had a boyfriend in Paris. She had the one that she really loved, who also lived in our building. Then there was the movie star—who is a known movie star now, but he wasn't then. I won't name him, but Rebecca was having an affair with him. That's three. Then there was a very sweet guy, who I ended up having coffee and commiserating with, who was literally stalking her. And she had a guy from high school who was still obsessed with her. That's five. And I was clearly sixth. At best.

So we had this developing friendship. We went out to dinner, we went to the beach, we watched a lot of *Star Trek* together. At some point mid-fall, Hannah and Rebecca and Dan, Hannah's boyfriend, said, "Why don't you come out with us? We're going to get high." This came out of the blue, because I didn't really think things were going anywhere.

I'd never smoked pot before. I had like two hits, and I had this tremendous paranoid response. I felt I was going to die. Classic, right out of a teenage movie of the week. Rebecca was like, "This is too much for me. He's freaking out!" She knew it was my first time smoking. I made Hannah and Dan take me to the university health services, where they gave me Benadryl and said, "You're high, go home."

Luckily that didn't interfere with the development of our friendship. Meanwhile, I was trying to date all these girls and the disconnect was so apparent. With Rebecca, it was immediately comfortable and informal and there weren't these barriers.

Then something happened on October 27 of 1992. I still remember that date. There were these three kids that my roommate and I would hang out with, helping with their homework one afternoon a week, like Big Brothers Big Sisters type thing. My roommate couldn't do it that week, and Rebecca wanted to photograph the kids. We carved pumpkins with them and we had a great day. It was kind of like a flash of domestic life— digging out the pumpkins, pulling the seeds out. She was taking pictures and it seemed so natural.

We made out after. For me it was like, "Wow, it's happening! I am winning!" Rebecca immediately said, "It was awful, I regret it. It was so bad. We're not doing that again."

Because, you know, I was not the only person obsessed with Rebecca. Her worry was that she was just leading people on, she was hurting people. But I couldn't believe that she wasn't on the same page as me. I really tried to argue it out. I tried to show her the evidence: "Look at how much time we're spending together. Look how much we're enjoying each other." How could she not see this? I was becoming obsessed. Clearly.

After that there was a lot of pathetic begging. We had the election, I mean the election fiasco. It was '92, Clinton versus Bush. I wanted to watch the returns with her. I made a bowl of guacamole and we were going to eat this bowl of guacamole and chips, just the two of us. But when I went up to her apartment, she was with a friend from high school, the one I put in the category of being obsessed with her. I stayed over there for a few minutes and it was kind of embarrassing—here I was with this guacamole. Once I realized that they were sort of ignoring me, I just left this bowl of guacamole outside her door.

It was a really rough time, months and months of it. I don't remember all the things that happened. It was just a lot of me feeling frustrated and talking endlessly to my friends and them not being particularly sympathetic. Rebecca was perfectly happy that we had become friends. She just didn't want me to be constantly calling her.

Then Rebecca decided to go to Paris for the second semester, to study photography and live with her boyfriend. And so the night before she was leaving, we said our goodbyes. It was her last night and clearly I was one of her best friends despite everything. I gave her all of these *Star Trek* figurines and related gifts and it was very, like, just the two of us. I was really sad.

And then the next day, I saw her on the street. I couldn't believe it. There she was. I said, "Wow! This is great! Do you want to go to the movies with me tonight?" And she said, "No, I have other plans." It was very unsettling because I had already gone through this whole goodbye with her. She was supposedly gone but there she was. I felt sort of betrayed—again.

I still wanted to go to the movies. I was done with my final exams and I invited all of these friends. One after the other, they all had other plans and I finally decided to go on my own.

So I went. This was a suburban Connecticut theater, not where the Yale students usually went. And when I got there, I saw her in the back row of the theater—with the future movie star.

I was enraged. I was never somebody who punches his hand through the window or something. But when it was over, I stormed out of the theater, and on the highway I roared past them in my car, like ninety-five miles an hour, and pulled in front of them and slammed on my brakes. Not trying to cause an accident but make myself known to them. I followed her to where he parked his car, and I was like screaming, yelling at her in the parking lot—not, like, names, but more like, "You really hurt my feelings!"

But while she was in France, somehow we quickly went from that moment in the parking lot to writing these letters. That pleasure we shared talking got put into this tremendous correspondence. I wrote her these postcards virtually every day that were so melodramatic and cute that apparently she and her boyfriend would read them together and laugh.

I did finally lose my virginity. I was seeing this girl, it just happened. It seemed very much like getting the job done. She also was very inexperienced. Once it was finished, it was immediately reported in my next letter to Rebecca.

And then summer happened, the summer between my junior and senior year. I went to Los Angeles where my dad was living. I worked at the Gap, and I was dating these girls who were not like the girls who went to Yale. You know, I was really playing the field. I didn't end up sleeping with anyone else, but it was a very exciting summer for me. I was experimenting, I was smoking cigarettes, I would sit till midnight at the coffee shop reading Dostoyevsky. I came back in the fall, ready to just be Rebecca's friend. I felt different. And I told her that and she was very pleased.

Within about a week of senior year starting, that plan totally fell apart. I was obsessed as ever before. We would often meet at the library and sort of study in tandem, but I wasn't doing much of anything. It had just gotten too painful. I couldn't concentrate. I felt like a crazy person.

The dishonesty of saying that it was okay to be her friend, it overwhelmed me. It wasn't fair. She was getting something that she valued—but it was no longer okay with me that that should be available to her while it was making me so unhappy. I couldn't have her go on with this friendly banter and pretend it wasn't wreaking havoc on my whole life.

Finally, in mid-September, I said to her, "I can't just be your friend. We either have to move to the next point, or I just can't be with you." It was clear that she was not going to move to the next point. So I said, "Well, then I just can't be with you," and I left the library. Both of us were crying.

It was like quitting an addiction. I really had to force myself with tremendous willpower to not contact her in any way.

For about two months we didn't see each other. I remember walking down the street on my birthday and seeing her. We looked the other way. She used to wear this perfume that was very appealing to me—I don't remember what kind—but I was just pining for her, and I remember passing someone who was wearing the same perfume as her, and I felt this serious jolt. (*laughs*) It turned out to be some elderly lady.

Then Hannah, her former roommate, came back into the picture. This was not a strategy of mine; they had had a big falling-out. They weren't friends at all anymore. I wasn't looking for anything, but I started spending a lot of time with Hannah. She was filling the role of Rebecca—the big gap. It was just someone, the kind of friend you also want to sleep with—and we were, within that month.

We ended up going to one of these formal senior balls, because we were now approaching the second semester of our senior year. It must have been November, the week before Thanksgiving. We drank a lot and we were dancing and I looked across the room. It was one of these moments where across a crowded dance floor, a channel opened. And there's Rebecca. She is staring at us and tears are just streaming down her face. There was no other way to interpret it, this reaction: She was having a moment, a realization.

I called her the next day. And at Yale, you get the whole week off before Thanksgiving. Everyone leaves. But by some wonderful coincidence, both Rebecca and I weren't leaving until Wednesday. We had all of New Haven to ourselves. We got together—in bed together. Here we were, suddenly, after a year and a half of on-and-off-again pursuit.

We were mostly secluded indoors. It was clear that we needed to be separated from the rest of the world because everything was so fragile. She was feeling really afraid.

A lot of resistance had built up to Rebecca with my friends and family. They were very protective of me because this woman seemed to be ruining my life. Her big worry was that if she got involved, everybody would blame her for restarting this horrible chapter of my life. So she forbade me to speak of it. Usually it would've been very difficult for me to keep my mouth shut about anything, but it was easy. I think we both knew that those first few days were either going to make it or break it.

Once it took hold, we were basically just together all of the time. We would forget to eat. We were in bed all the time. I was blissed out.

There were a lot of embarrassing attempts to say, "I want to say I love you," or "What would you say if I said, 'I love you'?" Talking had been instrumental in building our friendship, but the talking just got in the way now. The words came from a different part of the brain than the feeling part.

If I had been a cool character, we might have had a torrid affair right when we met each other, and it would have ended. It's hard for me to remember this now, you know, twelve years into marriage, but the fact that it took so long might be the reason why we ended up together. It's really been the key to our long-term happiness. With all that talking and all those twists and turns, we spent a lot of time together practicing for our domestic future. We just didn't know we were practicing for it.

RUSSELL GORE, AGE 52

NEW ORLEANS, LOUISIANA

"Love is the feeling that you get when you're with somebody,
and it's like a brother-and-sister relationship. But when the
weekend come, you might not be brother and sister
for a little while."

I met her seventeen and a half years ago when I was helpin' a
friend get his driver's license. I fell in love the minute I seen her.
She looked good! A hell of an attractive lady. A friend of mine
worked at the driver's license place, and I said, "Who is that
lady? Please, man, look, you gotta give me her number." He
said it was confidential and he couldn't give it out, but he said,
"Go follow her and see if she give it to you herself!"

And so I kind of like trail her outside to a sandwich shop at
the Kenilworth Mall. And I never forget, Sally Jesse Raphael
had a good program on that day and everybody was sitting up
there looking at the program that was on TV and I eased over
there to start talking to her.

She was reluctant. She just stood back and looked a little bit.

But we went to talkin'. She came from the St. Bernard housing project. I'm from the St. Thomas housing project, which is
one of the toughest ones. I just came on out and told her the
truth, told her the type of life I was livin'. I was a hustler. Cynth

was in the corporate world. She was the special-events coordinator at Harrah's Casino.

I was ready to change my life. And she told me that the relationship she was going with was kinda rocky. She looked at me and she said, "I'm just tired, Russell, I'm ready to get out." And I said, "Me too."

A couple of days later she called and invited me to dinner at her sister's house, and everything else was history.

At that time, I didn't trust nobody. Me, I was a Mike Tyson character. Love? Man, fuck that! I didn't care about love! I didn't even believe in that. I was there with the gang of dudes. Do what you have to do and move on, that was my thing. Until I met this woman, and I found out what love was about.

I just felt that this was the right person. When my mama first met Cynthia she also knew. She said, "Cynth, Russell is kind of mean but through it he's got a heart of gold. If you can put up with him and don't give in, you can break him. You could make him become that man that you want." And that's what Cynth did. She done broke me in.

Man, they used to call us Beauty and the Beast when they first met us. They couldn't believe a woman that pretty got somebody rough and tough as I looked.

I started playing the whole role, bringing flowers to her, bringing little presents, little gifts, taking her out for lunch. I just started giving it up from there. It's very seldom that you'd see most black guys do what I did. I'd start to have a flower for her at work every Friday.

A month or so after we met, what I did was, I gave her part of the money that it took to rent an apartment. I didn't really know the lady too good, but I told her, "Well, if this is gonna

work, you know, Cynth, here go the money to find an apartment, let me know where we livin' at." Next thing I know, she
called me up and told me that she got the apartment and that I
can come over now. You know, this woman could have ran off
with my money, but she gave up a house to come live with me.

She just left all her furniture in her relationship. We really
just had the apartment—no bed, no nothing. We laid on the
floor. But you know, love made us feel like that house was fur-
nished. I'm serious. That's how much I was in love. Made it feel
like I had all the furniture in the world in there.

About six months later, she laid down the law. I had a decision to make: Do I want to be with the gang, or do I wanna be
with her?

And you know, it's funny, man, I had gone to Victoria's
Secret and bought her so many fancy lingerie and stuff—for
Valentine's day, her birthday. So one day she sit me on the side
of the bed and she open up her drawer and said, "You know
what, Russell, if you don't slow down or try to do something
with yourself, suppose you go to jail? Some other man gonna
see me wearing these underwear." And then I started to think
about it. And it motivated me.

'Cause I knew where the gang was headed to—I was either
going to be dead or incarcerated. I didn't want to die. I wanted
to live. So I made a decision to take a chance and be with her.
That's what love do—make you want to live, make you want to
move forward, make you want to see your next birthday.

I learned a lot from her. I believe this woman changed my
life. The project that I come from, you couldn't afford to laugh
or show kindness or friendship because they'd think that you
were weak. This woman learned me how to laugh.

It was a transformation. She started with me, man, from knife, fork, and spoon, showin' me how to live in the white-collared world. She came from a world where you know what side the fork is supposed to be on, or this is the salad fork, this is the dinner fork. I came from a world where you just pick up your meat or just grab a fork and a fork do everything. One fork for me was every fork!

I had to put on these suits, and I had to have these shoes, and I had to figure out what side did the man walk on and what side did the lady walk on, even how to grab a paper sometime and how to look at the news. I had to get a whole new hairstyle, man! In fact, my whole look changed when I met this woman!

At first, I really didn't want it. To me, I was looking like a sissy, learning how to drink wine and eat cheese and talk about the current events of the day. I didn't like going to some of the places that we went out to eat or those balls at Harrah's casino—I didn't want to hang with these guys, with their little suits on and all this and they scared to death of me like I'm John Gotti. They're lookin' at my wife and they wanna clown with her like they clown with her at work, but they was scared, so I gotta walk over and tell them, "Guess what? You clown with her at work. Clown with her right now! I'm not gonna do you nothing."

She got me doing things that even I couldn't believe. I never thought that I'd see the day that I'd play golf. When golf come on on Sundays, I thought it was the most boringest thing in the world looking at this TV. But this woman got me—man, I'm chasing a golf ball!

My partners look at me sometimes and say, "Where's Russell

at? He ain't shootin' pool, he ain't clownin' no more? Look at him, that woman got him henpecked." Man, no, I'm in love.

Back in school I was an artist. I picked up photography from high school to college. I majored in commercial arts at Delgado. I went to make my mama happy. I was living in the projects, and I turned my bedroom into a darkroom. I failed all my classes except for art and photography.

Cynth brought out of me that I had talent and didn't have to do what I was doing. She showed me how to get a business license. I'm an artisan; I'm a licensed photographer. I've got a table at the French Market. I make pins, brooches, and earrings, and sometimes I make these plaques that go on the wall for Jazz Fest and stuff like that. I owe all of this to her. If it wasn't for that lady loving me the way she loved me, I wouldn't be here. Cynth was my motivation. I went to go work, man! And I would give this woman all of my money because I know that Cynthia take care of business. And business was taken care of. You know, like if Michael Jordan take a shot and miss it, it would be Dennis Rodman's job to rebound it back so he could take another shot. That's the way our life was: If Cynth came short of something, it was my job to go out there and make sure that it was on the table!

I don't think I've ever been in love like that before—you know, outside my mama. But that's a natural love. And then you got God. That's a natural love too. But that third love—she was the first person that I met besides my mama that I let inside—inside my heart. I was vulnerable. It's hard for a man like me to open up my heart and give it to you, because you gonna break it.

I was afraid of getting married. I was scared because it was like handcuffs, you know? It took like—whew—seven years before we got married. We went to the justice of the peace. It cost me fifty dollars. I couldn't afford to go out and get the diamond rings that I wanted, so I went to the flea market and got the rings. Them wedding bands weren't gold! They shined like gold just enough to go through the ritual of getting married. 'Cause see, I think love and trust don't come in a ring. I could wear the ring twenty-four hours a day and I could still sleep with a person with the ring on. The real ring is inside your heart.

I always call her Fat. See, my mama was kinda stout, and we used to call her Fat, meaning that we loved her. Cynth thought Fat mean she was getting overweight, but she learned to accept it as a way of me saying that I loved her. After we got married, we said it every night before we went to sleep. My last thing was a kiss on her jaw; she'd turn right and I'd turn left: "I love ya, Fat"; "I love you too." It become like a work clock.

When you say you love somebody you gonna listen to the good and you gonna listen to the bad. If I think that day, "Hey, Fat, I don't like that dress, blah blah blah, in the back"—'cause you can't see yourself in the back of the mirror—she doesn't take offense to it as far as me trying to make her feel degraded. She knows that I love her and that I'm only going to tell her the truth. And she could tell me, for instance, "Russell, where you goin' with them pants on?" and you know I'd go pull them off and put something else on and say, "Well, how that look?" and she'd say, "Oh, that look better," and when you talk about love, that's what love is. It's not to say that I'm degrading you—it's just that, when you walk out that door, I want you to represent me as much as you're representing yourself.

She met my every need. And I think if a man really got love at home, you can let him go—'cause he don't see nothing else on the street that he wants. With Cynth, we had grown so much, she wasn't jealous. She knowed exactly everything about me. These days, they don't have that. It's like you—how would a guy put it?—it's like you're a prisoner, "Where you goin'? How long you gonna be?" And to me, that ain't love, 'cause you really don't trust the person.

Love is the feeling that you get when you're with somebody, and it's like a brother-and-sister relationship. To be in love and have a brother-and-sister relationship, that mean you can tell her everything. But when the weekend come, you might not be brother and sister for a little while. (*laughs*)

We never argued too much. Sometimes when I'd get upset with her, I'd grab my golf clubs and go to the driving range and hit me some golf balls, and by the time I come back, if I'm wrong, I say, "I'm sorry, Fat." Sometimes, if I was still mad, I used to go into my room, my extra spare room, and go to sleep. She'd turn the air-condition on, up, up, up. And once I get cold, I'd get in bed. (*laughs*) We tried a lot not to get into big fusses.

So. Time went by, and rent started going up. We said to ourselves that it was time to own a home. I called my brother up and asked him to help get the money together. I had no idea of what house she was getting. Man, I didn't even know what street I was gonna live on.

Well, she got the house, and during hurricane Katrina, we

were right here in it, in New Orleans East. We weren't worried
too much. We got us a bottle of Absolut, and we thought when
the storm was over we were gonna celebrate, we was gonna beat
this.

Everybody started evacuating the city that Saturday. She said,
"Well, Russell, what do you think?" And I said, "Fat, I ain't
goin' nowhere, I'm gonna stay here. If God wants to take this
house, let him take it." We had life jackets, and the interstate
was crowded, man! I mean the traffic wasn't even moving. It
was a fairly new brick house. If push came to shove, we were
going to go to the strongest part of the house, which they say is
the bathroom. We had it all figured out; we had water, we had
food, we had everything.

That night, I went to sleep, and when I woke up, it looked
like the storm had done passed.

If you've ever watched the movie *The Perfect Storm*, that's
what happened to us. In *The Perfect Storm*, it's quiet, and in a
matter of minutes, all hell breaks loose. It was quiet and we were
celebrating. I was in my golf room and she passed by me with a
drink. I looked at her laughing and I said, "Fat, where you
going with that drink?" and she told me that she was going in
the bedroom and I said, "Wow." I thought it was time to make
love.

I told her that I was going to fix me a drink, and as I came
into the kitchen, something told me to peep out the kitchen
window. And I thought I was looking inside of an aquarium
tank.

All that water in the backyard. Nothing had come in the
house yet, but it started seeping in.

I tried not to panic, because I didn't want to panic my wife.

I tried to play it off as a joke, and we started to move a lot of artwork, a lot of expensive artwork. She got up by the attic and I handed her water and food and a lot of things. Out the front window, it looked like my house was sitting inside of a river. Man, when that window broke, water was coming in like a tidal wave. In less than a couple of minutes I had ten feet of water in my house.

We were in total shock. I was standing right there in the attic with my feet in the water. I knocked out a little wind vent and started choppin' in the roof to get out. I chopped out a big old hole, and she had to tell me to stop. She said, "Fool, you choppin' up the whole roof!" All you could hear was helicopters flying around.

She was up there trying to flag for help and I'm sitting on the steps with my feet in the water, and I said, "Cynth, do me a favor. If push come to shove, you leave me. They ain't gonna pick us up if it's the two of us." I figured there was a good chance for them to pick up just a woman, but if they saw there was a man, then they'd skip over us.

She looked at me, and she told me that she ain't gonna leave me. That night, we put a pallet down and we both slept inside the attic.

Next daybreak, I made a little flagpole, like *Survivor*—we loved *Survivor*. We was clownin', we was crackin' jokes. The woman was putting on makeup for the helicopter! My wife always dressed real good. They used to say, "Wow, Ms. Cynth!" at Harrah's casino, about how pretty she dressed. So after she got to lookin' pretty and all that, she climbed up on through the hole in the roof and was waving the flag.

Do you know, the helicopter hovered over her head like they

were going to pick her up, and then they took off and didn't pick her up. She got worked up about it. I said, "Cynth, don't start fussin'. It ain't time to fuss. Just sit down and relax. Do me a favor and just be cool with it. It's gonna be all right." I found out later that they were only picking up elderly people and children.

I'm sitting there worrying about her and I just kept telling her that it was going to be all right. And then, almost out of nowhere, she went to talkin' like she was talkin' in tongues or something like that. At that time, I knowed that something had really took an effect on her. She was lookin' in the corner like something was coming after her in the attic, and I was looking too, but I didn't see nothing. She was hollering, "No! No! No!" and I said, "Cynth, don't do this to me," and she was still hollerin', and in a matter of minutes, I pulled her to me and she leaned across my lap, and she died.

I tore her shirt off, I tried to beat her in the chest, I tried to breathe in her mouth, I tried to give her water, I did everything in the world . . . everything that I'd seen on TV to try to revive her. But she was gone.

I believe due to the heat she had a heart attack. They had an autopsy, and that's what the autopsy said. That due to Katrina.

She was the center of my life. And I just watched it go within a matter of minutes. I hollered, I panicked, I tried to motion to the helicopter to stop, but they didn't stop, they just kept on going. I had to tell the people around me what happened, 'cause they heard me hollerin', and I just tell them my wife is dead. I stayed with her, a day and a half, dead.

I spent that night on top of the roof all the way until the mid part of the next day. I just trying to keep on saying what I believe in: Absent with the body, present with the Lord. I kept trying to say to myself that what I'm looking at, it ain't my wife. I felt my wife, when she died, I felt that everything left when she was in my arms.

There comes a time in your life where you question even the strongest of your beliefs in God. I was up there asking God, "Why don't you take my life and let her live?" Man, I was just up there trying to bargain. I thought the whole world had come to an end.

When the storm was finally over, they came over above my head to pick me up, and I said, "I'm not going nowhere, my wife is dead." They tried to get me, but I wouldn't leave my wife's body.

The next day two guys that were Christians in a boat, they convinced me that my wife wouldn't want me to commit suicide or do something stupid. They said they were coming to get me away from there. They brought me down to the bridge, where we had to walk into the city.

I found some wet shoes and I put them on. I walked from New Orleans East all the way to Harrah's casino, looking outside the casino like I was waiting for her to come out like she was getting out of work. But she never come.

I didn't have no idea in my mind that the Lord was going to give me only eighteen years with her. Sitting out there at my shop at the French Market, listening to people when I asked them how long they'd been married, they'd say thirty, forty, fifty years—I really thought I'd have a forty-, fifty-year experience to tell everybody about.

I have this statue, it's called "The Joy of Love." She died right about up there. (*points upward*) And I haven't moved this statue since I came back to the house after the hurricane. And in the morning, when I get out of bed to go to work, I kinda say, "Come on, Cynth, let's go," to really motivate me to do what I have to do. I really feel her presence with me.

I thank God for my eighteen years that I had with Cynth. I realize now that the Lord put her in my life to get me straight. And then Cynth moved on to better places.

I wish I could lie to you and tell you that it's easy—it ain't easy. I still struggle with it a little bit. But through prayers and religious things, you know, I just recently learned how to not cry so much. Because my wife is with me every day of my life. I never did lose her. She's with me right now! And she's gonna be with me like that for the rest of my life until I meet her again. That's the only thing that keeps me on the straight and narrow and keeps me doing what I'm doing, because one day I'm gonna meet her again.

I really think God left her as my angel to kind of help me out. I believe He said, "Well, I don't want that problem, Cynth. You know him better than I do. Take care of him." I really believe that she's there for me. I do believe there's somebody out here that's gonna fill her shoes. But she's the one who's gonna show me who's gonna fill 'em.

CRAIG JOHNSON, AGE 42

HOUSTON, TEXAS

"I wasn't going to let my circumstances destroy the
tremendous love that God gave me."

Sam and I met when I was eighteen and she was fourteen. My
dad went to speak at Sam's church in Visalia, which is in central
California. We lived in the Los Angeles area. And I came down,
I sang at her church, and then the pastor, who was my dad's best
friend, introduced Sam and I. At the time I thought she was too
young, but she was really a sweet person. Her dad was a pilot
and his airplane crashed off of Catalina Island when Sam was
ten. He died, and she basically helped raise her brothers and
sisters.

We kind of hung out. I think all the youth groups went out
to pizza, and then every once in a while we'd talk, 'cause our
families knew each other. And then time just passed. I was
going to college, and about four years later, I got a graduation
announcement in the mail from her. I guess she hadn't forgotten. And I thought, "Wow. She's grown up." (*laughs*)

She had blonde curls. Kind of sandy blonde, green eyes, perfect teeth, which I love, and a smile that blows you away. For

me, she was beautiful inside and out. Really, really kind heart. There was just a gentleness to her. When I saw her picture, something just clicked. I felt a connection.

We went out on a date. We went to Mann's Chinese and saw a movie and we went to Miceli's, one of the oldest Italian restaurants in Hollywood. It was an awesome night. I remember putting our hands in the middle of the stars' handprints in the cement outside the theater, and she picked up her hand from one of them and our hands just kind of came together.

We kind of knew that night, like, this was planned out, this was supposed to happen. Like divine intervention. I believe that. I believe God wanted us to be together. I was dating somebody else, but I knew after our first date that it was over with the other person.

So. Then things just kind of accelerated 'cause our families knew each other, and we had some history. We got married ten months later.

There were some tough things at the beginning. Her family gave me a couple of challenges. One was that I needed to go find a good job. If I was going to be in the ministry, I needed to have a good job, which I didn't have yet. So I went out and got a youth pastor job. And when it came down close to the wedding, they didn't want to let go of Sam. Sam was eighteen, so I kind of get it. But they basically talked Sam out of getting married and sent announcements out to everybody to call the wedding off. This was about a month before the wedding. And I'm just like, "You gotta be kidding." (*laughs*)

Sam called me like nothing had even happened, "Hi, Craig, how are you?" And I'm like, "Well, I'm just a little devastated." She started crying, and I told her, "Sam, you know, if I'm the

right one and if you love me and you want to get married, you
know what to do." She wanted me to come up and get her in
Visalia, and I said, "No. If you want to get married, you need to
get your stuff together and come down. If this is what we're
supposed to do, let's do it. But I'm not going to come get you
and make you get married." I didn't know what was going to
happen. But about seven hours later a car drove up.

We went ahead with the wedding at my dad's church. A lot
of her family didn't come. And that was devastating for all of us.
We patched it up. But interesting enough, it made it so much
deeper as far as our love for each other. Even though I had great
support from my family, it was her and I for a couple years. I
think couples go into marriage with a false sense of what it's
really like, and they don't realize that it's a commitment. You
have to stand by somebody. I think it made us say, "You know
what? No matter what we face in life, we're going to do it
together and we're going to stick together."

We've been married nineteen years. I mean, we were really
blessed. We had Corey and Courtney—Corey's seventeen and
Courtney's fourteen. Corey and Courtney are just awesome and
great grades, great hearts. Just awesome.

It's kind of a funny story. When Corey was twelve or thirteen, we felt like, hey, this is all you can want right here as far as
kids were concerned. They were getting older, and we were
looking forward to doing more things as a couple, having date
nights. We were doing okay financially by that time, but in the
ministry it's not like you're making a ton of money, so we were
excited that we were going to be able to buy some things, go
traveling more together, and different things like that.

I went to go get a vasectomy on a Thursday. And then Sam

called crying on the phone on Saturday and said she was pregnant. And our whole world just changed in that moment.

In the beginning, Connor responded just like any other baby. I could talk to him and he would respond. He had eye contact. He had everything. He was as normal as any of our other kids. And we're not blaming this, but obviously, you know, there's a big debate about it: Shortly after he got his vaccination shot, about two months later, he got an ear infection, and it just started changing, where he wouldn't look at you. He hardly made any eye contact. When you said something to him he wouldn't respond. He would begin to go sit by himself. Kind of became distant in ways. He started rocking. And what was really hard for us was: How does a baby go for a year and a half from being totally responsive and then all of a sudden it just shifts?

You know how a lot of kids can walk up to you and say hello. Tell you what they want, tell you what they need. It took my son till he was at least three and a half to give you an idea of what he wanted or needed. When he got hurt, we weren't sure because he would give no reaction. He would have to really bang his head hard if he fell or something like that.

From the beginning, Sam was right there, maternal. That just seemed like that's how moms are built. She was just going to hold him. The mother usually automatically connects, and her life becomes that child. And Sam was the same way, connecting with parents through the Internet and trying everything from diets to you-name-it.

But dads connect emotionally. So I would say, "I love you, Connor," and he would just look at me, or he would look away. I come from a family that hugs a lot and is very expressive in how we feel. It was probably the most devastating thing that's ever happened to me. Because dads, what they want is what guys try to do in general—they want to give the answer, solve the problem, and stuff like that. And when they can't necessarily solve the problem, and the mom is so engrossed in finding that cure, they pull back. A separation begins to happen and arguments begin to take place. And unfortunately, it's affecting families in such a huge way. The last statistic I heard was that 80 percent of parents with autistic kids end up getting divorced. And that one out of one hundred sixty-something kids are born with autism. So this is becoming a huge primary epidemic.

About four years ago, I got the call from Lakewood Church here in Houston—it's the largest church in America. Joel Osteen is the pastor. He's the most watched pastor in the world—about nine million people watch him every week. So they were building this huge children's building and they needed a pastor to come in and help design that and build that, and so we came here.

And it was valuable for me to be here at the church, to be around somebody like Joel that really lifts people up and brought hope. Joel has key phrases he uses. He'd say things like, "You're a victor, not a victim." And what he's saying is, "You know what? You've got to believe that you can overcome this. Don't be a victim. Don't look at issues that way. Keep moving forward."

And that was right around the time we got the diagnosis. I remember the day that it happened. Connor had been tested and everything. I remember I was driving home from work and my wife called me and said, "I just got back the diagnosis and they said Connor has autism. He's in the middle of the spectrum." You never know until you get the diagnosis. It's like until you hear the diagnosis you're still not sure. And there's this kind of finality with that when you hear it. And I started getting all these thoughts, like, "Your kid is not going to be like the other kids. He's going to always have problems. He's not going to be accepted."

And I remember just going, "No! I'm not going to entertain these thoughts." I remember hitting the gas, driving home, going in the driveway, and I ran up the stairs and I picked up my son upstairs in his home and I just held him. I looked down and I said, "Connor, you're a victor, not a victim." I said, "You can do all things through Christ's strength." I just started speaking words of hope into his life. I wasn't going to let my circumstances destroy the tremendous love that God gave me.

After we got the diagnosis, I was determined never to walk backward and experience death in this relationship. I was determined to always bring hope, always move forward. So what we did, if we had an argument or frustration, stuff like that, we never let it go on. And that might have started from the very beginning, when we first got married. We never let the sun go down without saying, "I'm sorry." The Bible talks about that. Even though we might get into an argument or get frustrated, or I'd feel a disconnect, I would always turn back around and say, "You know what, we're going to work through this." Because if I kept on pulling backward, then I knew there was going to be death—not physical death but death in the relationship.

What people do when they get in hard situations, they get fearful. And that's death, because that stops whatever is trying to connect or come forward. Pulling back makes me feel desperate, like there's no hope—until you engage again and walk in that situation again and work through it. And it's the reason why marriages fail, because one person gave up or stopped feeling hope. Only takes one, you know, in that situation. And this is the quintessential thing—it really comes down to how you're going to respond. Are you going to let fear and insecurity and anger and all those things pull you back, or are you going to choose to move forward?

Obviously I have a great faith in God. Because it always seems like God gives you enough so you can keep going. There's one thing that He gave me from the very beginning. A lot of autistic kids don't respond. To anything. Now I could ask Connor, you know, questions. I could ask him for a hug, and he wouldn't do it. But then I learned that if I asked him, "Connor, give Daddy a kiss," he would turn and give me a kiss. No matter what, Connor would turn to me and give me a kiss. And it's almost like . . . God knew what I needed, you know. (cries) It's still hard for me, right now.

It's kind of turned around for me and Sam, where what was originally pretty devastating has also been the greatest gift, because, man, our love is so much deeper than I ever could imagine. I thought I loved pretty well. (laughs) But with Connor, you celebrate every little moment. Every little time he kisses me or every little time I get a hug . . . We do this kiss with Connor. It's called the Connor sandwich, and Sam kisses him on one side of the cheek and I kiss him on the other side. And when we do the Connor sandwich, man, that's just showing him we're right there—we're going to get through this together, and you're going to live a good life. It's incredible.

There are times, obviously, just like anybody else, where I

go, "Man, this is really hard." But it's less than before. Where before I might have dwelled on it longer, I don't dwell on it as hard. I go, "No. You know what? We're going to work through this."

All my kids have different challenges in their lives. Corey's going to have a different challenge, Courtney is going to have a different challenge. That's just life. That's just kids. And if I had a choice with Connor having autism or being strung out on drugs, let's say—I mean, is that any harder? Would I want that to happen to one of my children? Absolutely not. So I don't have to face those obstacles that other parents have to face, and they don't have to face some of the obstacles that I have to face. I just need to thank God for the blessing I have with him.

It seems like God's always testing you, just refining you. And that's been the greatest thing for me and Sam—we're such better parents today. Connor's made me a better person, and I think God allows you to go through those things so you'll love deeper. And care stronger. And learn to hope for more.

After we got Connor into a specialized school and saw what they were doing, we looked at different churches to see what they were doing, and they're basically just babysitting these kids, letting them watch a video, different things like that. And I said, "Man, why couldn't we do that in the church?" So Sam started a support group centered on special needs and autism. And she's reaching out with Texas Children's Hospital, and we're reaching out to families all over. And we've also launched a prayer chain where any time any child comes in or any time there's a need, we'll let one person know, let another person know, let another person know, and before you know, you could have one hundred people praying for that child.

You realize how desperate the other parents are that you come in contact with. You come together and you see: This isn't just about our family. And you realize, "Man, I'm here for a bigger purpose. Connor's here for a bigger purpose. It's not just for us, it's to impact others." And now it's going to impact hundreds if not thousands of lives.

I mean, we're still going through it. But now that we know that every little thing we celebrate is another victory for us, it helps build our faith. For instance, in the support group that Sam launched, a young boy, fourteen years old, tried to commit suicide because he just couldn't understand why he was so different than the other kids with his autism. And here Sam is reaching out to this mom, trying to comfort her and build her back up and just speak words of life into her.

I have the greatest wife in the world. I mean, I just don't know of anybody who loves me any more, that loves my children any more, that is so giving and caring, and, you know, not a lot of guys can say that after nineteen years of marriage. (*laughs*) I love her more every day, and sometimes I don't even realize how much I love her until we go through some of these struggles. It's just so deep.

Twenty Years to Thirty Years

STEVEN HAGER, AGE 50

IDAHO SPRINGS, COLORADO

*"That was the first time she tried to commit suicide.
And that happened four or five times."*

We were remodeling our house and putting in a second story. Leslie, my wife, went up there to get something and stepped off the opening and fell about ten feet. She injured herself pretty bad. Nothing broken, but it ended up kicking off this horrible, horrible pain. We didn't know what was going on. She had back pain and then migraine headaches. The doctors are looking at the X-rays and MRIs and saying, "We can't really see anything. You shouldn't have this much pain."

She was starting law school at the time. She graduated and opened up a practice. But her condition got worse and worse. She ended up having all kinds of strange illnesses, a lot of them balance-related. Just stuff that was weird. She was driving back from visiting Oklahoma once and began to throw up—for about three weeks. The doctors never could figure it out.

She had periods when she went six or seven days without sleeping. There were times when she would just roll up in a ball with pain and zone out in kind of a catatonic state. If she was feeling decent for three or four days, we considered ourselves lucky.

The problem with pain is it's a downer. And the problem with pain medication is it's also a downer. So it was kind of a no-win situation. Her life would be tolerable, and then she just couldn't sustain the pain anymore, and she'd just sink into real deep depression. It went on for years.

She ended up in the mental hospital.

The worst day was sitting with my son and my wife and the psychiatrist in a room and her telling me straight up, as calm as you could be, "I do not want to live anymore. I have had all of this I can stand," and me listening to my wife and my best friend telling me that she did not want to exist anymore—and actually understanding what she meant.

One day, I heard her messing with my shotgun, trying to get it loaded. We had a big walk-in closet, and she was in there with the shotgun, trying to pump it. I heard it clicking. She was crying and telling me that she couldn't take the pain anymore. Thank God it was a pump, because they're noisy.

That was the first time she tried to commit suicide. That was about four years into it. And that happened four or five times.

It was the most awful feeling. I definitely felt like it was my job to stop her, but at the same time, I felt like I was prolonging her suffering. I had mixed emotions and mixed beliefs about whether or not that's right or wrong. I had discussions with my pastor about the validity of the Scripture that reads, "God will not trespass or let you get through anything you can't handle." Well, I thought that was bull crap because if she had been successful in killing herself, it meant He'd given her something she couldn't handle.

When I first met my wife, in 1985, she was the most vibrant, intelligent, fun-loving person I'd ever known. We were in Tulsa. We were coworkers. She actually told me that I smelled like antiseptic, which I kind of think was funny. We discovered years later that I was wearing Mennen deodorant. She didn't find that very attractive. Then she said that I wore dentist shirts, you know, those kind of shirts with the embroidery that you get when you go on cruises. We didn't really have any interest in each other.

I was on a different floor from her. We had two computers back then, so I had to go in her office to use her computer. And of course, you're sitting at an office with somebody, you begin to talk.

About a year after we met, Leslie was at a Christmas party and was by herself. She looked fairly sad even though she was putting on kind of a happy face. About three or four months into the next year, she was going through a divorce. I'd been divorced about two years when I met her.

We began to do things outside of work together—mainly going to church. There was this period of four, five months where we were absolutely just friends. Never had dated, never had kissed.

We probably had to wait on each other about a year and a half. We definitely started to have, I don't know, feelings for each other, so I asked her out for a date. We knew God had put us together. I recognize that people say that kind of thing when really, they just have the hots for someone; the difference between having the hots for someone and otherwise was that I felt an extreme peace of spirit. It wasn't verbal.

We got married on January 1, 1987. We had a dream of a

two-story house and a three-car garage and three children. We had two daughters from our previous marriages. She got pregnant and we had a baby boy on November 13.

My wife was pretty intelligent, and was well educated in a private prep school. But after she fell, because of the pain, I just saw her take a slow dive. It got to the point where she was basically stupid. She had all this schooling, and to see this just all go out the window . . .

I missed the woman that I met and fell in love with. That woman no longer existed. She was this person that's just in pain. There was no spark left in her eyes. We had sex once every two weeks, three weeks, maybe every six weeks. It just kind of depended, because she was in a lot of pain most of the time. It's difficult to be in the mood.

Because of the pain, my wife zoned out sometimes. There was a lot of conflict with the stepchildren sometimes that she wasn't aware of. And there were issues, one of which involved Leslie wanting to preserve some of her heritage.

You have to know her ex-husband. He got convicted of embezzlement. When he was young, his parents had given him this little bear. You pulled on a string and the bear would say things like, "You can do it. You're the best. Keep trying!"

This bear was sitting up on one of the shelves in our house. It was prominently displayed along with some other antique toys. And I think I had probably mentioned to Leslie that I didn't really like this bear. I had knowledge of what this guy was like and it irritated me and I told her once, "I want you to get rid of that bear."

I know this sounds childish, but she wouldn't get rid of it. Well, I eventually tossed that bear out the upstairs window toward the back of our house. And I had this really old picture from my childhood, and she took it and sent it sailing out the window, tit for tat. There was all this stuff, flying out the back window.

But for the most part, we had a really great marriage and we are best friends. When I ask people, "Who's your best friend?" if they're married and they don't say their spouse, it saddens me a little bit because I think that your spouse should be your best friend. Our definition of love is that you stick with somebody through thick and thin no matter how hard it gets. You want to be with your best friend and you want to live life together.

We went to what I refer to as "name-it-and-claim-it" churches, which is really not the best place to be, in my opinion. They're basically feel-good churches where the majority of the Scripture being taught has to do with healing, and there's a strong belief in the spoken word, in speaking good things into your life, like health and wealth. We went to these churches because my wife liked the worship and praise music.

But I would listen to what this preacher was saying, and then I would go home and I would read the Scriptures the preacher may have been speaking about and say, "Wait a second. He's not taking it in context."

There's a lot of suffering. And God does not promise you that you're not going to have suffering. God chooses not to heal most people. You know, this just feel-good interpretation doesn't conform with my situation and with the situations of people I've seen, Christians that I know who are sick and dying and not so wealthy. But because we do believe that there is a God, and we do believe that He's a healer, we struggled with the "Why?"

The main question I had was, why is there so much pain? I would be slapped in the face by somebody that had a child that was ill or dying, which put Leslie's pain into a whole lot of perspective. I don't know if there was really much self-pity, because we still believed that we were created beings. I thought, "I think this is what God's plan was for me and my wife."

In August 2006, she started the upchucking again, and this time it didn't go away after three weeks. She lost about forty-five pounds, and she started going to different doctors. And for some reason, they sent her to an ear, nose, and throat specialist. They thought it might be something like Ménière's disease, which screws up your balance. This guy couldn't figure it out, though, and sent her to get an MRI. She'd had at least five MRIs.

But in the beginning of September, one night, this doctor calls. Doctors don't call you at night. But he left a message basically saying it's very important. I thought, "Great, we've had eighteen years of pain, and now you're going to tell me that my wife has a tumor."

Well, he told her that through this MRI, he had discovered that she had a birth defect called an Arnold-Chiari malformation. It's this common malformation at the base of your brain in the back. You have these things that look like little tonsils. In a normal person, they're either nonexistent or curled up under the base of the brain. But in some cases, they grow straight down into the spinal cord, where they restrict the flow of your spinal fluid. Essentially it was squeezing her spinal cord. Some people go blind and some people have strokelike symptoms. And that jolt of falling off the staircase, it basically caused those cerebral tonsils to move just enough to kick off all this pain.

The neurologist looked at the MRI films and said he understood why they didn't catch this ever. Out of probably four hundred pictures, you could only see this condition on two of the pictures because it has to be a certain slice in a certain direction.

The neurosurgeon told my wife, "I cannot tell you that this operation will alleviate any of the symptoms. Nobody has any idea what might be fixed, if anything."

I think he was trying to hold her expectations low. Our attitude was, "If an operation fixes anything, it's better than what we got."

Here again, we felt the same peace that we felt back when we got married. I believe that God chooses to heal very few people in a very direct manner, because there's so much suffering that goes on in the world. But we felt that this was God saying that He is going to heal my wife.

They did what's called a decompression surgery. They go in and they cut a big area out of the back of your head, probably about two and a half inches across, and they pack material back in that's more elastic. They're just making more space for this brain tissue and your spinal cord. She was in surgery for eight hours.

When she woke up she said she could tell she did not have tension in her back specifically. After seven days, she went home. Her migraines stopped. Her back pain went away. She's not on any pain medication. My wife was healed. After eighteen years.

When we first got married, we had four dreams: We wanted to move to the mountains; she wanted to go to Europe; I wanted to work for myself; and we had a dream to open up our own law practice together.

All right, so now we're sitting here, we bought a log cabin at eighty-seven hundred feet, in Idaho Springs, halfway between the ski slopes of Breckenridge and downtown Denver. Last August, we took a trip to Paris, Germany, Budapest, and Greece, visiting exchange students that we had a few years back. In September when we got back, I gave up a full-time, good-paying job to go out on my own. Five or ten years down the line, we might have a little practice in Idaho Springs, making some extra money here and there while we live in the mountains. Although I don't really know what might be in store for us.

Her being able to go to sleep at night is an amazing thing that most people take for granted. I've told her before that listening to her snore is like music. A few weeks ago, we hiked up to this glacier lake. We're just standing there, eleven thousand feet, and my wife realizes that she just climbed this thing with me, she's enjoying life, and she's not in pain.

We're twenty years older, so we both have a lot more wrinkles and we both weigh a little bit more, but I now have that woman with the spirit and the love of life back. And that's what I missed most.

I can find people every day with worse situations, but those eighteen years were hell. It got to the point where I was asking God for the strength to get through the day because I did not know whether or not my wife was going to be alive when I got home.

Our love is more like a superdeep friendship and it's less like a hormonal love, although our sex life is better than it ever has been before, and we just continue to be amazed by that.

But I think love is basically about action, about doing something for a person. It's about choices. If you're pissy, love is a choice to not take something out on your spouse. It's a choice to not jump on their case. If you're feeling tired, it's a choice to get up anyway and do things for that person. It's a choice to have fun with that person.

She has often said to me, "Thanks for sticking with me." But that wasn't a choice. We have a family and we're committed to each other. When the creator of the universe gives you to somebody, then, you know, in your time of need, how can I turn my back on you?

MARY BAIRD, AGE 69

MINNEAPOLIS, MINNESOTA

"One makes a decision in a marriage to enter into it through thick and thin—or as Joe used to say, 'Tru tick and tin.' And I would always ask, 'Is this tick or tin? It's really hard to tell.' "

One of the first things that grabbed me about Joe was a sense of physical presence. He was big and powerful, good-looking. And—oh, golly. He had an aura about him.

I took him to church with me, and everybody in the place turned around and looked at him. People came over and said hello. I'd been going to this church for years and nobody ever treated me like that. (*laughs*)

We met at an annual meeting of the Minnesota Press Club. He asked me out for dinner after the meeting. I was very aware of him because we both moved around in the same world, the public relations world, and he was well known and highly thought of. So I was real impressed.

And the story that unfolded was that he had left a marriage that was very violent and very isolating and very difficult.

I felt really sorry about that for his sake. It was clear that he was really very vulnerable in that part of his life.

So then he described his three children: Jeannie, who was fifteen at the time, and then Keith, who was twelve, and Mike, who was nine. He said, "I miss those guys. I just love them." And he showed me some photographs of these real fat, squinty-eyed, no-necked . . . they look like they came out of the—what do you call—the mountains where cousins marry cousins. He said, "Here are my little children." I looked at them, and I thought, "Oh, boy. These are really homely-looking little kids." And it was a long time before he told me that they weren't his kids, that he'd been on a trip, for work, down to rural Louisiana, and found the picture somewhere down there! (*laughs*)

He was so funny. I mean every day.

We did have a lot of fun. Joe loved the opera and I used to work for the opera. We had a lot of things in common. We had a social network.

He had a huge curiosity about the world and was well read, interested in politics, had a good grasp of history, all of which gave him a certain authority. He knew what he was talking about.

It was fun to get to know a person who has a lot to say.

And he seemed to be crazy about me, which I always found to be an attractive quality in anyone. (*laughs*)

I was thirty-four when we got married. We were just kind of getting used to it. I thought it was new and fun. But after six months, we get a call at midnight one night, in the middle of winter, from Jeannie, saying, "Mom threw me out. Please come and get me."

Suddenly, we had a teenage kid plunked in the middle of our marriage.

You can't have everything set up for a kid in three hours. And it wasn't just a kid coming along; it was a kid arriving in a really kind of heartbreaking way.

Three people is a harder relationship to work out, no matter who the person is. The dynamics change.

Joe was trying to be involved in a brand-new marriage. He never expected to be the custodial parent, and he suddenly was. And I mean *suddenly*. I had never been a housewife, and suddenly I was maintaining a home for three people. I overheard Joe say, "She never signed up for this kind of duty." He felt torn 'cause he felt responsible for Jeannie and me too.

Joe had real big guilt feelings about his kids that he didn't know how to cope with. He was not a good parent. And on some level he knew that. He had a wonderful mind and a strong sense of honor, but he was emotionally immature and defensive.

He had difficulty talking to Jeannie. And I put myself in the middle as an advocate for her. I meddled where I had no business meddling—still, one of my favorite characteristics about myself. (*laughs*) But it's a bad thing to do.

He was very short-tempered, very impatient. Looking back, I realize Joe never experienced any parenting himself. His mother died when he was five. And his father was a real martinet—a very difficult man. Joe was in over his head.

Two years after Jeannie moved in, Mike, the youngest, came to live with us. The doorbell rings and there stands this eleven-year-old child. A short time after that, Keith, the middle child, got out of drug treatment, and he came to live with us! The honeymoon, so to speak, had ended.

I said to Joe one time, in a long-suffering sigh, "If there were any more, you would tell me, wouldn't you?" (*laughs*) We thought it was pretty funny.

Jeannie lived with us for five years. Keith stayed for a year, and Mike stayed for three or four years. Our life went from being 90 percent tension-free to just . . . everything was hard. Joe had job pressures too. I think he felt like these responsibilities were all caving in on him. He weathered it poorly, and he started to hide behind being angry all the time.

Joe was in recovery from alcoholism. But I hadn't seen this other side of him before. It was probably there, but I was unable or unwilling to see it. I didn't know about myself that I was an untreated codependent. For me, that means attaching your worth to someone else's and trying to get them to change.

I developed a nickname for him, "Joe 'the-best-defense-is-a-good-offense' Baird." If anything came at him that he thought was scary, he would yell. A lot. Hoping to . . . well, send it away.

So I fell in love with this guy who was big and powerful and commanding. But when he used it in causing his own children to back down, the fun feeling between us just got inundated with stress.

I began aligning myself with the kids against Joe in the middle of their dustups. And his rage would get turned on me. I couldn't make him stop, and I kept getting pulled into his volcano. We were both so reactive. Joe was scared to death of other people's anger, especially mine. Any tiny hint that I might be angry, he got even madder, hoping that that would stuff my anger back down. Not fun. I don't mean that everything has to be fun, but it sucked. (*laughs*)

It wasn't all just 100 percent angst and horrible. We still had a very lively social life in the midst of all of this, and we still loved going to the opera and to the ballet. We were affectionate and still had sex. But when you're really upset with someone it's not exactly conducive to a romantic mood.

Even during the hard times, I remember a real close friend saying to me, "You should see how he looks at you. He just adores you." And I remember thinking, "Really?" That's the thing: People are complex. Relationships are complex.

The worst part lasted two years. And oh, gosh, it just got to the extreme of no-fun. I can remember yelling, "I hate you!" and thinking, "I hate my life." There were times honestly when I thought, "I would really like to get out of this," but I couldn't bring myself to do that to those kids again. Where would they go?

Luckily, we had a real big supportive community comforting and reinforcing us. We were in AA and Al-Anon, and were helped by the wisdom and spiritual power of the people there.

One night, we were having people from AA for dinner. And Joe said something so angry and inappropriate to one of the kids. I thought, "Oh, this is just abusive." And the guests said to me later, "This guy has so much anger."

They understood family dynamics of people coming out of alcoholism. And they joined me in saying to him, "You need to do something about this."

I finally said, "I'm over my head here, and I'm not gonna live like this. Some of this situation is you, something has to change, and it has to be you."

That really got his attention. Joe realized he needed help. And that's when he got into therapy. I felt like the mouse that roared!

When he came home from the first session, his face actually looked different. It looked softer. He said, "I had no idea what . . . I just didn't understand what I was doing. I really didn't. And I'm sorry."

It melted me into a little puddle. I hugged him and loved him up. And I poured praise on him for having the courage, because I wanted him to go back for the second one. (laughs)

He stuck with it and learned that his anger was not me or the kids doing something to him. It came out of his own self—the harsh emotional landscape from which he came. Then he was able to shower some compassion on himself, and it freed him up to be more confident and to realize that if somebody else got mad he could endure that. It wouldn't mean a devastating attack that he couldn't survive.

It helped him be able to love himself, and to be just basically kind. And have some patience. And talk about what was going on with him. He was able to open himself so much more fully to me.

It was really the beginning of a new era for us. I started recognizing some of this isn't me. I'm trying to make people be happy and get along with each other, and there's nothing I can do about that. Nothing, nothing, nothing. I had to get that through my head. "I can take care of myself, and that's a full-time job."

I stopped being reactive. Somebody tosses out a package and says, "This has your name on it," in an accusation or something. I learned to say, "No, that's not me and I'm not going there." I learned how to walk away, leave the room.

Eventually, we both got access to a healthy spiritual life. We had some higher authority to whom we could appeal. Joe would come at me with some angry statement, and I would just say, "Oh, God, help him. It's too big for me. It's too deep." We could emotionally unload in a safe way through prayer and meditation.

He showed great courage. I think I did too. Courage to see things the way they really are. And to change what we could.

After the kids left, it got even easier. Those are the years I mostly think about. All of these problems took place over six or seven years, and then we had another close to twenty years during which we grew closer and closer. They were so fun. We started traveling all over the world. On Valentine's Day, we'd be yammering away as if we were the only two people in the restaurant. We laughed about it: "Jeez, maybe we should quiet it down a little bit!" There was no life at any of the other tables, no sparkle. But there really was at ours.

One makes a decision in a marriage to enter into it through thick and thin—or as Joe used to say, "Tru tick and tin." And I would always ask, "Is this tick or tin? It's really hard to tell." (*laughs*) And I think that one thing that kept me going is I kept thinking, "Well, I'm gonna stick in here until I understand what I'm doing."

Love doesn't have to do with what mood you're in, or how you feel at one point or another. Especially if you're really emotional like I am. It's an honor-bound decision. I was grateful for his willingness to do the psychological and spiritual work. It freed him up to be this person I thought I had glimpsed and that was actually him. So the payoff was huge.

Early on, I found this description of love in the Bible: "Love is patient and kind, never jealous or envious, never boastful or proud, never haughty or selfish or rude. Love does not demand its own way . . . it does not hold grudges and will hardly even notice when others do wrong . . . If you love someone you will be loyal to that person no matter what the cost."

You read through that and think, "Wow, this calls for a grown-up. I don't know if I'm ready for that." (*laughs*) It's so disappointing. It's not romantic. But I decided it's true. Love is what I felt for Joe and the kids. I'm not saying I was perfect at this, but it's something you can rely on. It's always there. I stayed for love.

It might have been worse had the kids not come because we might never have had to deal with all this stuff. I never thought of that before! The same dynamics would have been there, but we might have just managed to limp along and never have to confront any of this stuff.

I think I became a more thoughtful and a kinder person because of all this. And so did Joe. We would encourage the good things we saw in each other. We had a lot in common. We really did. And it made our seeing of things so nice and deep and good because they were shared.

He started to write poems again. He had written things to me from the very beginning, and that was part of what really won me over. Because they were darling and so fun. I used to think, "Did I actually see that spark? Was it really there?" But oh, it was. He had the tenderest person inside. He would say gorgeous things to me, and it made me feel like I was blooming.

And I was.

Thirty Years to **Forty** Years

BAO-HSI WEST, AGE 53

BLOOMFIELD, MICHIGAN

"We not spoiled."

I'm from the northeast part of Taiwan, very close to ocean and very close to the mountain. It's a little town. My parents is rice farmer. We didn't have electricity. We usually wear wood shoe, and they have maybe four nails on the side to support to the plastic. I get the shoes left over from my sisters. We have eight kids. And at that time the girl don't go to school after elementary school. The boy is more important than the girl. The boy is the next generation.

My sisters and I go to Taipei to work any job we can get. I stay with my oldest sister at my auntie's house. And I worked. It really not called happy or not at that time. Maybe I consider happy because I was in city. It's not like countryside, you know? In the big city there, is all new.

My husband was twenty-six. I was sixteen, almost seventeen. I was walking on the street, and my husband also walking on the street. At the stop sign he ask me in Chinese, "Where can I get a hamburger?" I said back in English, "Right across the street there's a hamburger." And we began talking.

He studying Chinese, Asia studies.

He's half Greek and half Irish, from Detroit. At that time, he got dark hair, curly hair. I don't know you ever heard, in China, they usually call the foreigner "ghost with long nose." When I met him, I guess I just think, "Oh, somebody interesting." A curiosity kind, you know what I mean?

I never have boyfriend, so I don't know how, you know, a relation, I don't know that part. I was very innocent, I didn't know male female, how they (*laughs*), you know.

So he buy me a hamburger. But he's the one eating it because I don't grow up to eat those kind of stuff. He asked me to go out with him and to see his friend and I said, "What friend?" I'm from the country, so "friend" is my cousin in village. That's how we lived. All the village is blood related. In Taipei, I only allowed to go out with my sister. We just go shopping and eat. There's no other people call "friends." They are all strange, outsider.

I go with him and it was just a bunch of his friend. Some of them have Chinese girlfriend, some American, some long hair, some smoking, drinking—it's just completely black and white life I grow up from.

Maybe one reason I like him because my other two sister are more closer. Three of us always together and my older sisters always holding hands walking in the street. Because three people holding hand will be too crowded, I'm always the one walking behind or front of them. So I have my own eyesight to see things, making my own judgment, and I get more independent.

He do things different than what I'm doing. I start really see things different. He took me to this fancy hotel to go swim-ming, but I think it more like, how guy hang out with their girlfriend and looking other girls same time? He wanna eat two cake at the same time. I start learning little bit what is between boys, girls, the way attract each other. I see a lot of wealthy peo-ple there and I say, "Oh, that's how they act." I was like, I wasn't going to act like a country bunkin.

He and I know each other maybe one month. Then he left the country. He's a dreamer, you wanna say it that way. He like to travel. When he's three, he run away from home. Many times. His parents had to tie him up with the clothesline so he doesn't run away. They had to tie him up like a dog.

He came from poor family. He's the oldest and didn't get along with his dad. His mom wasn't good cook, and they were poor, they didn't have that good food. When he got drafted to the army, he didn't go to Vietnam, he went to Thailand. And Thailand was better life than Detroit. He got to learn languages, meet all different kinds of people. He thought he was gonna die in Vietnam War, but he was so happy because he got to get good food.

After we met the first time, he left for two years. He went to Greece, Egypt, Thailand. I was very lonely. I was too young, and I guess when it's puppy love, you just don't know the next step. I wasn't looking for another person. I have my sisters always around me and we had my aunt. But we still had contact with each other by letter. I guess at that time I'm not that bad-looking and he was not bad-looking. So we remember.

One day I was playing cards with my sister and my aunt and somebody knocking on the window. And I was shocked! He came back, you know? I don't know how many people he wrote letters to, but I guess he like my letters. We went out that night, then we were together for two months.

I guess he decide maybe I'm too young for him, or maybe he didn't want to settle down. He moved again. I'm pretty sure he had a Japanese girlfriend at that time. He had meet too many girls. He didn't know which is the one that he wants. He was a playboy. He was not stable. Guy don't even have a job, you know? All he does is traveling. What he makes, he has enough to live and that's it, he goes to next place.

But I guess he get scared because he was raising up with a Catholic family. And so he saw a problem; he had to settle down. He went to the church—it's called a retreat—and I guess the priest talk to him. The priest told him whatever one is the true love, you go back with that person. And then he came back to me.

My family, they were *very* angry. My older sisters both not married, both didn't have boyfriends, and I was the one first. I almost gave my parents a heart attack. I got slapped from my brothers, they told me I was too young, I shouldn't go out with a foreigner. He's probably just take advantage of you, I'm sure he have other. They ask me what kind of job he got, and I say he's a lifeguard here and teaching English a few weeks there.

The number one with Chinese, if you don't have a stable job, they cannot provide your home. Chinese always looking for homes before you can think about get married.

We lived together maybe about six months. We really getting to know each other. There's love, there's a hate, there's fighting. We both were stubborn that we would not rely on my family, and he didn't have his family in Taiwan. So he got a job in

Taipei Hilton hotel as the assistant manager. That gave my family more confidence.

My mom didn't want us to get married because I was only eighteen. I was under twenty-one, I needed adults to sign the court papers that we are agreeing for daughter to marry. My parents wasn't gonna do it. But I got pregnant. I didn't have a choice, put it that way. So they said, "This is what you choose. Your life. But remember you forced us into signing the paper." And then we got married.

I didn't have a high education, I wasn't getting hired. He wasn't getting a good job. We didn't ask our families for help, so we were living a very poor life. We didn't have any money. We were eating canned sardines. I mean, something that was, like twenty-five cents a day, a can of sardines, and some rice, and that's how we lived.

About five months later, my husband told my mom he can get a job in Indonesia for oil company. And that's a pretty big thing for my mom. She say there's no way, if you need help, even if you scream, we cannot help you because you're gonna be so far away. That's how my mom thinks. She will go to temple, to prayer, and make sure I get some soil and a little wood, to make sure I don't get sick. You know, like superstition stuff.

We got to Indonesia. I see people live in Jakarta. Very poor, sleeping on people's front porch. And he did not get a job. Now I know what my mom talking about! You cry, and if they wanna help me, I'm way outta there, on the other side of the world.

So my husband say, "Oh, maybe we can go to Australia. Australia is the closer country to Indonesia. We just had enough money to buy ticket to Australia." We didn't even have enough to pay the hotel! We are running away from the hotel without paying. I say, "God, I never done this kind of stuff." I was so scared.

The plane's supposed to leave and we couldn't get anybody to take us, so we hitchhiked. In the middle of the highway, this guy was riding a motorbike scooter and I didn't know what to do. He stopped in the middle of the highway and my husband begged this guy, please take us to the airport!

That's the first time that we had a talk. We got to Darwin, Australia, only had a few dollar left. We said, we cannot live like this. Finally, I telegram to my family and say I need money. I asked them for one hundred dollars U.S. At 1975, that is big money for my family. He asked his family for one hundred dollars.

We hitchhiked to Melbourne. It take us about four days. And sometimes we slept in the truck, like a homeless type. I thinking I'm married to this guy, this is the type of life I'm gonna live. But then I said to myself, what can I do? You have to keep going.

So we got into Melbourne, I got the money from my family, he got the money from his family. We found a place, just a little shed, like a toy shed with a twin bed. If we want to use the bathroom we have to go inside the landlord's house.

Then my husband became a teacher, and we got the papers saying we allowed to stay in Australia. Life started changing. We start working, and just tried to work hard and save money, and we went up higher and higher.

I mean, we do have problems. My husband is my first boyfriend, and I didn't have the experience. And you know, he had to stuck with me. I'm sure he can have better chance of other girl too. We had tons, tons of arguments, tons, tons. We have plenty of talking about divorce. We share lots of tears with each other. We lost the child I was pregnant with when we married. The baby's ready to be born and I feel the water break. Then I start bleeding. That was the dramatic type life we went through.

But I am sure we have love each other too, otherwise we wouldn't be together still now, right? There's lots of little bridges to make our life.

We stayed in Australia four and a half years. When I had my daughter, Kimberly, we have an apartment that had kitchen area and a bedroom. And that was big for us. That was the first thing we had. We would never forget that. And we had a cat! And then we moved to a one-bedroom apartment that was bigger. Maybe a year later we moved to a two-bedroom apartment.

Then we moved to Philippines. He graduate from dental school in '82. Then we move to New York, and he got in for NYU start school again. Even that he went to school, he work also part-time. I worked in the dental office and he's teaching and he also interpreter for the court. Life started getting easier there. He's a busy man, and also I was working full time, so that's how life became more . . . more family-type life, you know. More stable. And then we came back to Michigan and bought a house in '89.

We always, always together. My husband, I guess he got used to it as a family, you know, he's a family man, so he want to be with wife and kids.

We fight, yes, but we never do anything but talk. It's just argument. I came from a family there's no divorce. Divorce is like a bad thing to do. I'm pretty sure his family is the same way.

Catholic. Sometime you really wanna kill each other but you got a kid, what you gonna do? I mean, having a kids is about responsible. I always tell my husband, we the one that wanna have the kid, the kid don't wanna have us. Now, the kids is not here, they grow up, we argue and sometimes say yeah, we could get divorced. But we never do any of it, just talk.

Now I'm look back at it and I see his life and my life are completely different kinds. Grow up different kind of life.

What made me to stay with him? We went through a really hard life together. You know, if both of us have a good life I don't think we have that type patience. You know, we not spoiled.

When I was young, I didn't have a good life either. My mother wake me up in the morning, like alarm clock she use a stick. She would whack you on the leg. If I'm a spoiled kid, we'd be divorced long time ago.

We argue a lot, and, you know, and sometimes in front of the kids. And I always tell my kids, you know, if you have something to say, you say it in front of the person, you can't hide it. You know. We must did something right that makes us still together even we are argue a lot. But argue doesn't mean you hate each other, it just means you have different opinions. You know what I mean?

I admire him a lot of things. I have confidence in him. I don't need people giving me a sweet talk. I wasn't brought up like that. I don't need people giving me, "Oh, I love you," and then really I don't feel it. I'm more like, "What do you do? Show me what you do," and I can see what are you doing for me. I was brought up like you just do your thing, what is right, and then make that person happy. If that person cannot be happy, there is nothing you can do.

I would say love and support is the same thing. You don't talk about it, you just do it. Everywhere we go is always two of us. There was nobody else, because we live in a third country, not his family country, not my country—just us.

He let me do things I wanna do, like to create things in my house, garden, and if I wanted to work—even ten hours a day, he cannot complain. All these years—I've been with him thirty-five years now—it's flexible. I don't control him, he doesn't control me. Maybe that's why we get along.

He still do crazy things that made me mad, like planning to go overseas without asking me. But I can tolerate it. He's like a dog: he will go away and then when he is hungry he will come back. Sometime I have that feeling like he cheating on me. If I catch this, you'll be dead, and I'm not sticking around. Because I didn't do it. Why should be you doing it? But I don't think he's doing it. I know he like to talk to people. Okay. But doing it and talking about, that's two totally different things.

I couldn't imagine my life what it would be like without him. I'm not the type of person, adventure type, you know. I can stay in one spot, I'm happy with it. Probably I could have find someone more like local people, more matching me than the difference between me and him.

Now I have a house, I have tenants living in my house. We have two nice kids that any parents would want. It didn't come up from my family, it didn't come up from his family. It's all coming from us. So we must did something right, otherwise we wouldn't be having all this.

I look at my life. I have one, I think that's enough. I'm happy where I am right now. I'm comfortable. In a few years, I'll be gone, you know?

It's like this: If you're with your husband for so many years, you know every move that he did. He doesn't even have to open his mouth, I know what exactly he's gonna do. My husband say many time, "How do you know that's what I'm gonna say?" I say, "Even if you're in another house, I know exactly what you do. Because I know you like copy machine." So why would I want to go through that stuff all over, learning how to copy all those papers? I don't want to go through that. It's not gonna be perfect? No matter.

GERD KOHLER, AGE 66, AND
DINA KOHLER, AGE 79

VENICE, FLORIDA

"One day he comes in my house and says, 'What happened with your husband? He has an affair with my wife!'"

Dina: 1973, I was married twenty-five years. I find out my husband is cheating on me. I didn't know Gerd before. One day he comes in my house and says, "What happened with your husband? He has an affair with my wife!"

Gerd: I thought I was happily married. I met and married my dream girl. She was a beauty! A cover girl, you know. We had a baby together. I just could not understand how that woman could leave me with some other man. It was Dina's husband. And to repair the whole thing, I went to her house to ask her to take her husband back and leave my family alone.

Dina: This was still in Germany, in my apartment. I say, "Oh, he's a good-looking man." He was thirteen years younger. I was forty-four, and he was thirty-one.

Gerd: It's still the same, you know. (*laughs*) She's still thirteen years older than I am.

Dina: (*laughs*) He was seven years married and had a daughter of four years. And we come together, we talking and talking and talking. We were together the whole night.

Gerd: May I interrupt? The only reason why I stayed at her house was because she had a hidden bottle of Bacardi in the couch. I was ready to leave after ten minutes, but then she opened up the couch, and I decided to stay.

Dina: Yes, it's true. Then later on, maybe eleven p.m., my husband comes back. He comes in the door, and he saw Gerd and he say, "Ach! Good! I'm happy you are here! So. We can talk together." We were sitting the whole night.

I didn't know before. I didn't know anything. Gerd's wife was working in the same company where my husband was an agent. This was an insurance company. And I was twenty-one years by this company.

So this was very sad for me. Very sad. I was so sick and so terrible, I couldn't sleep in the night anymore. It was a very hard year. Every day was a new story from my husband.

Gerd: They told us they are so much in love with each other that they rather would die before they would come back to us.

During that time, we help each other out. I took Dina for dancing, dinner, movie theater. She help me with my little daughter, and so on. And it worked out so perfectly good that we started thinking we would be better off without them two.

Dina and I were so close already. We were not in love. We were just close.

And we invited them two later on to come and talk to us, and we told them, "Hey, no, we finally agree with you two. You can stay together. We both get divorced, we make you no problems at all." Because we have companionship, we found out we're getting along very good, you know. And they hated that. My former wife started crying, wanted to come back to me.

Dina: When they find out we want to stay together, they want to come back again. Then we say, no way anymore!

Gerd: I told them, "We can do what you do. Don't worry, we are adults too! We are able to love."

Dina: My husband say, "I don't want a divorce. I only want to go to her three times in a week." You know what I say? "You have to look for a stupider thing than me." And I go to the divorce lawyer right away.

But my husband and his wife, they never together. They started a little together, but the love was gone.

Gerd: Let's say, even if they tried to plunder our banking accounts they were empty and their love also was empty.

Dina: They had nothing, we had everything.

Gerd: At that time, in Germany, we had a law of guilty or not guilty. And when you cheat on your spouse, you get absolutely nothing. You have to pay for the lawyers, you have to pay the court, you have to pay for everything, and you leave the house empty-handed. That's why we are good off, you know? We ended up with two complete houses!

Dina: At the end of December '73, we both divorced. We were already a little bit together at this time. And we find out we have a lot of things what we like together—

Gerd: Bacardi—

Dina: And we like to travel.

Gerd: I needed somebody to take care of my little daughter, you know, because my wife left me with the little girl at home. Dina felt a little guilty, because it was her husband who took my wife away. So she was so kind to come to my house and help me out with the cooking and the laundry. And after a while my little daughter started calling her Mommy. Because I had to go to work, we spent the weekends together. And we became closer and closer. And the day came when we said, "Why don't we just try to stay together for good?" And now I see it worked out perfectly. Many, many times we talk about that, and we still are thankful that destiny turned that way for us.

Dina: We are married for twenty-eight years, but together thirty-five.

My first husband, he did nothing. You know, he don't want to go on vacation or something. And we, when *we* were together, we were every weekend away. We saw all in Europe.

Then we were in America, and we liked it so much. We like Florida. And then we had the idea we come here to buy a house. He always liked marriage. But after what I had before, I don't like this so much. But when we bought this house, then I say, "You know what? It's better that we marry."

So this was August '80.

Gerd: That was actually the official time we got engaged. It was one o'clock a.m. But where can you get engagement rings at one o'clock in the morning? We opened the refrigerator and pulled out two cans of beer. We pulled off the rings and exchanged it.

Dina: Yes, it's true.

Gerd: We still have them. It's our official engagement rings.

Dina: So we married and we bought this house, and we were both very happy.

Gerd: Love that grows out of something like what we have is stable and deeper than love at first sight. Some pretty face might turn out to be garbage. Sometimes when we watch TV, beautiful girls on *Judge Judy*, then they open their mouth, well, that's it. There is more than just a nice face and making love.

Why we are getting along so good is we . . . I don't know how to express it in English, but maybe you get the idea: I'm not living my life, I living her life. I try to do everything as good as possible to make her happy. If she tells me I need two pounds of potatoes, we go together and buy those two pounds of potatoes.

Dina: It's not a lie. We make everything together. He never, ever walk anyplace without me. Only to work.

Gerd: After all those years, we can honestly say we never fought. We just don't do that. There's no reason. We are both engaged in this marriage to make each other as comfortable as possible. And bad words, they don't work. Of course, we have different opinions once in a while.

Dina: But we say, never go in the bed before everything is clear. You know, talk. When you have a problem, talk.

Gerd: Of course we have days when we aren't agreeing about things, but before we start fighting, we shut up.

Dina: You know, we are so much on vacation together. We go eleven times on a cruise. We were four times in Las Vegas, not gambling but only look around in the nice casino. Sometimes we went in a new casino, I say, "Oh, I love this, it's so beautiful. I want to know the architect who did this." It was so beautiful. We never gambled. We only walk around and enjoy life.

Gerd: Another big moment where we really appreciated to be together was—I know it sounds like a cliché—when we were for the very first time at the Grand Canyon. We start asking, "Who is the architect on *that*?" (*laughs*) And we said, it couldn't be an American because if it had been American, it never would be finished! We hadn't to say anything, you know. Just arriving there, looking down in the big hole. I lay my arm around Dina's shoulder and looking at each other, and we both started crying. To be there together and see that. It was one of the moments where we really, really appreciated to be there together, because you cannot tell anybody how that feels.

What was our nicest day we ever had together?

Dina: Nicest day? Oh, we had a lot of nice ones. I can't say.

Gerd: Maybe it was when you told me oysters would help my sex life?

Dina: Oh, shhhh . . .

Gerd: I can honestly say it's a lie, because the other day I ate a dozen oysters, and only nine worked. (*laughs*)

Dina: You must be thankful to have each other.

Gerd: The love that was with my first wife was a very young love. It was more passionate. The second love, what we have now, was, let's say, born more out of common sense. We love each other more than we used to love our first partner. But it's in a different way.

Dina: When you're young, it's a different story. It's only, "I love you, oh, yeah, yeah."

Gerd: I'm coming home every night, not going to any bars, make no problems—this is a love sign. In my younger years, I liked to drink a lot. And if I didn't have her to hold on, maybe I had forgotten to control myself. She was a big help without ever saying anything.

Dina: And smoking too. He was also smoking, and I had a

problem with bronchitis. He stopped maybe fifteen years ago, and who knows, if he not stopped, he not alive anymore.

Gerd: I remember maybe twenty years ago, when we still had sex. (*laughs*) We just were engaged in that action and she said, "Do you love me? Do you love me?" And I said, "What do you think I'm doing here?"

I'm trying to be funny for the reason. We do this all the time. Our life is that way. We spend nights next to each other, laughing our ass off. Sometimes we sing opera during the night.

Dina: We went to Spain and we rent a house. It had only one bedroom, you know, but it's a nice house, we both singing opera all night. We can do that, you know. We can do that, and we like it. Then we laughing and happy.

Gerd: This is also something that keeps us together, you know, the jokes and laughing all the time. I really have problems to take life seriously. Believe it or not, I'm happy when it's raining. Because if I'm not happy, it's still raining. My whole life is like that, you know? I lost a leg to diabetes, and I'm happy. I never get cold feet anymore. I only need one shoe when I go shopping.

Dina: The last three years was hard time for me. When Gerd had lost . . . and then the other leg started . . . Then he had bypass, then kidney. He had a lot of problem and I'm only by myself with everything. Was not always easy.

Gerd: This is also big, big, big thing in our marriage, that she takes care of my handicap, without any question whatever. It is just there, every day and every day and every day. If I try to go to the refrigerator with my crutches to pick up a Coke, she's right behind me, "Sit down! I do that. I have two legs, you only have one, I do that!" And this is much more worth than say every five minutes, "I love you," which is mostly just said to say something.

And it's also 100 percent sign that she loves me because I might meet 250 people and I tell them all the same joke and she's still laughing. She doesn't have to yell at me, "I love you. I'll kick your ass, you don't believe it!"

Dina: So we are both a little older and smarter. Much, much happier than before. This was a very different life, and a much, much better life.

Gerd: We thank her ex-husband every day. Actually, every year on the divorce date, we send him a thank-you note.

AUBREY REUBEN, AGE 76

NEW YORK, NEW YORK

"I've dated three hundred women since my wife died."

In 1945, when I was thirteen, in England, my father died. And at thirteen, you become a man in the Jewish religion. So I took my father's seat in church, and I prayed day and night, and said the mourner's kaddish for my father. I felt that God was on my shoulder talking to me, and I swore that I would be ethical, never tell a lie, and that I would remain a virgin. I was going to be pure, and when I married my wife, I would be faithful to her forever, because I believed in all those values.

Then what happened was my sister married an American, and my mother and I came to America. And I came to New York and got a job at the New York Public Library part time and transferred to New York University.

And on the first day, I go to the library for my books, I hear a noise, and I look down and there's an umbrella. I pick up the umbrella, and I see the most beautiful woman I had ever seen in my entire life. And I said, "You are the most beautiful woman I've ever seen in my entire life. I want to take you out." She said, "No, no it's impossible." So she went her way, and I went my way.

The next day, I'm going to class, and I pass an open classroom, and there's that vision of loveliness that I had seen the night before. So I waited. She comes out of class, and I said, "Look, it's impossible that I could know you were in this classroom. It's fate. God has decided that we have to . . ." and I persuaded her to come with me to Chock full o'Nuts and I bought her a twenty-five-cent cheese sandwich with cream cheese and walnut bread, and I bought her a Coke. I spent like thirty-five cents on her. (laughs) Money was no object!

She was twenty-seven, I was nineteen. She was half Filipino and half American, and she was the most stunning woman you ever saw in your life.

She said, "I can't go out with you." I said, "Why not?" She said, "I'm married." She was married to a professor. I said, "I don't care if you're married." And we started an affair that went on for the entire year. I lost my virginity. Out went the Jewish religion, out went God. Everything went down the drain, because now all I cared about was sex with this girl. It was so great that I was annoyed that for nineteen years I hadn't had sex. I've been trying to make up for it ever since.

We had the most wonderful year. I remember everything about it. This was 1951 to '52. We'd walk around. She'd buy socks for her husband to show why she was late. We'd go to a movie occasionally. I can tell you the movies we saw. The best one was *Viva Zapata!* with Marlon Brando and Anthony Quinn.

My birthday, May 27, she meets me, she said, "Aubrey, it's over." I said, "What do you mean, it's over?" She said, "He's gotten a job with the secretary of the navy, and we're leaving for

Washington." I was brokenhearted. The love of my life. Anyway, I was drafted in the army in 1953, and guess where I'm stationed? Fort Belvoir, outside of Washington.

We met in Washington that night. We went to see *Julius Caesar* with Marlon Brando and James Mason and Deborah Kerr, and we started our love affair again. I got sent to Germany during the Korean War, and every day I wrote to her, and every day she wrote to me. And when I got back, I went to Washington, she meets me in a restaurant, and I said, "I want you to leave your husband and we're going to live together and we're going to be happy for the rest of our lives." She said, "I can't do it." I said, "What do you mean, you can't do it?" She said, "I'm pregnant." She never thought she could get pregnant. She had an upturned womb or something.

So I get a grant to go to Mexico City. I wanted to be a professor of Latin American history. I walk into my class on the Mexican Revolution, and this cute little brunette says, "Hey, you, you're not a Mexican, are you?" I said, "No." She said, "Come to my house tonight. We're having a Mexican fiesta. You'll learn all about Mexican customs."

She was gorgeous. She was five foot two, long hair, brunette, shiny eyes, cute little body, slender. She was an authority on Mexican history—oh, brilliant woman! The first day, I was in love with her.

It was different in those days. In 1956, we didn't have the sexual revolution that we have today. Every time I went out with her, I had to have a chaperone. All the good girls were chaperoned. But what we did was, we told her mother her classes were every afternoon at the Facultad de Filosofía y Letras. What the mother didn't know was that two days we didn't have classes, and we'd go to the movies. We fooled around a lot, but no sex, because she was a virgin. And, of course, I was in love with sex, and we hadn't had sex. So at the end of the year, in December of '56, I married Maria Elena, and we were married for thirty-nine years.

She got pregnant immediately, and nine months after we got married, there we were, father and mother. I was twenty-five, she was twenty-two. That was a little scary. We had no money. I got a job as a Spanish teacher in the New York City school system. My wife became a teacher as well. After ten years, I became an assistant principal. Twenty years after that, I retired at fifty-five, and I get a pension every month. It was wonderful, because you work six hours and thirty minutes, 180 days a year, and you've got all the time in the world at night.

So I would go out every night, every single night, 365 nights a year. She couldn't do that, because she was still a teacher. She had to prepare her classes. So I had to take other people out, and of course, some of the people were very good-looking women. And so, if they liked me and I liked them, since I'd already committed adultery at the age of nineteen, and I wasn't religious anymore, if you have a chance to sleep with a beautiful woman, it's very hard to say no.

I kept winning grants and so forth. I went to NYU on a National Defense grant, and so she went to Mexico for the summer. I had an affair with one of the girls in my group from Connecticut. Because, look, my wife went to Mexico, she'd be gone for four or five months. I wasn't going to stay a virgin for four or five months.

I didn't think it was harming. Every woman I had an affair with, I told her I was never going to leave my wife. If they liked my company, they liked going to the theater, they liked going to the opera, fine, come out with me. Otherwise, I didn't care, because I had my wife at home.

She knew that I loved her and I would never abandon her, and I would never divorce her. Because that's the way I am. And she was more important than any other woman in my heart. The other women were kind of cute and nice to have sex with, but they weren't important. I never let myself fall in love with them or have a passion for them. I had passion for my wife.

My wife was brilliant. Her brain never stopped working. That's why I loved her. We'd go to see a Broadway show and she would notice things that were on that stage that would escape me. Oh, she was brilliant. We were perfect together. We loved theater, opera, the ballet, cabaret. She never stopped studying. All the time. We had two thousand books all over the apartment. In the kitchen, there was no food—just books.

My wife was not that domesticated. She said, "Aubrey, when we get married, I can only be good in one room in the house. Forget the kitchen." We had sex right up to the day she died.

She was so full of life, everyone thought that our son and her were brother and sister. She was leading the conga line when she retired from the school system at the last party. She was beautiful. She was good company. I just wanted to be next to her all the time.

I know she never committed adultery, because it was against . . . she was a straitlaced person. Her pride would've been hurt if she had sex with another person. And she had her opportunities. Men were coming on to her all the time. Everybody wanted to have sex with my wife. All her life, everybody loved her. Everybody was charmed by her. She did all the Mexican folk dances. They'd make her dance at every party we went to. Oh, they loved her.

And then, one night, we went to the opening of Tito Puente's restaurant on City Island. It was an all-star gathering— Rita Moreno, Celia Cruz, Paul Simon. Elena had started writing for Spanish newspapers, and in the nightlife she got to meet all these people. Rita Moreno became one of our closest friends, and she always says she was with us on Maria Elena's last night.

So we get home and she goes to the bathroom and vomits blood. I called 911, and they come and take her to the emergency room. They pull the curtain. She's still lucid, and she vomited again and went into a coma, and they put her on life support and everything else, and forty hours later she was gone. Never said another word.

What had happened was a vein burst in her esophagus, and it was all based on having a damaged liver. When she was fifteen she was given a blood transfusion in Mexico, and she developed hepatitis. For forty-five years, that virus was working on her liver. When she died, the specialist said, "Your wife had a great desire to live." He was amazed that she had lived to be sixty with that virus. She retired June 28. She died July 27. She didn't even get to enjoy her retirement.

I was devastated. I couldn't believe it, because I lived always on the assumption that I would go first. My father died when he was forty-seven. I figured when I died, Maria Elena would be a merry widow. We had tons of money, because I'd started working as a photographer with the *New York Post* in 1985, even while I was still working at my day job. I photographed Britney Spears before she was Britney Spears. Bimbos like Lindsay Lohan and Paris Hilton. You take a photograph that nobody else has—it's worth a fortune. Anyway, I was shocked. It was I the merry widow instead of her.

I've dated three hundred women since my wife died. Some of them I date for one night and I don't want to see them again. Others I want to see. I love women. I love every type of woman. They have to have a brain. I've dated many very famous women, women married to movie stars. I like slender girls. I don't like buxom women, fat women, big busts. I mean, I was friends with Anna Nicole Smith and when she hugged me, my head disappeared in her breasts. I don't like that.

I have no wisdom to offer about relationships. I'm just very realistic. I think I've got both feet on the ground. I think I've got common sense. It's not wisdom. I'm a practical person.

I live for the day. The past is over and I can't change it. I mean, I was sorry to see her go. I grieved. I went through all her things—all the photographs and all the times we had together. You do that. There's a period of grief. But immediately, within a few days, I went out, took photographs and everything. I was out every night and that helped me get through it. I had something to live for. I didn't say, "Oh, she's dead. I'm going to kill myself and join her." That's nonsense.

About life and death, I'm very dispassionate. In 1939 and 1940, when I was eight years old, living in Manchester, we were bombed every night. In one night, eight bombs fell on my street. My father died when I was thirteen. It was a big shock to my family, because it changed everything—my whole life. So I can look at it dispassionately, because this is how I've looked at everything—dispassionately.

I don't want to marry anybody again. I've done it, and it's

enough. I don't believe in marriage. I married a sweet, wonderful, bright, intelligent, beautiful—always dressed perfectly—always looked like a million dollars, always wanted to jump on and have sex with. She was a wonderful, marvelous woman. It turned out that it worked out well. But I don't believe in marriage. I think it's a horrible institution—and who wants to live in an institution? Honestly, we just discovered the leading cause of divorce: marriage!

People marry for many reasons. Many people marry, and I truly believe it, because they fear being alone. Most husbands hate their wives, and most wives hate their husbands. Or, worse than hating, which shows a little passion, they're indifferent. Many don't have sex. If you go to a restaurant, there are couples that never say a word to each other. The whole time. Whereas at the other table there are two girls talking the whole time—because they're not married! But the married couple has said everything they had to say to each other. It's disgusting.

All my friends have taken Viagra. Don't be stupid. You don't need Viagra. Nobody needs Viagra. The dysfunction in sex is you don't like the woman you're with. You're sleeping with a fifty-five-year-old woman who's fat, who's repulsive, who doesn't turn you on, and you have to have sex with her because she's your wife. She demands it. So you do it reluctantly. That's not love. That's not pleasant.

If I'm with a woman that is angry or annoying or does things that turn me off, or says things that irritate me—what's the point of making a life insufferable? If a woman has a family that irritates me, or a mother or a father or children, or a brother or a sister, or friends that I don't like—why do I want to be with her? I don't want any other influences but me with that girl, and that's why I like single girls. I love it if they've never been married, because they haven't gone through the horrors of a divorce or the sadness of being widowed. I like a nice, single, beautiful, sexy, wonderful, bright, brilliant, sense of humor girl. I would never date an ugly woman. I mean, I have to find her beautiful.

What makes a woman special is that you just want to be with them twenty-four hours a day. You never get bored with them, and you'd rather be with that woman than any other woman in the world. When I want to be with her constantly, I enjoy her company, she stirs me up passionately so I want to have sex with her all the time—then I know this is the woman for me! It's better than jogging in the park, it's better than seeing a Broadway show, it's better than photographing a celebrity. If you don't have sex, you might as well—well, that's why I don't go out with old ladies.

I want to live the best life possible. If a woman contributes to my happiness, then I want to be with her. If a woman does not contribute to my happiness, I don't want her.

Forty Years to Sixty Years

DORY SPENCE, AGE 66

SCHROEDER, MINNESOTA

"He said he was leaving. And I said,
'Oh?' And I said, 'When?' "

It worked for a really long time. We laughed a lot. He was a really funny guy. He still is. And I admired his . . . he was a very hard worker. Our first years of marriage, it felt like we were real compatible, and we had fun together. We had a lot of friends, went to lots of parties. We didn't have children until after we had been married for four or five years, and so we traveled and did fun things together.

We moved out to Montana due to my husband's job in about 1983. And then we moved back three and a half years later. We came back to the Twin Cities. My husband was starting a new business. I was not seeing the great stress that he had during that time, and I wasn't in sympathy with that, I guess.

I was just kind of plugging along being a mom and being probably not the best wife in the world. I didn't take care of myself as much as I did during the early years of our marriage. I got just so into the children, and I was just so focused on them and doing all the things that I was supposed to for them, that I didn't do enough things like going to exercise class or just even going out and having fun with my girlfriends. I felt like I had to be the mom and be everything for everybody in that family. He wasn't very helpful because he had stresses. Over a few years' time, things were sort of deteriorating. It just sort of crept up on us. We weren't communicating.

There was one separation for a few months where my husband moved out. I can see myself and I can see him in the kitchen. I can't remember really what led up to it. We must have been in some kind of discussion, but all I remember was we were both standing in the kitchen. He said he was leaving, something about that he was leaving. And I said, "Oh?" And I said, "When?"

He told me later he was shocked. I probably was feeling some relief.

That lasted a few months, and then he was back, and then it was maybe a year and a half later he started a relationship with someone and announced that he was leaving again. I didn't know that he had another friend, but I knew I didn't really care, because things were not that good.

We were divorced a few months afterward, and it was then that I realized this was such a huge thing. I spent about a year sort of wallowing. I was devastated and really down on myself. It wasn't that I missed him or was sorry that he was gone, but I was born and raised Catholic, and for that marriage to have failed was just a huge thing for me. A failure of the dreams that you have when you're young, that this marriage that you got into was going to last forever.

In those first couple of years, so many things came up, things

I didn't give him credit for. Things that would happen around the house, and I'd go "Oh, my God. What am I gonna do here?" Things that, you know, he was always there to take care of. A lot of financial things. And different things that came up with the kids. I had a suspicion that my son was smoking marijuana, and I took these little weedy things that I found in his bedroom in a plastic bag up to the police station to ask if that's what it was. The guy said, "You and your husband need to have a talk with this kid." I guess Tom ended up talking to him. So that kind of stuff, everyday stuff of being a parent. I did miss that.

That same year a brother of mine died, and he was my favorite. He was an older brother and died suddenly, and I just felt, "Oh, there's a lot goin' on for me here. All my advisers are leaving me." Because he was another one I could go to and ask questions.

But then I started learning to do things, especially a lot of financial things. I had no idea about our family's finances, and that was my fault because he had always encouraged me to be more interested. So I learned more about that. I was pretty independent.

We were divorced for five years. During those five years I think I thrived. I did my job. I did a lot of studying and got a higher position. I was a nurse in the oncology system at United Hospital in St. Paul, but I got into a supervisory position. I was very content with doing the things I was doing for myself—as far as my job went, as far as maintaining relationships with my children, who were by then off on their own.

I don't think that I ever would have started a relationship

with someone else. I had a couple guys that asked a couple times to go out to coffee, go out for a drink or something, but I just wasn't interested in that. There are some religious values that I have, and unless I had a marriage annulled I would not have gotten married again to someone else. Or probably even have gotten into a relationship.

If someone had told me that we would ever get back together, I would have laughed. Because it wasn't just a separation. We really did sever the ties. Except that we did have to communicate about the children.

While he was seeing this woman, we would get together for a couple of hours on Christmas. He came to my brother's funeral. But there was nothing. He was there because it was his duty and I was tolerating his being there. We weren't unfriendly, but we weren't in any kind of relationship at that time.

Our first granddaughter was born about October of 1995. And there's something that happens when (*laughs*) you become a grandparent. It feels like your heart is just sliced wide open—or for me, anyway. I wasn't aware of what was going on at the time, but there was so much love for this child that I was opened up to be able to receive again.

It's probably similar to when you are first in love with a girl and you wake up every morning and everything is wonderful— that kind of thing. It does open you to other relationships, and you're a more optimistic and open person at that time, whereas when you're getting ready to divorce and things are falling apart in your life, you're more closed.

Looking back, that was the time when we began corresponding a little more. And then shortly after, I heard that he was no longer with this woman.

I can't pick out a minute. It just evolved over a year's time. We started visiting the grandchild together. And from there, once in a while we'd do stuff together—go to a concert or something. It seemed really natural. Then one day my daughter said to me, "Mom, are you and Dad dating?" And all of a sudden it occurred to me. "I guess we are." (*laughs*)

I remember the first time we kissed again after all this time. It was at his home and I was dropping him off after we had gone somewhere. It felt like I was a young teenager having my first kiss.

We weren't staying over at each other's houses or anything like that at that time. But then maybe a couple of weeks after that, I took him back to his house one evening, and we were just having another little kiss good night. He said, "Dory, next time bring your toothbrush." And I'm going, "Oh, my God." Here I am, a grown woman, and I'm feeling pretty much like a young kid.

I think he wanted it a little more than I did, to get back together. I think he was lonely. I had learned to accept myself. I could have been happy just going on the way I had the last five years. It didn't feel like I needed another person at that time. But, you know, we kept on; we had fun together.

We had talked about getting married again, but I still wasn't sure if that's what I wanted. We decided we'd wait until after our daughter's wedding because we didn't want to take away from her enjoyment. I guess we waited another six months.

Our second wedding, we had a mutual friend who's a judge in Pine City, Minnesota, and we got dressed up. Not in wedding clothes: he wore a suit, and I wore a bright red dress, and we had corsages. We went up to the courthouse and his friend married us. Our kids didn't come. We didn't invite them. And then we went and had lunch with our judge friend and went out for dinner, and that was it.

So we got married December 26, 1966. We divorced in, I think it was, 1991, and we remarried in 1996. We celebrate our anniversary on the day that we were first married.

I don't look back and have any regrets about anything that we did. We weren't the first people this happened to. And more and more I hear about other people getting back together.

I think we're in a really nice place in our lives now. We're ready to help each other through whatever might come in the next years. We're both getting a little older—any day there could be a health issue that could diminish one of us or devastate one of us.

We grew back into a relationship that I'm pretty satisfied with now. And I think he is. That feeling of failure is gone now. And I think we both admitted to ourselves—probably not as much to each other—all the ways that each of us needed to change to make it work again.

We're just so much more tolerant of each other. We've gone through a lot together and we're older, and I think that getting older makes you see that there's so much more to the world and to life than what you see when you're young. There's so much more to love. Accepting everything about the other person even though, in any relationship, everybody doesn't love everything about that person, and if they say they do, I don't think that they're being honest.

In my everyday living with the guy, you realize you just have to let some of this stuff go. Little things—they seem fairly childish to me.

We have our lake cabin on Lake Superior near Schroeder, Minnesota, like seventy-eight miles northeast of Duluth. We actually spend seven or eight months of the year here. And then we have a condo down in the Twin Cities, in St. Paul.

Okay, I'm looking out the window, and I have some beautiful flowers and pots out here and stuff. And my husband, for about two or three weeks, he's been running around the yard, buttoning things up for winter. You know, putting away hoses, putting covers on different parts of the house for winter so things don't get in there. And it's October. I'm going, "But we still have five weeks before winter. Do we really have to worry about this?" And he says, "Oh, no, I'm not going to be doing this in the middle of the winter." And I pretty much need to close my eyes to it.

Or: my husband has taken up cooking the last couple of years. I'm really thrilled about it now, but he's rearranged the whole kitchen. The first day I came in and couldn't find anything. I just was going ballistic. This happened a couple years ago. And now I just think, "Okay! He cooks! Let it go and just keep looking for the stuff that you need."

I guess that before, I was more controlling than I ever wanted to admit. I think I probably wanted things my way or no way a lot of the time. There was probably a lot of me overreacting, and him withdrawing. At the time you don't think you're overreacting at all. And he didn't think he was withdrawing at all. But that's what you learn after a lot of years of looking back.

When we were starting over, it felt like we didn't have any real attachment to each other except we had been married so many years before—like twenty-five years. We were both free. I felt I was a different person and I had learned new things. And surely he had too. I guess we had learned to be kind to each other again, or good to each other. To be more careful to listen to the other person. Listening. I guess that's a huge thing.

PAUL PESCE, AGE 83

MIAMI, FLORIDA

"I turned to her and said, 'Could I take you to your home?'
She looks at me and she says—with a pause—'If you got a
quarter you can go anywhere you want.' "

I was born in Brooklyn. My mother died when I was about nine years old. My father tried to take care of us. What he did was, he moved us in with a family. My brother and I. And he went to work and he paid them for room and board to take care of us. But then he would come home and say, "Did you drink your milk?" and I would say, "No. What milk?" He'd say, "I gave money to the people to give you milk." That was during the Depression when food and money and clothes were a little difficult to come by. And the family he was paying, well, besides the money business, other things happened. But we won't talk about those.

Anyway, he had to put us in the orphanage. Which was very lucky for me and my brother. Instead of playing hooky and not studying and becoming a street guy, the nuns took care of us. We had to go to bed at a certain time, we had to go to church at a certain time, breakfast a certain time, school a certain time, lunch, play, school. It was a regular schedule right through the night until it was time to go to bed with prayer. And when we got out of the orphanage, there was a war on. So I went and I joined the navy.

When I got out, the whole world had changed for me, because they were paying for education. What I did was, I went to pharmacy school in the day, I went to high school at night to finish up my high school diploma; I worked as an X-ray technician, I had an internship, which I was doing at Walgreens in New York. And going home one Sunday night, I go down on the subway and something happened that has never happened before—ask any New Yorker, they'll agree with me—there was nobody, I mean no single person on the subway platform.

It was maybe ten thirty, eleven o'clock. The train comes, and again, nobody is on the train, except for a woman sitting at the head of one of the cars. So being a young New York boy, I get on the train, I walk the length of the train to where she's sitting, I sit down right next to her, pull out a book, and start reading. And I peruse the page, or a half page, I turned to her and I said, "Excuse me, does this train go to Brooklyn?" She looks me in the eye and she points across the other side of the car, and of course, there's a big sign: "To Brooklyn." Of course I've only seen that sign like a couple hundred times. But I said, "Oh! Thank you! Goodbye."

Get back to the book. Couple minutes later I turned to her and said, "Could I take you to your home?" She looks at me and she says—with a pause—"If you got a quarter you can go anywhere you want." Which was what the subway cost at that time. And she got off at the next station, and I got off with her and followed her to the next train. I sit down next to her, pull out my book, I'm reading it. (*laughs*) She's standing here watching me tell this story again.

If you see a picture of her back then, you'll say she was a beautiful woman. But, I can't say exactly why I was doing this. It was just instinct. And if the train had been crowded that day, I wouldn't have seen her, or if I had, I don't think I'd do what I did.

We went from the New York train to the New Jersey train, and then at one of the stations, she changes to a two-tiered bus. She goes up to the top, and I sit down next to her, pull out my book, I'm reading it, and I turn to her and I say, "Excuse me, can I buy you a drink of coffee?" Pause. She says, "Okay."

Okay, great. So we go down, have a cup of coffee. And we sit there, and we don't say anything. And when we were leaving the coffee shop I said to her, "Can I walk you to your home?" She says, "I'd rather walk by myself." I said, "Oh. All right. Would you give me your phone number?" Pause. "Okay." Pulls out a paper and pen, writes down a number. And I go home. And her name is Eleanor, by the way.

Monday morning I call right away. And Eleanor comes to the phone and I said to her, "Can I take you out tonight?" And she responds, "No." "How about tomorrow night?" And she responds, "Okay."

So she gives me her address, and I pick her up, take her to New York, and take her to see a play. And as we're exiting from the play I turned to her and I ask her, "Will you marry me?" She looks at me—pause—and she says, "Okay."

You gotta realize that the time that we spent together was not really a communication of friends or neighbors or anything.

Even through the coffee—that was not the most intimate relationship. Through the play we're not talking to each other or, you know, we're watching the play. So when we walked out, I was standing next to a stranger and so was she. And I asked her, "Will you marry me?" Pause. "Yes."

Now she's left the room, but at this point, when she's listening, she usually says, "And what's the name of the play?" And this was fifty-five years ago. I always answer, "I don't know. I don't remember." Which I don't.

I really don't know why I asked her. I just liked her. Before I met her, I was just doing the thing that comes naturally to a young man. As far as I was concerned I'd be dead before I was thirty-five. Shot by a jealous husband. I wasn't thinking about marriage. It just came out. I think it was just instinct.

I think that people are tribelike. We're meant to be with other people. In a group. At least with two people. Like a marriage. If you look at it, you'll see that plants do the same thing, birds and animals do the same thing. They form a family.

To me, love is a chemical reaction that takes place, or a psychic reaction. I just felt like she was nice. And that she was beautiful. And that she paused and she contemplated anything she said to me. But like I say, it was just instinct. Like the bugs and the animals. What kind of courtship do they need? We had a fifteen-minute courtship!

After she said yes, she said to me, "Don't tell my mother we just met. Tell her we knew each other in grammar school." And that's what we told her mother. And her mother acquiesced. Her mother started making plans for her wedding, but her stepfather kept making excuses for slowing things down in his broken English. He was selling a car—a New York Chrysler—and her mother loaned me five hundred dollars to buy the car. I took driving lessons. But I didn't know anything about how to drive. I had to ask a cop once how to turn on the lights.

I wanted to get licensed in Florida, because I had been stationed in Jacksonville, and I figured that as a pharmacist I might someday want to go to another state. And I said to Eleanor, "I'm gonna go to Florida to take the state boards, and then when I get back, we can get married." She says, "No, you won't." I said, "No? What are you talkin' about?" She said, "I'm going with you." Her mother agreed. She said, "Go ahead. That's the best thing. Elope."

So one night we throw a couple clothes in the car, and we begin to drive from Jersey down to Florida. And as we come to the Pulaski Highway, which goes from Jersey, I drive directly into the median. On each side, one wheel on each side of the median. So I turned to her and I said, "You watch the gauges, and I'll watch the road." So I backed off, we took off again, and she watched the gauges and I watched the road and we drove through the night.

We went over to Tallahassee so I could take the state boards. And then we went to a justice of the peace and got married. And I told her, "Look, as long as we're here why don't we go down to Miami before we go back to New Jersey?" And she says, "Okay." So we're driving into Miami and I'm reading a newspaper and it says, "Pharmacists wanted. A hundred dollars a week." A hundred dollars a week! Goddamn! They're paying me only seventy-five dollars a week in New York. So I go to the address of the drugstore and I said, with the newspaper in my hand, "You uhh . . . hiring pharmacists?" He says, "Yeah." He flips out his pharmacy jacket, puts it on my shoulder, and says to me, "I'll see you tomorrow. I haven't had a day off in six weeks."

I went outside, and I said to Eleanor, "Find us an apartment. We're staying." I started working. She found a little house in Little River that we rented, and I worked two shifts every day for about a year without a day off.

One day one of the accountants comes over to me and he says to me, "Hey, Paul, what are you doing working for somebody else? Why don't you get a pharmacy or a drugstore yourself?" So I told Eleanor. And this is the way my whole life has been with Eleanor: I get an idea, I tell her, and goddamn if it doesn't happen. 'Cause she makes it happen.

We found this little drugstore way on the outskirts of Miami. And we worked in the drugstore for about five years. Now, because we were, you know, on the outskirts of Miami, we also put in a post office, a Western Union, American Express money orders; we collected bills for Florida Power and Light, Gas Company; we put in a beauty shop. We had a fountain, with hamburgers, soup, sandwiches, and the fountain itself. We had a freezer that we sold milk out of and we sold bread, cake, cigarettes of course, and Kotex. We bought Kotex and sold it at the wholesale price, which would bring people in.

And all of these were my ideas, but she was the one executed them. She was an accountant for Singer Sewing Machine before I met her. So she was good with money. And the marriage was always fine. Fine. Fine. I mean, we're too busy to fight. We were running the business. She's doing most of the running. All I'm doing is working as a pharmacist. But she's taking care of the business, taking care of hiring the help.

I had promised myself when I was in high school that I was

gonna retire by the time I was thirty-five. So we were very fru-
gal and we saved money and we had enough to retire. Which
we did when I was thirty-nine. I started taking acting lessons.
My doctor friends all said to me, "What the hell are you
doing?" So I went to medical school.

We sold the drugstore to a friend of mine. I became a physi-
cian, a family doctor. And Eleanor took care of the business
part. She was the boss of the office. And by that time we owned
the building and a strip center.

After trying for eight or nine years to have a baby, we finally
did—Paul Pesce Jr. We gave him the nickname PJ, which he still
uses to this day. And then we had Chris, and then Vicky. I
worked in the office, and Eleanor worked in the office and took
care of the kids.

And we never fought. Hey, I'm not gonna fight. Well, I can't
say that—one time we did have an argument and I left. That
was a while back, in my youth. I stayed with a girlfriend. She's
not in the room now so I can say that. I stayed away about two
days. When I came back she got so mad at me she hit me. She
punched me in the chest. And I slapped her in the face. And I
think PJ remembers that. I think he was about ten or twelve at
the time.

That was the only time we really got into a fight. I mean
we've had discussions and arguments about certain things but
not too much—we seem to think more or less on the same
plane. I think one of the key ingredients of our marriage is that
we agree on so many things. We're willing to give in to the
other. I think I was probably pushier than her about getting my
way—probably by a huge margin. But, well, even if it's not
equal, it's still satisfying.

Day to day, it's always been in my mind how lucky I am. We weren't shy with each other, we were very affectionate. Lovey-dovey. If I got upset, she calmed me down. Out of the fifty-six years we've been married, I've only been away from her for two weeks.

I think it has something to do with my generation. Because I think the natural thing for my generation is you stay with it. I don't know anybody of our friends that got divorced. Even if the wife knows the guy is foolin' around. She may not accept it that gracefully, but she accepts it. And the guys, if they were doing something like that, I mean nobody flaunted it.

Anyway. Now she's got Alzheimer's, which is heartbreaking for me. She's had it, I'd say, about four to five years now. I don't think she realized it when it was happening, and neither did I. It was her friend who said to me, "Hey, Paul, what's goin' on with Eleanor?" She would keep repeating the question—the same question—after you gave her an answer. I started realizing it. And when I spoke to the doctors about it, they agreed.

Mostly she doesn't communicate. She just sits and stares. Occasionally I'll get a giggle out of her. She's pretty well aware of her condition. Which is terrible, you know. If she didn't know, it wouldn't be so bad.

You're looking at a guy who delivered babies in the Cancún jungle, who scuba-dived the Great Barrier Reef in Australia, who climbed the Alps, the Andes. We've been to China, Japan, Italy, France, England. I was just looking at a picture of us when we were in China and we were dressed in Chinese costumes, as Chinese warriors. We've been all over the planet because I mention it and she makes it happen. If I thought that we oughta own property, all of a sudden we had shopping centers. She's handled millions of dollars. She was so brilliant. She took care of me all of my life. All our lives. From that one meeting in the subway.

And now we walk around the house. There's a law in Florida that says if there is a school that's receiving money from the government and there are any empty seats in the classroom they should give them to the senior citizens free of charge. So what I'm tryin' to do is find classes that have movies. She seems to enjoy watching them. Tomorrow, I've got to take her bowling in the morning with a group of women who have Alzheimer's. And that's what we do. And it's just heartbreaking. So in case I sound a little confused, or a little off, you'll know why.

I consider myself one of the luckiest people on the planet. I've gone through wars, depressions. Never been hungry. But this is horrible. I'm eighty-three. We joke; I'm supposed to say I'm thirty-nine. I will be eighty-three in August. And . . . all my friends are leaving. And now this. It's horrible.

We have a doctor's appointment today at about eleven thirty and she's been standing around here with a purse on her shoulder, which she's gonna lose, waiting to go to the doctor's. For over an hour now, she's been walking around with that purse. Doesn't say anything, but you know she's waiting to go to the doctor's or somewhere, she doesn't know for sure where it is. If she knows where it is she'll forget it in ten minutes.

She'll last longer than me. Even with the Alzheimer's. Eventually her brain will forget to tell her heart to beat, and she'll die. But she'll outlast me. Because women last longer than men.

I'm not sure that the Bible says anything real about heaven. I think that there is something or somebody that has created us. I think of like a guy who made a little miniature railroad track with a town and a train. And he watches what's happening as it runs. But if there's such a thing as an afterlife, I hope I can spend it with her.

ETHELLE SHATZ, AGE 79

DARIEN, CONNECTICUT

"I say to him, 'You really are gorgeous, you know?
You're the most gorgeous man here.' "

My mother, who raised us very strictly, told me, "Never wear red shoes. If you wear red shoes, you're fast." So the first thing I did when I got to Cleveland with my scholarship money was go out and buy a pair of red heels. (*laughs*)

This was 1951. I'm seventy-nine. I was born in Newark, New Jersey, 1929, grew up in Brooklyn. As soon as I finished at Brooklyn College, I went to get my master's at Case Western Reserve, in Cleveland.

Burt was in architecture school there. I was in social work school. We didn't know each other, but we had something in common: no money. My scholarship provided me with a big fat hundred dollars a month for all living expenses, rent and all of that.

At the time there was a cooperative house right on the edge of the campus, big old rambling sort of Victorian house. We were twenty interracial occupants. We all had jobs to do in that house to keep it going. Burt came in after the first semester to apply. He looked like an architect: tweed jacket with leather, you know, at the elbows. I came clunking down the stairs, dressed for a meeting in my red shoes, making a racket. And I'm not so soft-spoken at all.

He heard me and the first thing he saw was the back of me, and what he says is, "Boy, you have a great ass"—which he insists I still have. (*laughs*)

So that's the way we met.

He was so prepped out. I thought to myself, "Oh, my God"—"OMG," as my granddaughter says. I thought right away, "Oh, he is not going to make a good co-oper. He's not going to really pitch in and, you know, he's going to be one of *those*."

But he turned out to be a very good co-oper. He was a restrained person. We had a lot of emotional drama queens, men and women, and living together like that brings out a lot of the drama. But he really was very, very likable, and he didn't stir up any trouble. He didn't leave the dishes in the sink like some of the boys did, or run around asking girls to do things for him. And this was a very old house, everything was broken all the time, and he was very . . . well, he still is: he loved fixing things.

We hit it off because we had good senses of humor, and that just sort of did it. We appreciated each other's humor and then we just appreciated each other.

My darling roommates, two of them, started to date two of the fellows at the co-op, and so Burt and I, rather than sort of being pals, joined them in dating too. The dating was very, very mild because nobody had any money. It was going down to this coffeehouse kind of thing, I think it was called the Bottomless Cup or something like that. It was dirty. Just a grungy place, you know. We called it the "Bug and Germ." Everybody would have a beer, and the beer company—I'll never forget this—was Leisey Beer, L-E-I-S-E-Y. And I remember we called it "Lousy Beer" because it was cheap.

We sort of just knew we were going to have a relationship. But there was absolutely no plan. I was graduating and taking a job in Chicago at the Jewish Community Center of Chicago— an outstanding agency. I couldn't turn it down. And Burt had to finish up at architecture school in Cleveland because architecture school is five years. And we discovered that Cleveland to Chicago was not much of a trip. We could continue to make arrangements to see each other.

Then Burt got drafted. They were drafting people for Korea. The idea of being apart for two years seemed so long. So we just sort of said, "Well, I guess we have to get married when you get back." That was how romantic it was. (*laughs*) It just seemed logical.

Basically, I was a little girl. I wasn't a sophisticated young woman. I was interested in my work and I really loved school. I'd never felt in love before. But once he went to the army, it felt terrible for him and it felt terrible for me. We were very, very lonesome for each other. And fortunately, he never went to Korea; he was in Germany. And so whenever he could get a furlough, he would meet me someplace in Europe.

Both of us never having been there, never even knowing where to stay, where to meet, it was quite an experience trying to find each other and, you know, do the dumb things that kids do that we can't believe we ever did because we are such conventional people now.

I was a kid still, you know, with a rucksack on my back,

doing it on three to five dollars a day. Girls just didn't do that sort of thing. That really was the most exciting time of my life. It was 1955 and everybody in Europe loved America. It was nice to be beloved. And it's just a total memory bank for both of us.

By the time Burt was drafted, our relationship had grown to where we very easily got along and very easily argued with each other as if we had known each other all our lives. When we argued, it would be tumultuous. We were both so sure of ourselves; I was sure I was right and he was sure he was right. I'm very voluble and I can get . . . not dramatic, but loud when I argue. Emphatic. And Burt can get so stubborn.

It wasn't like we were saying bad words to each other or anything, but we would do this in front of people. So when we told everybody we were getting married, which was in 1955, some of them said, "We give them six months." And some other friends in New York said, "What? Why?" They said, "Because they fight, you know." (*laughs*)

Look, this is what has characterized us since the day we met. We really get along very, very well. But we each have a very strong streak of individuality, so, you know, when it matched, it was wonderful. When it didn't match, it was tumultuous.

Our styles are different, our temperaments are different. Our approach to solving things is different. You know, "No, no, no, that's not the way you do things! You don't fix things that way. First you fix this, then you fix this!" "No, I don't want to do that! I want to do the floors first and then . . ."

I mean, it's as stupid as it could be. All we were interested in was I'm right and you're wrong. (*laughs*) And then each of us would go around muttering, "We always have to do things your way, we never can do things my way." We were acting still as very individual people and not realizing we're part of a couple.

But we always had the comfort of not feeling threatened in the relationship, of being able to feel that yes, you can present your worst side and not have to worry, "Oh, boy, I'm going to pay for this." I think that feeling of utter naturalness with Burt is what allows me to feel free.

A dual relationship requires so many opportunities for self-sacrifice—as it should. But part of that naturalness and intimacy is, as trusting as you are with somebody else, you still need to maintain your own sense of self and your self-respect. Every relationship needs boundaries.

Sometimes it's just a question of standing up for yourself when your partner is doing something very different from the way you do it, or even think about it. Rather than do a phony thing like going along with him, which presents too much of a conflict inside of you, you just say, "I won't do it. I don't have to be like you." (laughs)

Burt and I used to travel before the kids were born, as much as we could. I would be very friendly and I would always initiate conversations with people. I would chat. Burt would really have liked me not to be like that, to be more reserved, because he was a bit shy. I knew he would be so much more comfortable if I was as reserved and proper as he was. But it made me feel, like, I can't do that for you. I love to satisfy you and make you happy and have your high regard, but I can't really change my nature.

But what I think is that as the love ages and deepens, the capacity to resent flaws, or times when you don't get your way, tends to diminish, because so many other things are in place, feel good, and are good. As we got out of our thirties, our forties, our fifties, life became so much more relaxed. There's a recognition now that what we share is so much more important, and the other things are superfluous to the relationship.

Now that we have figured that out, I don't give a fig when we disagree now. It just does not mean World War Three at all.

For example, Burt thinks that he has the last word on anything we do in the house. I am terribly aware that it can use a painting, and he says, "You're absolutely right. But first we have to put a railing on the stairs." That's what he thinks is best. I think it's the dumbest thing I ever heard. And it infuriates me because he'll say again and again, "I don't tell you how to wash the dishes. I don't tell you how to do the laundry. So don't tell me how we fix the house."

This is a very recent conversation. He has to do things his way, one step at a time, and I tend to multitask. And I say it in my head all the time: Stop taking it personally. It's not selfish, it's not inconsiderate—he just can't multitask! (*laughs*)

But, you know, here am I, I've been a therapist longer than I've been married. I've been doing it since 1953. So I'm supposedly so self-aware blah blah blah. But I'm not, not at all. All of that goes out of the window when there's a big emotional thing or something that's problematic for me. I behave pretty much like most people.

But I always ask myself: Is this going to matter when I'm lying on my deathbed? Because I'm very aware of mortality. I'm grateful for each day and I'm so grateful to have him.

We're numbering our days now. We're older. I mean, seventy-nine and seventy-seven, oh, my God, that's old. And the thought that one of us might at any time have to live without the other is paralyzing, just paralyzing.

Burt has stenosis; he has trouble walking and all of that. It's a blow. He always wishes he could still be what he was. When we're physically diminished, it doesn't feel good. I think the caretaking—the loving way we caretake each other and really help each other—is very much more a dimension at this stage in life than in others.

I once complimented a friend of mine on how she took care of her dying husband, how much I marveled at her dutiful nature, her loving nature. And she said to me, "Oh, Ethelle, it wasn't very hard to do. I realized my husband would do the same for me."

And I went home and said to Burt, "So, would you do the same for me?" And he looked at me so helplessly and so pathetically and he said, "I want to, but I don't do those things well." And I just looked at him and I said, "You know, you're right."

So that's why I got long-term insurance for me and not for him—because I knew I could take care of him, but he couldn't take care of me that way. He wouldn't know a thing about cooking and this and that. I wouldn't do that to him, because he'd really fuck it up. (*laughs*) And I was okay with it. You know? That's the way it goes. You sort of need to be a strong type about it.

At this point, you're not the same people you used to be. I mean, you're not going bike riding as much as you used to. You're not climbing mountains. You find different recreations. You've lost a lot of friends, you know. The grandchildren are adults. Things are very different.

We do a lot of reminiscing and end up having fits of giggles. And of course I don't remember what he remembers and he sometimes doesn't remember what I remember. So there's a lot of joshing about that.

I think the experiences of the generations are enormously different. With one relationship—one man, one love—there will be real and everlasting depths. It's a different experience than, you know, my daughter's generation, considering the depths of, let's say, six different relationships.

My daughter, I know she's very happily married, and I know that the idea of fidelity is probably as strong in herself as it is in myself. But I just couldn't imagine doing the things she did as a young adult. I'm glad I had it my way. (*laughs*) Because at this stage in life, what Burt and I treasure is the continuity of "You've been my one and only." The sense of faithfulness is very deep.

I think we're the only married couple who still has the same bed we've always had. It's a full bed, not a queen-size and not a king-size. I couldn't possibly sleep in a big bed like that. I'm so used to ours. We cuddle before bed. And we wake up in the morning and we always hug and kiss each other good morning. We've always been that way.

There's very small things that we do that are nice for each other. Like, he knows that I'm tired of cooking after all these years. I'm a good cook, but sometimes I just get so tired of the daily activity of menial work, you know? Shopping, cooking, cleaning, laundry, blah blah. And so he'll just say things like, "You really are such an imaginative cook."

It's nice to hear. And it's never phony. It's always something very sweet, and it's just every once in a while, which makes it real, you know.

Or we'll be at a party or something, and we're sitting down. Nobody sees Burt with his limp. And somebody will say to him, "Burt, you look so well. You're so handsome." And something tells me that I haven't been looking at him lately. And it will spark me to spontaneously say to him, "You really are gorgeous, you know? You're the most gorgeous man here."

We hold hands a lot. We smooch a lot. I remember one time, my daughter and her husband and our grandchildren and Burt and I had a picnic. And Burt ate well. The wine was good and I would say his senses were very fulfilled. He loves my cooking and he was so happy I made something good to eat. And so we were clearing the table, and he gave me a good smooch. And the grandchildren were fourteen and eleven, and they were like, "Oh! Look at them!" They were a little embarrassed.

I don't know how demonstrative their parents are. Maybe they think that grandparents hugging and kissing is funny. I don't know. But it was like, "Nana! Grandpa!" And we . . . frankly, Burt and I didn't give a damn.

More Than **Sixty** Years

FRED WHITE, AGE 86

MISSION, KANSAS

"She was quite a doll and I didn't want anybody else."

My wife, Helen, and I have been married sixty-five years. I met her in junior high school. And I think we figured it up. It's seventy-one years that she and I have been together. Practically. We weren't actually dating in junior high school until a little later, but I knew her and we were friends and so on.

We've lived in the Kansas City area all our lives. Back then it was like any other medium-sized city, everything was pretty smooth, there weren't a lot of the troubles that there is today. It was just a good place to be. My father run a bakery there and we just had a great time. Her father worked for Procter & Gamble. I think he was a soap blender or something.

We lived about eight blocks difference. I could just walk on over anytime. We'd talk, you know, and play together in school. I met her brothers and we got very well acquainted. They liked to fish like I do, so everything was hunky-dory. I did a lot of hunting and fishing with them and we got so we were, you know, kind of like family already, as far as that goes in some respects.

So, you know, the feeling—it kind of grows on you.

Girls back then, well, it was all different. It's very hard to even remember. Girls and boys. As far as dressing goes, there weren't any of this show this and show that. (*laughs*) There weren't any tattoos then, neither. None of that stuff. They just wore normal dresses and, you know, whatever the kids wore to school. The hairstyle was very conservative too. Nothing real fancy. Helen, she was really blonde and she dressed and looked like a blonde—very neat and very particular. Not one to show off. A regular good listener and just a nice person to be around.

It just seemed to be the normal thing, and we both understood it. She was quite a doll and I didn't want anybody else. That's the way it was. I've got good taste!

We were sweethearts for quite a while. I had a high school graduation and then I had a little bit of college that I didn't get to complete because of the war. I went and volunteered in Leavenworth, Kansas. Helen, well, she took it like she always does. Whatever has to be, has to be. Then I was at air force training in Sherman, Texas. She came down there. We got married. I wanted to make sure that when I came home that she was still mine. (*laughs*) She was my sweetheart and I wasn't fooling around.

We never did have any doubts about each other at all. Absolutely not. I knew I loved her and she knew she loved me and we still feel the same way. She's my one and only. I've never had another. I remember, it was hard when I left. The last time I saw her, just before we took off overseas, we was surrounded by a lot of people. Everybody was doing the same thing, really.

They had their wives there with them. I remember, I was trying to keep her as long as I could before I went.

I was a pilot stationed on Guam. I saw action in Japan mostly. It was about thirteen hours in the air, you know, back and forth. We'd bomb and then fly the six, seven hours back to Guam. Thousands of miles. Nothing but ocean and sky until you get to Japan.

I don't know how many missions I flew. I just remember I would sit there for thirteen hours in that airplane, you know, and you think about a lot of things. We had to worry about the weather along with everything else. That long time over ocean water, there's always some storms or typhoons. You had to be alert because there were no warnings what was ahead. It was a lot of worry. Just nerves. They did their darnedest to shoot us down!

But I'd think about her. She was in my thoughts every time. I'd be wondering how she was getting by, and how she was living with her folks, and just what the heck was good for her, really. It helped.

I worried about her a bit. That she might be meeting somebody else or something like that. The thought would cross my mind once in a while. But I trusted her and she trusted me and that's the way it was.

I stayed in contact with her by writing letters. You'd write a letter, and hell, it'd be a month before you heard anything one way or the other. But if I got a letter from her, I'd read it two or three, four times, just to think about her. And I'd look at her picture every day. I had her picture right by my bunk. It was a good one—nothing fancy or nothing, you know, suggestive or anything like that, just from the waist up and such. I still got it.

It stayed on my bed. I didn't take it on the planes. You were not supposed to take anything personal, you know, if you get shot down or whatever.

There were some rough trips. This one particular one, they shot up both my wings and part of the rudder control. We had one left in-board engine out, and I knew we weren't going to make it back to Guam. So I told my navigator to plot a course to the nearest island under our control. And it was one of those little islands that had runways on them but there was a cliff on each end of the runway. And it was five hundred or something feet to the water off the both ends. We got on the final approach and everything was going pretty good and I had the wheels down, and my right in-board engine quit. I just got the nose over the cliff and the landing gear hit. We made a big kind of a fishhook turn and we went on fire. I lost my belly gunner and waist gunner.

I didn't even know my head was bleeding. All I'm thinking about is how do we get out of this thing? Some of the guys got their outfit on fire. I was trying to beat them out and I got both my hands burned. There was twelve of us and we all got out except those two guys. The waist gunner, I saw his body, but the belly gunner he got ground up pretty bad, you know, because he couldn't get out.

This was in 1944. I was twenty-one. I know I was more of a man than I was when I went over there. When I came back home and saw Helen for the first time, I thought she was the finest thing that God ever created. (*laughs*) I couldn't wait to get my arms around her.

We lived in an apartment, then we found this little house, and my first job out of the service was with General Motors. I gave them forty-one years. I started out on the line as an assembler before they had the conveyors in and we built them on dollies and pushed them to the next station. Then they asked me if I'd be a foreman. And then I was general foreman, then shift superintendent, then superintendent, then director of quality control. I was that for twenty-one years and then, when they shut the old plant down, they wanted me to come over to the new plant, and I said, "No, I'm going to go home to my wife." And I retired.

Helen never worked. She raised our boy, kept our home. And she was very supportive of me. She agreed with whatever I decided that it was my job to do and she did her job and we didn't have any problems there. She has been a good, faithful, enduring person and I wouldn't trade for nothing. I'd do this whole thing over again in a New York second. I think it has worked real good. I didn't ever have to worry about any of the marriage problems. We understand each other, we know each other well, and it just works.

We argue. Sure. We get in our little discussions, arguments, what you will. Sometimes I get the better end of it. Sometimes she does. I quit counting a long time ago. Sometimes you win, sometimes you lose. You know how that is. There are times when, you know, we get mad and walk away or something, but hell, an hour later, it's forgotten and by the wayside. You make it work.

A lot of couples don't do that today. They miss out on the benefits. We've got one boy and he's sixty-two now. Fred Jr. Now, Fred has been through a couple of relationships. So maybe he didn't pick up enough from the old man! But, well, we don't know a whole lot of people right now that has been long together. There are some, but not many. I think it's personal to us. I'm just once and never again and that kind of thing. I still love her and she still loves me.

I don't have a lot of advice. Give and take. You know? You have to share. We both think the same way and we try to live by the rules. Death do we part. Oh, yes. And one more: True love exists. If you make it. It's a true thing if you make it true.

Multiple Relationships

FRANCISCO ARELANO, AGE 33

BROOKLYN, NEW YORK

"Love means . . . Maga moo!"

I had a kid. I was sixteen, she was sixteen. We had a baby. Then she aborted. That's when I started drinking. That's when I started smoking. She didn't leave me. No girl could leave me. *(laughs)* Lidia, she was a beautiful girl. She aborted my son. When she was, like, seventeen, she went with some other nigger and I got jealous. Then I shot him. Yep. "Tha fuck you messin' with her!" I shot him like this, in the stomach.

Love? Oh, man. There was a girl—she got some beautiful hair, eyes. She lives in Northern California. I worked for Fendi—and she understood me, you know? I love the way she acted and the way she carried herself. And it's all right for her. She was fine. Yeah, I loved her too much. She's not with me no more. I took too much, my job. I live here now. In Brooklyn,

(Yells across street) Hey!! Filipo!

You wanna know the real thing? I'm with my girl, I tell her not to pay nothin'. Her lease, the rent, I got that. If she works, it's all for her mother, her sister, whatever. But I pay for all of the bills. That's what I want. That's what love is.

Listen, I have a woman, her eyes is blue. Her name is Teresa. She had the most beautiful eyes. She was my girlfriend. I fucked it up. I ain't do nothin'. She was the most beautiful girl you've ever seen. I was a little conceited. About myself. I went over there and I was like, "Yo, Teresa, let's go over there to this uh . . . to the wrong bar." Well, we hooked it up. She was like, "Yo, nice, nice, nice, and *nice*." And then that's it. I never seen her again. I was like yeah, that's fucked up. I've heard about her. She's makin' mad blow. She's making a nice thing of herself.

Love means . . . Maga moo! It means to have a fucking girl on the side. No. Love is love. Love is love. Patience. Love is where you can't let your girl just go with some fucking nigger. Just ask me, man. I think love is forever.

He was working at a steel fabrication company and I was going in to clean offices. He started making sure he was around where I was, so that he can talk. I was forty-seven. He was one or two years older than me. I thought he was nice-looking. He had Navajo Indian blood, so he walked with that real easy Indian gait. Very long black hair, very brown eyes, very nice smile, and very gentle.

His name was Ron. He asked me out. The night that we had planned to go out, he was supposed to come pick me up. We were going to go to a movie. Only he didn't show up. I didn't hear anything for three days.

Then he called and left a message. I was ready to chew him out for standing me up, and I found out he was in the hospital. He was wounded in the Vietnam War, and the drugs they gave him addicted him to heroin. And he was an addict for like thirty years. He was one of the few people who went through the program and got off that. For years, he'd been a drinker. He had stopped drinking, but all the years of everything had taken his health. He needed a liver transplant.

We went to a hockey game. That was the first hockey game I went to. He was a big Blazers fan. And we had a blast. The T-shirts, the whole thing. We went to a lot of hockey games. We went to a lot of movies. They have a thing in Oklahoma City where the radio sponsors a whole weekend of concerts. They'll have two bands each night. So we saw—oh, my gosh— we saw Sammy Hagar and his band, we saw Steve Miller, Mötley Crüe, the Scorpions. We went to White Water Bay all summer. It's like with water slides and a wading pool and all that. We bought season tickets. After work, we'd meet each other in the parking lot and go relax in the water for a couple of hours until it closed.

He was really my first adult, deep love. It was gradual. I was watching and watching. But I think it was the weekend we went camping. We went down to Robbers Cave and spent the whole weekend climbing around them rocks and hiking and looking in the caves and swimming. He had a little dog, a little bichon frise named Fancy Bee, and she was the cutest thing. We took his little dog prancing everywhere. She'd take off some- where and be doing something she wasn't supposed to be doing, and she would look back at him, and he would go, "Okay, little whitehead." You know, because she's just solid like a cotton ball. And she would just flap all over.

It just felt good to be with him. We had fun, we cared about each other's feelings and likes and dislikes. He always wanted to make sure that I was happy doing whatever it was we were doing—whether it was going to a concert or just renting a movie and staying in. At his house or my place, it just felt relaxed. And comfortable. And good.

My first husband and I, we were young. Eighteen, almost nineteen. We didn't know each other very long. Home life wasn't right for either one of us. We wanted to strike out on our own.

We muddled through like most young couples. But when you're young, you jump the gun and you think, "Oh, this is the one." You don't know the difference between the infatuation stage and real love. I stayed not because I loved him so much as I felt honor bound. Especially after we had our kids and all that, it was more that I'd made a commitment.

There were a lot of bad things going on. He liked to drink and he liked to hit me. He liked to go out with other women. Sometimes you're blaming yourself and you're wondering, what did I do wrong? And you're so hurt because you're thinking, how could they do that to me? You lose all your self-confidence. You hide everything because you're ashamed.

I was such a different person by the time I met Ron. I knew who I was. And we had so much in common. He had lived in Northern California for years and I had spent my growing-up years in California. So we knew a lot of the same areas, and being close in age, you know, we liked the same kinds of music, the same kinds of movies, same kinds of foods. It was like we just blended.

With Ron, it was not just a mental choice; it was a heart choice. He taught me one thing that was very, very important, and it has always stuck with me. He said, "I don't need you. But I want you." I couldn't understand that for a long time. Because you know, when you love somebody, you think you need them. But of course there are different kinds of need. But the wanting, the desire means worlds more than need.

One day in May—we'd been together now for about five months—he asked me to meet him after work. He had went to the doctor that day, and they told him that he had contracted MS. Which meant that he was no longer eligible for a transplant. It was like a death sentence.

We still did a lot of things together, but that first joy of life, the joy of being in love was gone. Because he knew he was going to die. With no hope of a transplant, he knew it was only a matter of time. You know, we still had hope. The heart hopes forever. But, of course, the sadness tempered everything.

We continued to see each other for the next few months, but he kept pulling away. And finally he told me, "You need to be with somebody who can offer you a life." Of course, I didn't want that. I wanted to be with him. Because I loved him.

He told me that he loved me too, but he loved me too much to put me through that. He wanted me to go on and be with somebody else I could have a life with and be happy with. He didn't want me to see him go through the things he was going to have to go through. That was the worst part for him. He wanted me to see him as a whole and healthy man, not as a sick person.

So we broke up. We didn't see each other anymore. For six months, I couldn't eat, I couldn't sleep. I worried myself sick about him. I realized he did it to spare me, but it put me through the worst torture of my life.

It would have helped my heart to put things to rest. The way it was, you know, I think back and I wonder, could I have helped in some way by being there? It hurts me that I wasn't. If he had allowed it, I would have been there, and I'm sure he knew that.

We stayed friends. A year later, when my mother passed away, he was the one who I turned to. He consoled me. We would talk for hours.

I was working in a dry cleaner's doing alterations, and I had taken a second job working nighttimes in a bar. First time I ever worked in a bar, and I was kind of freaked out. It used to be an old biker bar, and it's kind of a little run-down place. But I needed to keep myself occupied because I was still at loose ends, hurting.

The first time Barry came in, I don't even remember. But he came in. He started asking me out. I told him no, because he's younger than me, sixteen years younger. I kept telling him, "No, you're too young. I'm not going out with you."

He came in every single night for a week, asking me out and staying until I closed. Made sure that I got in my car safely and all that. And so finally, one night, I said, "Okay, we're going to have coffee."

Well, he moved in. And we got married.

Of course, you know, it's bittersweet.

Barry and I respect each other. We're friends. A lot of times we spend all weekend without ever even leaving the house. Just watching movies. Or we sit and talk for hours. I can be myself with him. To be with somebody who accepts you totally as you are—what more can you ask for?

I told him all about Ron. Everything. It was cool. And I told

Ron all about Barry. Ron said he was very happy for me. He wanted to meet him. So Barry and I, we went to visit Ron. We just sat and talked. And when we left, Barry said, "You know, he seems really nice. Under other circumstances, we could have been friends."

A few months later, Ron called me and told me not to worry if I didn't hear from him for two or three weeks, because he was going down to stay with his brother and visit with his family. Well, I didn't hear from him for a couple of months, so I got worried.

I called and called and called and called. Finally, I drove over to his house and his house was all dark and cold. I knocked on the neighbors' door—people he had been friends with—and they told me that he had passed away two months earlier, three weeks after I talked to him. He didn't want me notified. He wanted me to go on and be happy.

But it just broke my heart. The night that I found out that Ron had died, I got home and, of course, I was upset. I was crying and wondering why nobody let me know, and how could I have not known. I should have felt it. Or something. Barry came home from work and saw I'd been crying. He came over and put his arms around me, "What's wrong?" I told him Ron passed away. And he just hugs me up and says, "Oh, I'm so sorry, honey." He just held me while I cried over another man.

LISA NORGAARD, AGE 44

MINNEAPOLIS, MINNESOTA

"She was out—and I was married."

Peter and I married because I was pregnant. I was twenty-four. I was working at a health club and hanging out with his sister, who taught aerobics. She introduced me. She would gather up a bunch of girls for him to meet and then he would pick who he would hang out with. We dated over the summer on and off. He was dating other people, as I was, and we were having sex. I got pregnant in September.

He didn't think I was really pregnant, and I was like, "Well, I'm pregnant."

And he said, "No, I don't think so. I want you to go to this doctor."

And I said, "That's not a pregnancy test, that's a marriage test." Because he would only marry me if I was pregnant.

I did love him. I loved his intensity. At the time, when I first met him, he was so confident. He knew all of this stuff about horses and machinery that I didn't understand and that was interesting to learn.

But, you know, you want someone to love you, and *then* you want to commit to them; *then* you want to make decisions about having children and how you are going to do that together. So I said, "Let's wait. We'll get married after I have this baby," and he said, "No, no, no, no, no." We got married in December. And then we had two sons and a daughter.

We were a lower-middle-class family in a very wealthy community. Very involved in the school. Very sports oriented. Peter would coach sports that our sons played. My daughter rode, so every weekend was devoted to either doing horse shows or watching the boys wrestle or play football. I would do chores; I would volunteer at school; I ran this thing called Art Adventure, where kids took tours of the Art Institute. I did Junior Great Books, a book club for kids. I would drive into Minneapolis and teach my aerobics class at Northwest Athletic Club.

I didn't think I was marrying his family, but I was. I did not realize how enmeshed they were. The word for them would be "culty." That's how other people described them. Very, very, very, very, very family centered. (*laughs*) Peter's family owned a hobby farm with horses, chickens, and ducks. And it seemed like the Norgaards only liked you as much as you do what they want. So I did what was expected of me. That meant get up, drive to the farm four days a week, clean stalls, feed the horses.

I worked there constantly, to the exclusion of activities that I wanted to do. It was a point of contention that I taught aerobics. Peter's mom, when I was talking about my job, she said, and I quote, "Working is a luxury." It was a struggle. They were born-again Christians, Republican. I didn't really fit. They would always tell me, "You're not this," or "You're this," or

"I think you're crazy," or "How could you be a liberal?" (*laughs*)

I think Peter did love me—in his way. We cared about each other. But it was a bad thing that I was different from him.

In love, you want this person to look at you for all that you are. Not necessarily blindly accept it, or simply tolerate it, but not deny it either. I wanted to be seen. I wanted Peter to *see* me for teaching dance, *see* me for being a liberal.

At the core, he just didn't approve of who I was. And I wasn't being who I was. So it was a tough marriage. I was sad. I was lonely.

I was mother first, I was womb first. I'm not kidding. He said to my son once, "Date this girl. Can you imagine the kids you would have together?" What? That's just gross. Now I see how it was when he met me. I'm sure he looked at me like breeding stock. That's not hot, not hot at all. Yes, I want to be so desirable that you can't hold yourself back, but that's different from breeding stock.

As our kids got older, Peter didn't spend time with me. I would try to be really direct with him, like, "This is what I want." Very specific: "I want us to go out on a date so that we can go together alone." And "I would like to go to this restaurant." I wasn't asking him to Magic 8 Ball it and find an answer. I gave him an answer. I gave Peter the answer to my heart. And he didn't listen.

I was moving away from him anyway. One day, in 1997, I was teaching my class at the athletic club. The Twin Cities aerobics world is very small; I had seen her around before. And I knew the second she walked into my class: this is not good.

She walked right up to the front of the classroom, to the

front row, which is usually for people that are pretty strong, pretty competitive. She came in with this swagger. She was confident, comfortable in her own skin.

I knew that if she stayed, I would have trouble. Because here would be this woman that I find attractive—every day, in my world. I remember thinking, "Oh, God, not her, not that one. Not that one."

I did not think of myself as a lesbian at that time. I had had feelings that I was gay before. I kissed a girl when I was nineteen. It did not rock my world. (*laughs*) Right before I was married, there was a girl I worked with at the club who . . . I don't know . . . she had a mullet. She worked in the maintenance staff. We're sitting there one night in this lesbian bar, and she said something incredibly racist. And I went, "Are you kidding?" And that was it. I said to myself "I can't be with her." I made the mistake of thinking because she was a racist, I wasn't a lesbian.

Looking back, I can say that I was completely denying. But I just never had the moment where I went, "Duh! You're a lesbian!" And then I guess it's interesting—through the filter of hindsight, of course—well, ironic or tragic, that I chose a born-again Christian, hard-core supermacho guy to marry. Who would make me straight.

When Sue came into my class, I knew I would be with her somehow. I was nervous because she was out—and I was married with three kids. I liked her energy, I liked everything about her. But then I thought, "What the fuck are you doing?! You can't think this, you cannot do this!" It was excruciating.

She kept coming to my class. After class we would talk and we just . . . we just slowly gravitated toward each other. Watching her move, listening to her speak, seeing her in the world—I was just drawn to her. Emotionally and physically.

She liked me. I liked her. As simple as that is, it was a novel concept. And after two or three years, we started what I would say was an emotional, intimate love affair. We talked a lot. Nothing physical happened. It wasn't a flirty, touchy-feely kind of relationship. We would just seek each other out and spend time with each other and talk and talk and talk.

I loved Sue's intensity. And she loved mine. I think our whole lives, we were both told that we were too much. "Stop!" "Calm down!" "Settle down!" We shared this love for movement, aerobics. I would choreograph for her so I could watch her and see if she liked it, see if it would make her happy. With Sue, I felt that she accepted all that I am. I didn't have to edit. I didn't have to apologize. It was very freeing.

She would invite me to parties that she would have at her house with her partner. Those were tough. It was like, "Ughhhh. I gotta go!" (*laughs*) I felt very conflicted.

The revelation for me was going to a wedding and seeing a woman there that I felt obviously attracted to. I told Sue. I remember crying on the phone, "I don't know what I'm doing. I don't know if I'm straight. I don't know if I'm gay. This is overwhelming." She was jealous about it. We didn't talk for a month after that.

You have this quiet, still place inside you where you can look to the heart, to the truth of things. It's what you see when you peel away the distractions and expectations. Most of the time, we don't acknowledge it, because we're distracted by what I call the screaming monkeys. (*laughs*)

I think most people don't like to go to that place. But if you go there, and you pay attention, you know what you want and who you love. And if you have something in your life that isn't true, that's obvious too. So sometimes you might end up looking at the person that you're with and realizing, "I cannot do this. This is not who I am anymore."

I knew that if I chose to follow my heart, it would be bad with Peter and it would be bad with my children. But by staying, I would have taught my daughter to not see the possibility of living the life that she wants. It would have sent the message that the individual person is not as important as preserving a contract that you signed. And I feel very strongly: we are here to be cherished, not owned.

I knew how I would be treated by Peter and his family. But I also knew how I was currently being treated, and I felt that the consequences of inaction were as great as the consequences of action. I had to hope that my children would know the love that I gave them. And know the truth of that.

I remember there was this sign on Patrick's Cabaret over on Hiawatha and Lake Street. A big sign. It said, "Love," then it had a greater-than sign, followed by the word "Fear." "Love is greater than fear." I would drive by that fairly often, and every time I saw it, I thought, "I cannot continue being disingenuous about who I am and how I feel."

I remember the next time, after that wedding, having coffee with Sue, and I looked at her and I said, "I love you." She had a partner, and I was still married, so she wanted to run away, screaming. (*laughs*) But I said, "You don't have to tell me you love me, because I know that in my heart I love you."

After my thirty-ninth birthday, there was a surprise party for

Sue's fiftieth birthday. All of these aerobic people were at a funky little coffee shop. The music was on, and it was so fun and freeing to be able to dance and not be teaching a class, telling everyone what to do with a mic in front of my face.

Sue and I hadn't been dancing—on purpose. I was like, "Do noooot do this!" (*laughs*) Her partner was there and all of her friends. She looked at me and said, "Come on." And I said, "I will." And that was it. I let go. It was evident to everybody: the heat between us, the desire. There was no tamping it down or hiding it any longer. We'd acknowledged it in public.

It was about a month later that we became physically intimate. This was in August of 2004. By deciding to be physical with her I knew that I had crossed the line. That was my turning point.

We went to her apartment. There was nothing veiled about it. The whole point was, okay, we're going to have sex. I think I was hyperventilating. I couldn't believe I was doing this, I was just so nervous and scared.

And it was lovely. She's a really good kisser. Listen (*laughs*), good kissing is important!

I had never had an orgasm. Never. Because you have to trust someone to have an orgasm. You have to be able to let down everything. All my life, before, I might have gotten close, and I would think, "Well, that must be it. Yeah, I think that's it." With Sue, I had one on Day Two. It was just so easy to let go. I went (*gasps*) "Oh, my God, *that's it!*" (*laughs*)

Three or four days later, we were in bed for seven hours. We just reveled in each other's bodies. We would have coffee and scones and then have more sex. I had a lot of catching up to do.

At some point, Peter started to pay attention to the hours and hours and hours that I was gone. And finally, he's like, "What's going on?" and I said, "I'm in love with Sue."

He said, "Well, have you had sex with her?" And that was it. He punched the walls, took away my keys, my ID and credit cards. I said goodbye and tried to kiss him goodbye, and he pushed me down. So I tried to run away. He came after me with the car. And then, basically, I was in what I called lockdown.

That went on until October. I thought he was going to kill me. My parents thought he was going to kill me. Sue thought he was going to kill me. I would wake up in the middle of the night and he would just be staring at me. He was so mad.

Because he had put his fist through the wall and had broken things, you know, the kids had noticed. They were twelve and fourteen or so. So we sat down with them, and I said, "Okay, things are bad." And my eldest son said, "Well, it's not like you had an affair," and I said, "Well, yes, I have. With Sue." Peter couldn't believe that I had said that. He thought he would get control over me by holding it over my head.

Over those months he would wake me up saying, "Why are you doing this? Why did you do this to me?" He would be there with that hate. He drew in all of his sisters to try and talk to me, and then he would say, "Let's go out and have dates!" For those months he was going to win me back, but it was too late. And in no way could he see that it had everything and nothing to do with him.

I brought the kids to a regular, non-Christian counselor, who began to call Peter on some of his behavior, but then Peter brought me to a Christian counselor who decided to make me straight. He asked me, "Well, do you look at porn?" And I'm like, "What? No. I love her. This is not about titillation. Or sex."

It was awful. It was awful for everybody. And I can't sugar-coat it. I mean, I took a marriage vow. I broke the contract. I wasn't proud of how this impacted my children and my friends and family.

But if I stayed I would not live an honest, aligned life. And I think maybe that's one of the greatest sins. I am who I am now.

For two years, I would twitch all the time in my sleep, because I would be remembering the lockdown period. I really couldn't sleep. I can laugh about it now, but I spent that first year after I left just crying.

I still have to defend myself to the children. They are trying to reorder Mom as lesbian and how it fits with what they've learned about love, and what other people think about it, and how will they see themselves, and how do they want to be with their mom? I mean, it's messy. Born-again Republicans are not super supportive of the "lesbian lifestyle." (laughs)

My daughter has an ultimatum from Peter: talk to me, get kicked out of the house. She has met Sue a couple of times, and it went quite well, but my sons do not want to meet her. They actually said, "Well, this is a lifestyle, and you're a sinner."

I go to school, I work, I care for my children, I ride a bike. I don't go out dancing. I love someone and she loves me. And I'm happy with her. (cries) She likes who I am. What is the "lifestyle" that I lead?

In their worldview, the only place you can enjoy anything is heaven, and when you die, things will all be fine. But in the meantime, you mouth the words and quote Scriptures. And I think that's a small, mean existence.

My parents are neither Christian nor conservative. I think they understood the heartache, and they did not want me to be sad. The first time I introduced my parents to Sue, we had dinner. When I talked to my mom later, she said, "You were talking with Sue and she reached over and touched your hand and looked at you. And you touched her back. In all the years that you and Peter were married, I never saw that."

I am lucky. I am very lucky. There was never sharing before. And now, her joy is my joy.

I'm much happier. Much more whole. It isn't that I became someone new. I became who I always was. It's like your life just gets boiled down to the simplest thing. Like in cooking. A reduction. A reduction is much more intense. Take out the extraneous. Find the purest form.

KRISTIAN HOFFMAN, AGE 57

LOS ANGELES, CALIFORNIA

"I love insane people."

I thought gay people were stupid. Gay people didn't like rock and roll. They were into disco. They were boring. They were clones. I didn't want to identify as being gay. But being gay and not identifying as gay made it hard to find love.

When I was young, everyone assumed my boyfriend was Lance Loud from *An American Family*, which was this famous documentary on PBS in the seventies that Margaret Mead called one of the most important events in television history or something like that. He was the lead singer of my band, the Mumps, and he was a sexual expert—at least, compared to me. He loved to go and have all that anonymous sex with gays who were into the "sexual revolution." He was having sex two or three times a day, for all I know. And he had a whole variety of boyfriends in tow, some he actually seemed to have affection for, and other ones he was just exploiting to get things like fancy dinners or clothes.

We never had sex. We were never lovers. We were best

friends. We did everything together. People just assumed, "They're gay. They must have fucked." It doesn't really work that way.

I met Lance in high school. I was from a family of seven, and we were very insolent and nasty to everybody. We thought we were the best and we didn't need any other friends. But when I met Lance, I thought, "Oh, other people *can* be fun."

Everyone in my family told me my music was horrendous and I should give it up, which was another reason why I guess I stuck with it. I was too shy to be a lead singer, but I wanted to be in music somehow. Lance supported me and gave me the vehicle by which to express myself. We moved to New York together to start our band. It took us three years to get it going, and there were all the usual problems, like finding like-minded musicians.

Even though we weren't boyfriends, he was my first love, I guess. We were obsessed with each other, and we were just as needy with each other as if we were lovers. When I finally decided to break up the band and move on, it was like a horrendous divorce where he didn't speak to me for years afterward. It was like I had betrayed him.

To get away from Lance, I decided to move in with this guy named David McDermott, a fantastic, eccentric artist who had a whole floor of this beautiful brownstone on the Upper West Side. He was very extreme. I kind of had a love affair with him mentally because he excited me about art. This is like 1976, right when punk is all about to start. We would go to a lot of parties together and meet all sorts of artsy people and it was one of those glamorous things where you get your picture in *Esquire* for being odd and eccentric. So. I'd been telling him my problems with Lance, and he said, "Well, why don't you move in with me?"

I thought it would be really fun. I wasn't interested in him sexually. I just thought, "What a fantastic new adventure with a great roommate."

Well, it turned out he sort of assumed that I was going to be his boyfriend. There was only one bed in his apartment. Surprise! It was just one of those weird things and I thought, "Well, I guess this is okay."

He had this whole "time travel" ethos where he lived like it was 1895. He would wear vintage clothing, like a straw boater and these little spats. There was no electricity in the apartment, so we were living by candlelight and he would read to me at night. We read books I never would have read and then he had all these crazy people come over and we'd have these dinner parties that were like 1895 formal salons.

For weeks, whenever we went to bed, he would tap me and say, "Are you asleep?" and I would wake up and go, "Oh, my God." He did this to me until I would give in and let him give me a blow job. I got sleep deprived for weeks on end. I felt like I was losing my mind.

I don't think he loved me, but he loved the idea of me. He had a huge fantasy which didn't have anything to do with who I was or what I wanted. He just liked it that I was tall. I was reasonably attractive when I was young. Youth is beauty, whatever.

Things kept getting more strained. One day, he made this pound cake. And it was an 1895 recipe, so it was really heavy. I couldn't really eat it. And he pulled out a knife, and I said something, and he started chasing me around the apartment with the knife, and I thought, "Well, this isn't good." Then I left and he took an overdose of aspirin.

So he went to the hospital, and his mother called me and told me to leave the apartment. I guess that was my first love affair.

In the family I grew up in, there wasn't really a good template for love. There wasn't any example of love by which I would measure how to look for love or experience love or hunger for love. My parents didn't get along. It was a long, slow rehearsal to a divorce. And I thought people who were in love were stupid. Every example I had of love was either from boring movies or from people in high school that I thought were really stupid.

I was a professional sourpuss. That was my mode, which was acceptable in the world of punk. Punk was a bunch of people whose favorite thing to do was say, "I hate you." We were encouraged to regard love with cynicism. After a while, it got a little boring. I finally realized that maybe companionship and being nice, well, you know, maybe I better try that before I die.

I met this guy at a Pere Ubu concert at Max's. His name was Bradly and he was eventually a drummer for Teenage Jesus and the Jerks. I thought, "God, I met a gay person in the punk rock milieu. Maybe we should try and hook up." It was almost that clinical. Punk was not particularly gay-friendly, so it just seemed logical that I should experiment with this conveniently placed other gay.

So we hooked up, and it was crazy. He was my first alcoholic, my first drug addict.

We decided to move in very quickly. Since I had no way of judging what love was, I could only measure whether we were "boyfriends" with superficial things: We had a lot of fun together. Being in the middle of the punk era, you would go see a new band every night, and every time they would be fabulous. And you would be getting into trouble every night, meeting wonderful artists, and everywhere you went in America, people welcomed you. We did have sex, although he would usually just pass out and I would fuck him. At first, it was a little more romantic than that. We'd coo along to Lou Reed songs.

We were together for seven years and it was very colorful, and I have to say I loved him as I came to understand love later. I cared for him. I hoped well for him. I found him really attractive. I found him hilarious. I thought he had a lot of charisma. I thought he was talented. He liked to have all our friends over and cook for them, and that gave me this artificial feeling of family. And he adored me. He adored me in a very needy, broken, alcoholic, and romantic way, but he absolutely adored me.

I don't know what this has to do with love, but the way it ended up is that we had loads of great times. I had the most fun in life I ever had with him. But he had a very predictable, cliché descent into heroin and everything got worse and worse and worse. I slowly withdrew from him and offered him less and less comfort—which, of course, he could sense, which made me feel lost for both of us.

About the seventh time we had to carry him up seven flights of stairs because he had passed out, or peed his pants at someone's barbecue while everyone laughed, I was like, "Hmm, maybe this is an issue!" It finally clicked with me.

I actually tried to go to Al-Anon. I went for one meeting. It just felt like this bunch of old, whiny fishwives. I hated them.

Things got bad and I didn't know how to extricate myself. I had surrounded myself with piles of collectibles, this whole loft in New York just filled with antiques and crazy stuff, and Bradly said, "If you ever leave me, I'll kill you and destroy everything you have." That didn't sound good.

So I had two friends hire him for one night for something—he wasn't ordinarily hirable because he was such a big drunk. My brother flew out from California, and in one night, we packed up all my stuff and I moved to California. He came home and I had moved. That must have been a shock. That's a nice love story.

What did I learn? Nothing.

Within a week, I was having an affair with this guy Moe at a club where I was playing in L.A. He was an artist. I didn't want to move in with him right away. He had a boyfriend—that was a healthy sign! So I began an affair with him. But finally we did move in together for about two years. He had a college educa-tion, he wasn't in punk rock. He had a great job designing album covers. He was handsome in an all-American way.

It was another case of me making this kind of detached cal-culation: "He's an attractive boyfriend, and I'm going to go for this because of A, B, and C. He doesn't seem to be a heroin addict. He has an education. We connect on a more intellectual level. The sex is better." So I thought, "Well, let's just try this!"

I wasn't mean. I was in my head. I liked these people enough, but I was having my own life separate from them, and they couldn't ever get in there.

So, anyway, I broke up with him after finding him in a bathroom having sex with someone while we were out having dinner.

I had already met this other guy who was really cute, and he also already had a boyfriend. We started having sex and I thought, "Oh, my God, I've done what I hate the most. I'm a home wrecker. Twice!" The difference with this one was he was The One. It was the only time I felt this. I was addicted to him like a drug.

I was with him for ten years. I was hopeless. I thought he was the most handsome, the most wonderful, the most charming, the sexiest. The sex was insanely great, and we actually continued to have sex for, like, a couple of years after we broke up. It was always incredible, hungry, passionate, which can be quite a trigger for a person who hasn't had any good sex in their life.

We made bands together. We went across the country together. We did all sorts of stuff together. At first it seemed really sensible, but I do remember the first time I took him up to meet my mom. She looked at him and she said, "Who *is* this raggedy man?"

He definitely was not into dressing up or being presentable. He was really over the top, you know, vintage suits, old ripped-up jeans, and shaggy, multicolored hair. It was just of the era, sort of postpunk. He was wonderful.

But my Al-Anon nose had smelled out another heroin addict. I believed in my heart that no matter what the problems were, we were going to work them through together and grow old together. I didn't count on heroin being such a big competitor for his affection. I really thought I was going to win and we were going to go to counseling and everything would be just peachy.

There were, you know, the usual recriminations: He robbed me, he started having unsafe sex with people that I didn't know. I guess he was doing that for drugs. He lied about where he was and all that kind of stuff.

Then after a long, downward spiral, he finally went to rehab. I had just bought this house. We were going to try and start our life anew in this house. I said, "If you don't stay in rehab, you can't come home." And he didn't stay in rehab. So I said, "You can't come home."

It was the hardest thing that I ever did. And then two years later, of course, he got clean and sober. And didn't need me.

So I went back to Al-Anon. It was mind-bogglingly difficult. I would wake up every morning and wish I was dead. That was what Al-Anon helped me through. They said: You can't give someone else the responsibility to make your life, your well-being, your happiness. That's unfair to make anybody have that responsibility. They finally hammered that into my head.

It was funny, like there was one morning where I got up and I made the bed, because I thought, "I like to see the bed made." I had never done that before. I had only done it to keep the house neat for the relationship. It had to look nice by the time the boyfriend got home from work. When I finally made my bed for myself, that was a real realization: that I could do it for myself. I got to this position where I felt like I had a little perspective on my own behavior.

Later, I meet this handsome Teutonic guy in a meeting. At Al-Anon we were encouraged to go to AA meetings, to learn about the alcoholic. You know, like it never occurred to me that I was just cruising in the junkyard of train-wrecked souls and that maybe I should try and meet somebody out in the real world.

In Al-Anon, they say your picker is broken. I hate that line, but it's true. I just picked a guy. Only this time he was straight. Once again, he was a painter, incredibly exciting intellectually. We would talk until four in the morning.

It was like a mind fuck, and in a weird way, the mind fuck is the hottest fuck of all. If they're telling me something I don't already know, that excites me. They take me on a trip to someplace I would never have gone intellectually, and they show me something that thrills me; that's so charismatic I can't resist it.

We talked and talked and talked; then we kissed little inept turtle kisses and all this kind of stuff. He was conflicted by the sexuality, but then he still gave me a blow job. It's confusing: "You're straight but you blew me." But he really was straight. He really wasn't good at it. But this was another time I thought our love would repair all this and suddenly the blossoms would arrive.

He broke up with me on Valentine's Day. He said, "You know, this isn't working."

I said, "Hey, you're right. It isn't."

After that, I had a pretty long bachelorhood. I think I was a bachelor for almost two years. And that was exciting. I was totally ready to go on another ten years.

And when I was really ready to be alone, I met Justin, my current boyfriend. I came to this relationship with a lot more ease and a lot less neediness. I said, "We can't move in with each other for at least a year. We have to do a lot of dating and thinking about stuff and talking about stuff."

We did all that.

It isn't this shrill, white-noise high pitch of the other relationships where, if it wasn't going to work, everything was going to be over. He has his own wonderful, exotic, creative existence, which was well in place before I met him. We didn't come to each other as empty vessels that needed to be filled. We came to each other as full vessels . . . that could sit next to each other at Starbucks.

The coolest thing about him is my friendship with him. We're really superclose friends. We love to argue with each other, but we also love to spend time together and travel together. He's insane, and I'm insane, and I have to realize at this point: I love insane people.

I really don't think I knew, or know, what love is. But I think I'm more loving than I used to be. I think my definition of love has shifted away from obsession and control and more toward an emphasis on companionship, actually caring for the other person, trying to stay happy together and not putting too much of a burden on each other.

Intellectually, I can grasp that love is about neediness. It's about lust. It's about desire. It's also about empathy and wanting the best for the other person. It's some sort of mixed-up thing there, and you have to find a balance.

I found that kind of love. I think he's very lucky—because I *don't* think he's The One.

In 1972 the Catholic high school I was going to merged with the Catholic boys' school because of money. The boys came over. And so this guy, Brian, walks into homeroom, and when I saw him come in, it was love at first sight. I don't know how I knew, I just knew. He was tall, he was thin, he had long, light brown hair. He was looking kind of lost. He would always do things like close my locker when I was trying to get stuff out of it. Eventually we started going out, and I fell head over heels in love. But I was all of fifteen.

This is in Massachusetts, and in the summertime his parents would go down to Cape Cod. So we had to not see each other, and I was still madly in love. I was ridiculous. I was sending these love letters every day. I was really smothering the kid. When we came back to school in the fall, he broke up with me.

And then I met another guy, Gary. He was three and a half years older than I was. He was nineteen and I wasn't even sixteen. And that didn't go over real good with the parents, I can tell you. We started dating pretty heavy and steady. But it was such a tempestuous relationship. We would break up often. And Brian and I would kind of pick up where we had left off. Then Gary asked me to marry him.

I had a horrible life at home. Didn't get along with my mother at all. She didn't trust me. I couldn't do anything. I'm sure that had I had a more stable life at home I would have probably gone on to college and gotten married later on, when maybe I was a little more mature, a little smarter. Brian and I had dated and broken up and gotten back together, and blah blah blah. I told him Gary had proposed, and he asked me to marry him. But I knew he wasn't ready, and he was doing it so I wouldn't marry Gary. So I ended up marrying Gary when I was eighteen.

I saw Brian once within the first couple years of marriage. We got together for a cup of coffee or something. And then, you know, life went on. I didn't invite him to my wedding because it ended kind of badly when I said I wouldn't marry him. He got married three years later. I ended up going to his wedding. And I don't remember anything about it, but I could tell you exactly what he looked like that day. He looked beautiful.

When they say, "If anyone knows any reason why you shouldn't get married," I wanted to stand up and say, "Me! Me! I'll divorce Gary! I made a mistake." But I didn't, of course. I danced with Brian. Do you know the dollar dance? You pay a dollar to dance with the groom, and boys pay a dollar to dance with the bride. And you just dance for a minute. Heartbreaking. And after that we didn't have contact for fifteen years.

I was married twenty-nine years. I cheated throughout the marriage. Fairly often. I felt like something must be wrong with me because Gary's a good man. He's a great provider, great father, loves me to death, treated me like a queen. And it wasn't for sex. We had really great sex. But I wasn't happy, you know. Wasn't fulfilled. I think I just wasn't in love.

I mean, I would rather be with my friends anytime than be with my husband. The few times that he would go out with me it kinda put a real damper on things. You know? If he wasn't my husband I wouldn't have hung out with him. I didn't like him. He just wasn't my type of person. It's not like it was a horrible marriage. We made money, we spent money, we built a house, we had nice furniture, we bought a boat, spent a lot of time on that. I think I just knew in my heart Brian was the one I should be with.

For the first five years of my marriage, I hadn't thought about him that often, but after that, I started to think about him all the time. At least once a week. I would wonder how he is, I miss him, what if . . . blah blah blah. Couple of times I'd get drunk and I'd call. I'd get his wife or a kid would answer—he had three kids—and I would say, "Oops, wrong number!" I did the drunk dial maybe three times.

After fifteen years of not seeing each other, Brian stopped into where I worked, 'cause I've worked at the same place for twenty years—a bank. I was a banker, which really didn't fit with the way I felt, either. We went out for coffee. I still felt exactly the same way. But I didn't say anything, of course. We kissed goodbye—a friend's kiss.

The last ten years of my marriage, I started to think about

him a lot. All the time. To the point where I was really quite sick of it. I didn't want to be thinking about him. I was holding myself back from calling. I would dream about him. He was just in my head all the time, you know. Still, life was going along. I had my son when I was twenty-eight.

But I had a late adolescence. Jeez, it's embarrassing to say, but all my thirties, into my early forties, I was going out to clubs and partying and just doing things I really shouldn't have been doing. I used to live in an area of Massachusetts that was only forty-five minutes from Boston and twenty minutes from Providence, so I was always going out without my husband and getting into trouble, doing drugs: coke and Ecstasy. I have a lot of gay friends, and Gary thought that going to gay clubs was a safe thing. If you've been, you know it's really not. It's always straight guys or bi guys at these clubs and it's, you know, it is a pretty drugged-up atmosphere.

And Gary was pretty cool for a husband in that he would let me—and I hate to use that word "let" me—but he wouldn't give me a hard time about going away for the weekend to see my friends. Or when I started going to these clubs all the time he would even help me pick out my dresses. He didn't know about the drug stuff or the sex stuff, obviously. And sometimes it blew me away that he didn't know because I would come home so fucked up. But either he chose not to see it or I was a really good actress. And I'm not.

It got to the point where I was doing too many drugs, and I told Gary. I really kind of cleaned up. I had been seeing a therapist to talk about this. She thought I was crazy. Of course. What therapist is gonna say, "Oh, gee, you should put your thirty-year marriage on the cutting board and call this guy that you haven't seen in forever and . . ." you know? The therapist tried to discourage me. "It's all in your head. He's not thinking of you." That kind of stuff.

So I went on to Classmates.com somewhere around that time. Not looking for him because I knew he would never be on there. He didn't go to any of the reunions and that kind of stuff—which I did. I just went to see who was on. And there's Brian. His bio, the only thing it said was "divorced," and it had a smiley face.

Well, my heart stopped. I thought, "Oh, my God, he did that for me. He's trying to get ahold of me. Oh my God. Oh my God." But my mind said, "Oh, for God's sake, Louise. If he was trying to get a hold of you he would pick up the goddamn phone." Not knowing that he actually was trying to contact me, had been searching on the Internet trying to find my e-mail. I mean, my name was in the phone book. The same phone book his mother had. His mother had told him, "You should call Louise! You should call Louise!" But he didn't want to disrupt things.

I didn't know what to do. I was scared. I was thinking about him, thinking about him, thinking about him. And it kinda came to a head one day. This is like a year later. I could not stand it anymore. I was freaking sick of thinking of him. So I called. And he answered the phone. That was July 19 of 2003. I just poured out my soul. I said, "This is Louise and I think you're the love of my life. I can't stop thinking about you. I know you probably think I'm out of my mind but I just have to say this because I can't take thinking about you anymore." And I kind of blabbered on and on like that for a little while. We talked for an hour and a half. And we exchanged e-mail addresses and I was in heaven.

I remember now: It was a beautiful day. Sunny and hot. I was down at the beach. I was sitting in the sand, and as we talked on the phone, I kept digging and digging and digging a hole. By the time we were done talking I was in this freaking crater. And after we talked I got up and I ran five miles like it was a block. That was the most I ever ran. I stopped and it was like I could turn around and do it again. You know. Just a feeling of floating. Just not being real.

We started e-mailing back and forth, and then he pulled back and said, "You should try to work things out with Gary," and nah nah nah nah and we didn't e-mail for two weeks and then we started again. It was about a month before we talked again on the phone.

There was some sexual flirtation. And a lot of remembering the way we felt about each other way back when and he admitting that he did think about me while he'd been married but he just . . . he's very conservative as far as, like, he would never have cheated on his wife even if a woman had thrown herself naked in front of him. That's not the way he is.

So that went on for about a month. I pretty much lived on my boat in the summer but my husband lived in the house because of his work. He was in business for himself, so he needed to be around the phone and the fax and the computer and all that. And I wasn't working at this time. I had quit working in '98. Brian worked nights, so he would get home at one thirty in the morning and we'd talk for hours.

And then on September 6 of '03, we decided to meet. Physically meet. I was waiting for him down at a beach that we used to go to as kids. It has an old building on it, like a fort. When we were kids we used to climb up inside. So I was waiting for him, and there's like a causeway between the mainland and the beach. And I was standing there and he stopped the car, all these cars are behind him, and he jumped out of the car and grabbed me and gave me a big hug. He lifted me right off the ground. And then he parked the car and we walked around holding hands and lying on the blanket on the beach. We kissed and that type of thing, but we didn't have sex. I went back to my life and he went back to stay at his mother's and I saw him again the next day. And then after the next day, we had seen each other that whole weekend, and I went home and I told Gary. I said, "I saw Brian. We've been communicating and I think I want to try things with him, and I'm leaving."

That didn't go over too well. He was very upset. He kind of screamed with like a shocked scream, not a loud, yelling scream. He went to the living room and started crying. It was horrible. Oh, I felt terrible. I felt guilty. But I just couldn't not do it. On one side there was this great excitement and this great happiness and fulfillment, and on the other side was guilt and dread. I was so excited about the fact that Brian felt the way that I was always hoping he felt. That basically took everything over. That overshadowed anything else.

I left that night. I went to live on my boat for a couple weeks, and it started to get cold, so I moved in with my friend in Warwick, Rhode Island. And then I officially moved in with Brian in the middle of November of '03. And now we live in the middle of the woods in New Hampshire.

I would certainly hate for anyone reading this to think that it was an easy thing to do. That it was easy, that it was pleasant. Or that it's something that you should think about doing 'cause you're unhappy. Because I wish I had gone about it a different way. The grown-up thing would have been to leave Gary and then start a relationship with Brian. That would have been the nice, clean way to do things. But I don't know if those kind of things can ever really be clean and nice and tidy.

Especially when we first got divorced. Lots of guilt. There were many days when I didn't like what I was doing. I felt icky about it. When I first got divorced I was very, you know, "Are you sure you love me? You're not just with me because I left Gary, are you?" That kind of thing. You go through that horrible period of first feeling so guilty about what you've done to someone who really did love you. But I just . . . I had to. I mean I just had to. I only have one time, you know? I only get one time around.

I almost went back to Gary a couple times. The guilt really overcame me. I think twice, maybe, six or eight months apart. Gary and I tried a reconciliation, like going out to dinner. And I would realize I was nuts and come flying back up here, you know. I think it hurt Brian. But he'd been through a divorce too. I think he understood a lot of the feelings that you have.

We went through a period of adjustment, because I'm the one with the money. Not that I have a ton left after the divorce! We had a very fair divorce because I was guilty as all hell. But Brian's a janitor, which like, you know, gave my ex lots of giggles and laughs, "Oh, you left me for a janitor!" Which was very uncool.

Brian hasn't done a lot. Didn't go beyond high school. He's

always been strapped for cash. He and his wife both worked. They always worked. Didn't make a lot of money, you know. Brian often worked two and three jobs at a time. They had three kids. I think it was hard for him just because, you know, the man thing. And for me it was maybe a little difficult because I'm one of those people that needs the security of having some money.

I've been with Brian now for five years. He asked me to marry him in February in 2005 on Antigua. We had gone for dinner on the beach in one of the restaurants at the resort and we were walking along the beach and he grabbed me and said that he wanted to spend the rest of his life with me and that I was the love of his life. And I married him.

I'm as happy as I can be. I'm very happy. Very relaxed in my life now. I can't even imagine cheating on him. Brian has told me that if we had been married and I tried any of that shit with him (*laughs*) he would have kicked my ass out the door. And I wonder if I would have gone through that if I had been with someone who I liked. In the beginning, I would say I wish we had been together these past thirty years. And he would say, "No, I think it happens for a reason." You know. I wouldn't have my son. And I love my son.

I think I wanted to be with someone that I wanted to be with every minute. And that's how it is. I want to be with him all the time. I still go out, but yeah, no, I don't go down to Massachusetts very often anymore. I'm going down next weekend for a party, but it'll be low-key. I might smoke a little pot. And even if I did do a little coke or something, it wouldn't be like, "Oh, now I'm gonna go out and get in trouble." You know

what I mean? Like, I'm looking forward to going to Massachusetts because I haven't seen my friends in a long time. But I
won't want to do it again two weeks later.

Brian isn't into going out. It's not his thing. He hates to get
dressed up to go out to eat or anything. I mean, getting dressed
up for him is a clean pair of jeans and a clean T-shirt. But that's
just the way he is, and it's okay. That stuff just doesn't matter.
Because I just love him for the way he is. He's silly. He's like a
little kid. His sense of humor. The way he sees the world. He
sees all the good. Very optimistic. Hardly ever down in the
dumps. Although just after summer ends he has a bit of a
period. But he's very laid back. Very affectionate. Although my
ex was very affectionate too. Which I need. I need a lot of reas-
surance all the time.

How do you describe the person that you have found? He's
my best friend, which was a new concept for me. Not just loving the person you're with but liking them. You know, you've
probably heard people say, "You should be friends first." It's so
true. He's the love of my life. It doesn't depend on whether he
has been nice to me that day or did he buy me some nice Lindt
chocolate or jewelry. Or did we have good sex last night. It's
because . . . just because I want to be with him. I'm like a little
puppy. I just want to be with him all the time.

LEONARD PELLEY, AGE 40

BROOKLYN, NEW YORK

"I *know* I'm going to die alone."

When I was a kid in Atlanta there was this one girl in my junior high school named Elena. She was kind of like my first girlfriend—very pretty, just a nice Southern girl. I think her dad worked for Georgia Power. He never liked me for some reason, but that wasn't an issue. Because Elena liked me. I didn't have to push on after her. It just sort of flowed naturally. We ended up going to our end-of-school dance and off to high school and had some great memories. And then in my first year of high school, my family moved here to New York. Even then, we kept the relationship going. We'd write letters and I would go back and visit in the summertimes, all through high school.

So then we're a couple years into college—I went to the University of Missouri—and for Thanksgiving break I go down to Atlanta, and she's home and we decide to go out on a date. We went to see *The Adventures of Ford Fairlane*, starring Andrew Dice Clay. And I had some gifts I wanted to give her. So we came back to Elena's place, and we're sitting in the back room off the den and we're talking. I said, "I love you." And she said, "Well, I love you too."

I said, "We've been writing these letters and dating for so long. Do you see any way that once we're done with school, if we're still feeling the same way about each other, that we might . . . ?" And then there's a pause. And she just looks at me and says, "No. No." And I said, "No?" And then she goes, "No. No." She got up and went into the kitchen, and I guess she got a soda.

I laid the little gifts that I had out for her, a couple sweatshirts and a pen-and-pencil set and a picture frame, you know, junk with the University of Missouri logo emblazoned on it. And fifteen minutes later I called a cab and I left. But in the cab I'm thinking to myself, "She just told me that she didn't want to marry me." I wasn't asking her, "Will you marry me *now*?" I laid it out there logically, you know, we're too young, we're still in school. If she had said yes, then maybe we could think about it. But it was just a no. After that I got a couple more letters from her, and then she stopped writing and stopped responding altogether. I was just left thinking, "What the hell did I do? What went wrong?" To be the one for her . . . for her to be the one for me . . . and then it's just nothing.

And I guess the pattern was set right there. You know, there's no beginning, middle, and end to that story; there's a beginning, middle, and then just, you know, a blank page.

A few years after Elena and I broke up, I was living in Brooklyn. And my roommate at the time—my friend Patrick— we had started going to Iona. It's the local bar in my neighborhood. And there was this lady named Esther who'd come by the bar and drink, but she was also a musician, teacher, and vocalist.

She played the piano and was just out of sight. She was tall and had this really long brown hair, kind of streaked with gray, and these gray-blue eyes, with just a lot of sympathy and kindness. And she put those qualities into the songs she sang.

One song that always kind of sticks with me is "The Best Thing for You Would Be Me." It's a standard but it has a lot of weird little progressions in it, and she sang it at Iona once, and I was kind of blown away. After she finished her set I went over and I asked her, "Oh, do you live in the neighborhood?" And she said, "Yeah, I'll be singing at the Lucky Cat in a couple of weeks." So I went to that show, and kept . . . not tracking her down, not looking for her or anything, 'cause she made it pretty clear that she was in a relationship. But I just wanted to be around her and hear her sing. So I'd go to her shows. And she was always dating somebody else. And this goes on for, like, three years or so.

Then one Halloween I was at Iona and I got this stupid costume together with a Mets baseball jersey and a bat, where I pretended to be Mo Vaughn's younger, slimmer brother. Esther was there. And at some point I went to the bar, and her friend Leslie said to me, "Oh, man, you're going to get lucky tonight 'cause Esther just said, 'I'm going to take him home with me.'"

So we went home and had a very passionate night, and it was fun, and I left the bat in her house. A couple days later, she came marching into the bar with the bat over her shoulder, like she was going to whack me with it. We dated for a year after that, and it was good. Very good in the sense that, you know, I'd go to her shows and she would read my work—I write poems—and we would talk every day, and share things, and there was lots of e-mail back and forth.

She'd mentioned this other guy, Craig, who she was still kind of dating. Or she had dated him before and the relationship had never really fizzled itself out, even though we were dating. So, you know, there was something of a block there. Anyway, one night about a year into our relationship, we're at her place, listening to classical music—this beautiful piece she wanted to share with me—very quietly, listening to the music, holding hands, facing each other in these chairs. And she puts her head forward toward me, and I put my forehead toward hers, and her hair kind of spills over and covers most of us, and we're in this kind of prayerful moment.

The song comes to an end, and I say to her, "Would it be all right if I told you something?" And she says, "Yes, you can tell me anything." So I said, "I love you." She let go of my hand, her eyes flew open wide, and she sat back almost bolt upright with this look of utter confusion. It was like a bolt from the goddamn blue, like, "What? You love me? What?"

It confused me, because I thought we were on the same page here. I'd thought this was what people do. We should make it official by expressing our love. I mean yes, we can have sex, and I can tell you I love *this*, but I never told you I love *you* for being able to give me a moment where we're completely transported into another realm of sensual delight and perception. And because we're sharing it, because you and I are the ones here together, that's why I love *you*. That's what I was expressing. I was in the moment, I guess. But she squelched it. So I got another drink and I went to bed and that was it.

Over the next few weeks, everything became contentious. "Why do you call me all the time? Why do you send so much e-mail? Why are you always after me?" You know—"Come on, this is too intense!" Then after a while she just wouldn't return my calls. There was no more e-mail. I didn't see her in the neighborhood anymore.

So I waited a few months and then finally left her this voice mail. I was like, "Just giving you a call to say hello, how're you doing? Hope everything's all right." She calls me back and says, "Don't just call to say 'How's it going?' I don't want to hear from you. Leave me alone. Get my number out of your book. Just let it go. I don't want to have any contact with you." No explanation.

I would still see her around the neighborhood and sometimes on the subway, at the end of the car that I was in. When that happened I would just get off at the next stop. I couldn't bear to even think about it. I still remember her touch, I remember the way she would tremble a little bit in bed when she talked to herself. She had this thing where she would wake up fighting herself in a dream or something. I still remember. I knew then and I know now that there was something very, very right about us together.

But I still don't know why it couldn't work out. There was no end. No real end. I saw her recently at Iona. She was with this guy Craig, the same guy she was hung up on before we were together. And she came up to me while she was getting a drink at the bar and she goes, "How are you? How have you been?" And I couldn't not be honest with her. I said, "Well, I guess I'm doing okay, but I've never gotten over you." And that same look of shock and surprise came into her eyes a little bit, and she said, "We can't talk about this now," and I said, "I guess we can't." And then she walked out of the bar with the other guy.

I really tried to move on. I became interested in another lady who spends time at Iona. She was maybe a year or two older than me, maybe forty-two or forty-three, but pretty well kept. She's small and wears this short, dark haircut and has this kind of quirky, odd sensibility about her that's like, you know, somebody I'd like to know. So I ask the manager about her and she goes, "Well, she's into poetry." And I think, "Oh! Maybe I'll give her a piece of my work."

She's talking to two or three other people, this generic kind of bar conversation where if someone's sitting two or three feet away, you can kind of throw in your two cents' worth. I give her my poem and I go, "I heard you were into poetry. I write, and if you're ever interested in being one of my readers, here's the content that I do." She didn't look at the poem, just stuffed it in her bag. So the overture was rebuffed—I get it. That was maybe a year and a half ago.

After that I'd see her at Iona every once in a while. And one day she comes in and starts talking to this guy sitting at the end of the bar. But she just gives me this kind of perfunctory kind of quick wave and goes out to the deck. And she's out there playing Scrabble with these people, and I'm thinking, "What is it about this woman that she can't even be friendly?" It just rankled me.

Without being angry, without being in any way aggressive, I'm just thinking, you know, let me try and smooth this over, let me tell her, "Look, I'm just trying to be a human being, and this is the human being I am. I understand if you're not interested in me. That's fine. But there's no reason for any chilliness. We know a lot of people in common here. There's no reason that we shouldn't have a common feeling ourselves." That was my intention.

I go out on the deck and stand near where she's at, and I happen to notice that in her Scrabble hand she has letters that could give her a double-word score. And I was going to point that out to her. But before I can do it she looks up at me and says all this stuff. "You're hanging over my space! I don't want to talk to you! Get away from me! Just leave me alone!" Really vicious. Her pupils were so dilated, like she was just really mad. That's what shook me up. I couldn't understand how I could make somebody so mad by just being the way that I am.

But again, that question hangs at the end of it: What the fuck happened here? Where did I run off the rails? The whole thing just put me in a bad little spin. I didn't go straight home; I stopped at a couple other places like restaurants and bars that I know people at. It was a Saturday afternoon. And when I got home, I started crying. I wasn't crying for what happened, I was more crying for what hadn't happened. For all those other times with Elena and Esther and . . . Everything else where it just ended on this weird, discordant note and goes through time, just echoes through time and seems to affect everything going forward.

It makes me feel like a piece of shit. It makes me feel like I'm not deserving of love, not worthy of affection. If there was something I had done or said, some choice that I'd made years ago, or maybe even tomorrow—but I don't know what it is.

I sometimes wonder, for instance, if my family hadn't left Atlanta, who knows what would have happened between me and Elena? There wouldn't have been years of letters and that stilted scene where I'm fumbling around toward the idea of marriage that wasn't accepted. That might not have happened because I would have been there all the time. Just by familiarity, it would have grown and evolved into something different and more beautiful. But I'll never know that because that's not what happened. We did move.

I hold my mother responsible for some selfish choices she made. I still maintain the reason we moved to New York is that she thought she was going to get married to some guy who actually had no interest in marrying her. But regardless, she just up and ripped us out of school.

My mom was very young when she first got pregnant, about fourteen years old. At the time my father was still in the Army Air Corps, traveling around the country. He was cheating on my mom, and basically had another family, and that's what eventually led to them breaking up. We were living in Miami when they split, and by that point, my mom had a job as a licensed nurse.

We kind of fell on hard times. We were living in this apartment building on Northwest 56th Street. My older brother was in high school and was working some bull job. But no one was making enough money and we got behind on the rent. And there came a day, when I was five, that the marshals knocked real loud on the door. I remember they kind of pushed and banged on the door, and they came in and they started picking stuff up and just literally taking it downstairs and putting it out on the street. We didn't have anywhere to go. They were just putting our shit out on the street.

I remember figuring out what was happening—that we didn't have any money and we were getting thrown out. And I picked up these pennies and change that I found, and I remember going to one of the marshals and I said, "Sir, I have this. Will this help us? Will this let us stay? Can we not go if you take this?" (*cries*) He said, "I got a job, kid. Just put that in your pocket. Just put it in your pocket."

So that was that. The last of it was that I had this Snoopy, this little stuffed doll, and I really loved my Snoopy. And I still have a really deep soft spot for the old specials, like the Christmas special and *The Great Pumpkin*. But I had my Snoopy doll by all our stuff and I look out the door and I see one of the workmen throw my Snoopy over the railing, and he floated down and he fell in the dirt, and I went over and picked it up (*cries*) and then we left.

We moved into an another apartment for a couple of days, and then into some other shitty house. Then we moved to Atlanta. My mom was from South Carolina and her sister and brother were in Atlanta, saying, you know, there's plenty of hospitals up there, you can get a job up here. So we moved. And I kind of hold that against my mom—the fact that we moved around so much.

Lately I've been comparing what's happened to me in my life to other people's situations. My friend Justin, he's a child of divorce, and he has a relationship going on three years now. My brother Scott, he's had girlfriends over the years and relationships where he gets what he needs. My uncle Dennis lived with his wife for all the time I've ever known him. That's what people do. You find somebody, you live with somebody, you take them for the good and the bad, they take you for your good and your bad, and you get through it.

But those kinds of relationships, they're just never something I've been able to find. And now I'm coming up to forty and feeling like if it hasn't happened yet, you know, it's just not going to happen. I've established who I am morally, politically, artistically. And if that doesn't mesh with the one who is out there—who may not ever be out there—it's probably not going to happen. Coming to terms with feeling like I'm going to die alone—it's not something I feel like I have a choice about. I *know* I'm going to die alone. This is where it goes.

I'm never going to have kids. I'm never going to have a happy home and the weekend getaways and the vacation pictures of me and blank: me and blank at the Eiffel Tower; me and blank at Yosemite National Park; me and blank at the Golden Gate Bridge; me and blank at the Chinese place up the street. No. It's me and nobody. Just me, the good-hearted goof that can't catch a break, hanging out in the back of the frame of a picture of a bunch of couples.

I was walking down the street the other night and I happened to notice this couple having a little kiss. I'm thinking to myself, "If that guy was feeling something that nobody else in his life could understand, *she* still would." Or she might. It's just the possibility that makes the difference. And that possibility's not there when you're alone. I just have to eat the pain and eat the suffering, and maybe go home, write it down, and hopefully it will turn into art someday. And that's the situation.

While there's life, there's hope. I do hold out some hope. I feel that it's not likely to happen. But it *could*.

I want love. And I want to give that love to someone else. I don't just want it to be given to me; I want to share it. But for now, when I wake up in the morning, I'm alone. And I don't know what anything else would feel like. Being alone is really all I know. I mean, what do you feel when you wake up? Because in my world, there is nobody else. At the end of the day, and at the beginning of the day, there's nobody else beside you. It's just you.

KARLA COGDELL, AGE 49

MALVERN, ARKANSAS

"My husband can growl and drool just like
a rottweiler—exactly like one."

I met my first husband at Cloverdale Junior High in Little Rock, Arkansas. I was fourteen, and not knowing the facts of life or anything, I did have a child with him.

We were both from Indiana. His mom dropped him and his brother off at their grandparents' and never returned. We were both from the North—it was kind of a common bond. We walked to school every day and helped each other out on lessons, and before I knew it I was getting involved with him.

I didn't even realize that I was pregnant because I was so naïve as to what actually takes place. I was really, really scared and didn't know what to do. I really wanted to not live because my parents were very strict Catholics, and if they found out about it my life would be hell. Our time of going to bed, our time for eating, was so controlled. My dad was very strict with the belt and you had to come home and go straight to your room.

I told a friend, who started telling everybody at school.

There were a lot of black and white riots going on at that time at school, and you had to have gangs in order to actually survive. The leader of the black gang had got me cornered in the school courtyard and got me down on the ground and examined me to see if I was pregnant—in front of everybody.

I kept on going to school. My boyfriend decided to quit. He didn't want to be involved in it. By the time I got out of school, I was showing.

I didn't ever tell my parents. I just started showing and then my dad asked me and I said yes. I was the shame of the family so I had to stay in the house all of the time. When I had her in August, my parents forced me to adopt her out—that was the law then.

At the hospital the nurses were kind of mean. Of course back in those days they weren't used to young girls having children. They played this song, "Wildfire." I was in the delivery room and I remember hearing that song when they took her from me.

After I had her, I never really was a child again. I just sat and cried most of the time or I'd be in my room and I'd do a lot of mural paintings on my wall. I made this sun that went in the corner—it was huge and yellow and black—and then I made some moons and some eclipses and stuff on the walls. Then on the other side I made like a diamond-type shape with an EKG coming off of it across my bedroom door and those are the things I used to do as I listened to Pink Floyd.

When I came back to school, people would talk to me and say, "Did you kill your baby?" I just had to ignore them and go on. They held it against me until I graduated.

I wasn't with her dad until probably the fall after that. I

started seeing him on the side. I wanted to see him like normal people do, but my parents wouldn't allow it, so I ran away from home.

We ended up getting married when I was nineteen.

Scott, he was kind of a romantic guy—he used to carry me over mud puddles and carry me through ditches and stuff. He was a Native American, and he had the features of it but he was platinum blond with blue eyes. I always wondered if his mother might have been albino. He was that type of guy that was so beautiful that all the heads would turn. I looked like Cher and he looked like Sonny—it was funny.

I took a job so we would have money to buy a home and everything. I was a nurse. He ended up being a machinist. We actually had everything bought and paid for by the time we were twenty-three because we were both really hard workers.

I was extremely in love with him. We did everything together—whether it was housework or it was fun. We were kind of crazy. We rode on the motorcycle with shorts on and no shirts—bandeau tops, halter tops. I'd sit there on the back with no hands, just relaxed on the sissy bar. I didn't put my arms around him or nothing. He might have been doing ninety miles per hour, but I didn't really care. I trusted him completely with my life.

He was such a perfectionist. He would clean everything on that bike using little toothbrushes. He would dress so meticulous—he stood out in everything that he did. We were really multitalented. I had sewn all of my life and painted and cooked, and he made things out of wood. He was an artist too. He makes carvings out of wood, like Spider-Man, and he paints them by hand and everything.

We were married for probably about four years. But then he turned to drugs. He abandoned me so many times, cheated on me once, he left me—I mean he threw me out of the house, saying that he wanted to see other women. I had to move back home, which was only about one mile from our house. He would come down there, chasing me, and I was so much in love with him and I was so upset that I finally . . . I finally ran away from him on foot. I just told him I couldn't take it anymore because our whole relationship was so tragic all of the time.

After we divorced in 1983, he tried for probably five years to get me back. I didn't want him because I was scared. I was paranoid of him.

For quite a few years I really didn't have any good relationships. I couldn't seem to find the right person.

For sixteen years, I worked at a hotel. All I did was go home and then go to work. I was pretty much happy with that. I had a girlfriend that worked with me. She kept telling me about a guy named Mason Cogdell.

I was real leery about meeting people. I said, "Mason Cogdell, that's a weird name." She wanted me to meet him at a bar, and I go, "No way! I've been to three bars in my life and I never liked any of them."

One day I was over at her house and she was talking about Mason.

I said, "Well, why don't you call him up on the phone? I'll get on the other line and I'll just listen to what he says."

She got him on the phone. He had this real deep, low, masculine voice. He got to talking about his life, which wasn't good at all, and his past life with his former wife—he had a couple wives. He sounded kind of depressed, but everything he said, I knew he was telling the truth. I thought, "This guy is really honest."

She told him that I was there and he says, "Well, let me talk to her."

I said, "Well, I'm already on the phone!"

He said, "Well, I'll tell you what. I'm gonna come over and let's make a deal. If we don't like each other, that's it! We don't have to be with each other."

I said, "Okay, that'll be fine."

He pulled up in a cowboy Cadillac—the big dually—with the big lights over the top of the windshield and lights all down the running boards. It was lit up like a Christmas tree. It had these big, deep chrome wheels on and it was ruby red. I just went over and sat down on the couch.

He walked in the door wearing a black Stetson hat and he had on a big, long Texas duster with a turquoise bolo. He had on this big cowboy belt, and the boots were black with the chrome tips and the chains and the Indian bones on them. He had curly black shoulder-length hair, a beard with a mustache, and his eyes were light blue.

I turned and looked at him and I said, "Oh, my God, there's my husband!" And in my head, I said, "What did I say?! What am I talking about?!"

He came around the couch and he kneeled down on his knees, and he took my hand and he started talking to me. He kneeled there for probably a whole hour. I was giggling like a little sixteen-year-old girl. It was totally awesome.

He took me out, and we went on a drive up on top of the

mountain. Then when he kissed me, it was just like . . . I felt electricity go through my body. These bumps, you know, these little goose bumps they came up on my skin and my hair started standing up—it was electrifying. I thought, "Oh, my God, I'm with my soul mate." He felt the same way. We started seeing each other every day. I was thirty-eight and he was forty-seven and he asked me to marry him and that was in two weeks! I was like, "Maybe we should wait a little while!" We got married in two months.

It was a cowboy wedding. It was in November and it was kind of a cloudy day. The grass was just as green as if it was summer and the leaves that fell on the ground were yellow. His two sons made a little thing of macramé or something like that with little hearts and bells hanging from it. His stepdad was the minister. One of his stepsons were there running the camera.

When we said our vows, he said, "I'll marry her if she doesn't run up the credit cards," and he started laughing.

Then he talked about not spending any money on me, that he was only going to spend a dollar on me, which kind of threw me off. I'm sure that was from his ex-marriage, but I flicked him off, and they got that on the camera! And he said, "Look at her! Look at her! She's already giving me the birdie!" and everyone started laughing.

He was holding me in his arms and everyone was talking to us and we came in the house and we had a Kroger cake and muscadine wine. We had George Jones on, that song called "We Can Make It," about how much you've gone through, and now we can make it. He danced me around and kissed me and told me that he was going to make my head tingle, and everybody was laughing.

He was very skeptical about relationships with women. His first wife and him got together under pretenses that she had no place to live. She was never faithful. As a matter of fact, she was going with every guy friend that he had. Like, his best friend was in the house with her once—intimate—while Mason was sitting in the backyard. This was back in the seventies or eighties. He put up with her unfaithfulness for eighteen years so he could raise his kids, yet she was never, ever home. She would run off for weeks at a time and wouldn't come back.

When we were first married, he would leave me at two o'clock in the morning. He would pack his bags and say it wasn't workin' out. We wouldn't be arguing or anything. We really didn't have any arguments at all. He just didn't trust anymore. I always got scared that he wasn't going to come back.

This went on for two and a half years until I finally told him, "I can't take this anymore. The next time you pull that, you're not coming back." I said, "I'll divorce you if you walk out that door one more time."

And he did! He packed up his stuff and he left.

I decided right then that I was going to divorce him, and I did.

He made a lot of phone calls to my neighbor and my mother. He tried to come back over one day. His eyes were just red and he'd been crying all the time. He was tore up. My life didn't seem to be anything, either. I didn't feel complete or nothing. But I didn't trust him to stay.

Then about nine months later, I turned on one of my music boxes that he gave me. And it was just like God was telling me it was time for us to get back together. So I called him up and I went over there to his house. He had grown his hair halfway down his back and he was really skinny. He looked terrible. He was depressed and he told me that he prayed every day for me. It was pretty upsetting.

I took him out to JCPenney's beauty salon and got him all cleaned up and we were back together again. We decided to remarry.

When my daughter had turned twenty-one years old, I told God, "I can't wait any longer to meet her," and I kissed the Bible. The phone rang two days later and my mother told me that my daughter had called and she wanted to see me.

She was in Little Rock and I decided that I was going to go down and see her. For days we talked for six and seven hours at a time. I was so excited I couldn't sleep. I went down there on a Sunday night and she was waiting there with a rose in her hand.

When I first met her, it was so shocking. She was a platinum blonde, like her father. Her eyes actually kind of looked like a lion's, the way they were shaped. They were a cross between mine and Scott's eyes. They were real pretty.

A little over a year ago, I asked my daughter, "Do you want to meet your dad?" We went down to Little Rock to see him. I hadn't seen him in about ten years. His hair was total white. I could tell from his waistline down to his feet and his hands, but I didn't know him otherwise. He had been into drugs and his whole appearance in his face had changed. I was kind of scared, actually.

We went to a restaurant together. He sat across the table kind of stiff and rigid. I was playing with my daughter's baby, and he looked over at me, and I looked over at him. Our past was still there, but it was so sad. He was not living in a life that he should be in.

They talked amongst themselves. I went to the bathroom, and when I came back, she said that he said about five times, "There's nothing between me and your mother." She said, "Well, if there isn't, why do you keep telling me over and over again?" And he didn't say anything.

When we left from there, I sat in the front with my daughter driving and he sat in the back with the baby. He started crying and he said that he had never told his family that he had had a child. How could you do that!? Here you are walkin' around school with a pregnant girl and then you are married to her! How could you not tell somebody that you had had a child? I never showed any anger toward him, I just held it in. I was trying to make it pleasant for my daughter. She said that he scared her.

He gave my daughter a picture. He was standing beside his Spider-Man all cut out of wood and painted like a real Spider-Man, and he was just like a statue—no smile, no happiness. It just totally freaked me out.

And he said to my daughter, "You know, the day I let your mother go—I've never been the same since, and I've never amounted to anything."

You know, people, they choose their own roads. He wanted me to leave so he could party. What was I supposed to do? He could have changed, but he didn't want to.

If you ever have a child with somebody, you always share a connection with that person. I felt a deep sadness. I told him if he wanted to get in contact with his daughter, then he could call me. But he hasn't called.

My first love was definitely a first love, I think. And my marriage with Mason is more of a mature love. 'Cause we didn't start out with nothing. We already had houses and cars and furniture and all that stuff. We had to combine our lives together, we already had kids before. You carry baggage from your other relationships into your next relationship, which can be very hard on a relationship.

Over a ten-year period of our marriage it's been a transition, a building period where you build trust, you build love, you build everything back to what it's supposed to be. It's a lot of hard work. I wouldn't jump back into another relationship because I know that relationships just don't happen. Not real ones.

It seems like the first five years are always the roughest, but I think after ten years you just start to blend together. It seems like we are just kind of meant to be together, like it was a destiny thing. The days we have together always seem to go by so fast. I feel a lot of passion and connection with him. But I really wish it would have happened many years ago (*laughs*) like, you know, when I was nineteen and he was twenty-nine. We wouldn't have wasted so much time. But good relationships sometimes never happen. Some people never find love.

My husband and I fix everything together—the cars, the house, everything we do together. We work on cars a lot. He rebuilds everything by hand, even a piece of junk. He can fix and make anything run. I don't care how run-down it is, he can drive it all around Arkansas and it'll never break down. We decided that we wanted to have a backhoe, so we bought an old one. Me and him broke it down together, the whole thing, and we rebuilt it—together. We painted it and rebuilt the whole engine.

He's kind of like my hero, kind of like my buddy, my pal, my friend, my lover. I call him Hercules. My husband does everything really in a very big way. I got my first flowers about nine months ago just because he wanted to. They were very big flowers. They were red and white roses and they had those lilies, you know they smell really heavy? It was huge, like two feet high. He gave me a Corvette. How many husbands give you a Corvette? He just gives me really big stuff, stuff you're not expecting to get. He got me a violin for my birthday. I told him I played it as a child and I was wanting to get back into it, and all of a sudden he came home one day and he had this violin and I cried.

He just said, "I love you and thank you." How many people say that? He's just extraordinary.

My grandpa was a very loving man, and he made everything from junk, just like my husband. He was like an inventor-type man and he was a master mechanic, electrician, and carpenter, and my husband is too. I think I fell in love with my husband because he was like my grandpa. He was funny, he was witty, he was kind and loving. All of those talented things that I grew up with, I learned from my grandpa. I really do think I married my grandpa.

My husband had a mean father and a mean grandfather. Back in the day, in Hot Springs, when there was gambling and moonshine and hit men, well, my husband's dad was a moonshine runner and a hit man. My husband didn't want to be like him, and he didn't want to be like his grandpa either. His grandpa had a junkyard dog, and he would give the dog ice cream—but he wouldn't give the grandchildren ice cream!

My husband loves ice cream. When he comes home from

construction, he gets his ice cream bars out of the refrigerator, and he gets in the bathtub and he eats his ice cream bars and he sings his little songs, and he slides down the bathtub with his legs straight up in the air, under the water, and then he squirts water out like a fish. He does that every day!

My husband can growl and drool just like a rottweiler—exactly like one. He loves to do it. He loves to scare people. He does it all the time. It's absolutely miraculous. He likes to come up behind me and do that. And I find it to be kind of romantic for me. I don't know why!

People in the neighborhood probably think we are nuts. I chase him around the yard—I chase him! Then he comes after me with the lawn mower! We'll, like, do dueling lawn mowers, we just do some crazy stuff. I'm always wrestling him. He'll try to get me in a hold but I can hold him off with one leg or one arm. (*laughs*) I'll throw him on the floor—he loves it!

He doesn't set any boundaries in my life. I am able to do whatever I want to do at any time, he don't care. But of course no cheating, yeah, he would care. But I'm just talking about, if I wanted to go with my girlfriends or if I want to do a project, whatever it may be, he don't care. He lets me do what I want to do.

He's a lot more calmer. He's not upset or depressed anymore. Sometimes he tries to run from me when I got a new project to do. He's goin', "Oh, my God, what does she want to do now?!" But you know, he comes around and we do it together. You get in the routine where you know what to do. It's smooth.

When I married my first husband, I married to be married forever. And because he was a womanizer and a weekend alcoholic, that changed that whole theory.

Clyde.

The son of a bitch.

I remember the day—this was years after we divorced—my daughter called me and says, "I know you don't care, but Clyde had a heart attack and died when he was out jogging." And honest to God, I thought, "Son of a bitch, I'll never be able to run him over."

He was so bad. Bad about his own kids. He's not even worth talking about.

I met Bill at Domino's, a nightclub. The owner took me over to introduce him. What can I say? I knew I loved him the minute we talked.

We left the bar, and I said, you know, "I'm separated, and I have four kids, and I won't go to bed with you tonight."

And he said, "Who asked you?"

And I said, "You will."

And he did.

And I didn't.

But we sat in the car and necked until I thought our skin was going to fall off.

I came home that night. And the next day, I told Ruth, my neighbor lady friend. I said, "I found him." I said, "He's a combination of"—I don't know if you know who these are—"Alexander King"—he's a writer—"Jack Parr"—the host on a talk show—"and Captain Kangaroo." And that's what I got. That was Bill.

I don't know if you have this, for your freezer, the food salesman—there were guys that went into homes and sold people food plans. You order, reorder to fill it. Well, he was in that. And the first time he showed me the pitch that he gave to people, I was enchanted. I just thought, "I'll buy one now!" He could sell snow to Eskimos.

My oldest girl couldn't stand it, because I was bringing him into the house. She was thirteen at the time and she says, "I don't want you to marry him. I want it to stay the way it is. You, me, and the kids."

And I said, "Okay. If I can't have any friends, then you can't have any boyfriends." So *that* closed up. I said, "First of all, I don't care whether any of you like him or not. You will respect him. I'm marrying him for me. Not for you."

· · ·

I was about thirty-three or thirty-four. We didn't get married until '62. We saw each other every day from our second date until the day we got married. And he was my husband of twenty-four years. I was so blessed. He adored me and I adored him. It was just a mutual admiration society.

He was built like a gorilla. I mean, he was really built like a silverback gorilla. He wore a size 52 coat. Let me tell you, he was a big man. He wasn't tall. He's just six feet, but he was big. And he was just so cute. He was just so cute.

Love to me was being a responsible person. To someone and for someone. Bill was a rock. He was like a father, a brother, a lover, a friend, a pal, a buddy, and would do anything for me. It was always very safe and very secure. And I needed the emotional security that Bill could give me. I didn't care about finances.

I used to tell him, I said, "Look, I don't need your goddamn money. I didn't marry you for your money. I married you to love me. That's it. I don't care about all this other stuff." Because he was always wanting to buy . . . if there was an appliance out in the market, I had it. He was so good.

Bill was steady. But he was never boring. No, no. He was too intelligent to be boring. He was Italian-Irish. I'm Italian-Russian. And we could argue about how to boil an egg. Our house was always in an uproar. We fought about everything— except important stuff. Never fought about money or anything like that.

He died of cancer.

Four months after he died, I was sitting in a bar. I used to always sit by myself at the table. Because even when I was fifty-something, I was pretty hot. I wanted to select who sat down next to me. And that's how I found Edward. He came over and asked me to dance. And then I invited him to my table. That was the beginning of it. I said, "I like your face. I'm going to take you home with me."

Ed had been married for twenty-five years and he had stayed with his wife—I forget . . . Daisy? Daisy—until all the kids were grown up. They had a house out in Palm Springs. He said he was sitting in the Jacuzzi and some guy on the radio said, "Is this the way you want to live the rest of your life?" And he got up out of the Jacuzzi and took his clothes and left! (*laughs*) Which I thought was great!

Oh, he was crappy dressed. I had to redo him. My husband had some beautiful clothes, which I gave to him. My daughter-in-law said, "Doesn't that feel strange seeing Bill's clothes on Ed?" I said, "No, you're wearing one of his Hawaiian shirts. That doesn't feel strange to me." It's a piece of material! It's just a fabric. That's all it is. It's not the man.

I know my kids were just horrified. Four months after Bill died, I'm out honking around in bars. And I wasn't . . . I guess I was. When I told them that Ed had this '67 Ford truck, they were convinced that I was either going to get killed or robbed.

And then after we'd been going together about three weeks, he says, "Would you like to go on a fishing trip?"

Yes! (*laughs*)

When we left, I'm going down the freeway and I'm thinking, "What the hell am I doing? I've only known this man for three weeks and I'm going off to Idaho and Utah in this horrible truck I wouldn't let anybody catch me dead in." But he was so different and he was so . . . he was more poetic than Bill.

When he was fourteen years old, he was a wrangler. He'd say things like, "You never heard anything until you've heard a cougar scream at night." Or he'd say, "Watch a snowflake kiss the ground." What am I going to do but fall in love?

Bill was my knight. But Edward was the man. He was a cowboy. I would say that he was the most exciting. When we made our trip to Utah, I found a postcard and it said, "When I grow up, I want to be . . . " and I checked off cowboy. Mailed one to each of my four kids.

They were horrified that I was doing this. I had been an executive's wife, with the cocktails, and all that shit-ery that goes on with that, and now I'm with this guy that only owns a truck and the clothes on his back. And they just know that he's going to do me in. I said, "Look, I'm fifty-seven years old. I'm not some eighteen-year-old kid. I know what the hell I'm doing!" Really, how can you be upset about a man that's making me so happy? They eventually fell in love with him just like I did.

I had to make some adjustments in my thinking because first of all, he was a mechanic. He was a handyman. So his hands were always grubby-looking and I used to say, "You can't touch me until you go scrub your hands." I would make him go scrub his hands with a brush. And I'm an organizer, so I had to get him organized. His truck—the dash looked like . . . he was a redneck! He was born in Idaho and it was just crap everywhere.

Bill was such a fuss-ass. The biggest fuss-ass in the world. The mailman would come by and drop off the bills and Bill would meet him across the street and give him the bills all paid up! (laughs) That's the way he was. Oh, yes, I never had to pick up anything after Bill. Never—except cardigan sweaters. He had an aversion to putting his cardigan sweaters away. But his closet—we had this huge walk-in closet. His side was always . . . shoes were here, this was there. He was just so. He'd wiped the tub down. Wiped the bowl off in the sink. Wiped the shower walls. He was absolutely meticulous about everything.

And Ed just was an absolute slob. Which is why I needed to make sure that I could live with it. Like, what if I couldn't change it? So then I thought, "Well, okay, if I'm going to do this, let's face it: It's going to be your money that does every-thing. Are you going to resent it after a while? You're going to have to handle it in such a way that he doesn't feel like he's being kept, like a gigolo."

I said, "Here's what we're going to do. I've got the money, and you've got the time. We're going to fix up the old Ford truck. And I'm going to sell the house and the Continental. And we're going to hit the road. And become gypsies."

Which is exactly what we did.

We did that for nine years. We became prospectors, panning for gold. We did swap meets, we sold solar panels, we went to school. We got drunk and danced every weekend. It was just an incredible life.

I was just hot for his body. He was glorious. (*laughs*) I mean he really was glorious. He had a big head of hair. Salt and pep-per. He looked like the Marlboro man. And he was about six foot two. And he kept me laughing all the time. What was he? My boy toy? (*laughs*) No. No, no, he was a love.

When I got the face-lift, I'll never forget . . . I'll never know how I ever did that.

I go to see the doctor and he says, "Well, first of all, I want to know why you want one." I said, "Look at my face. Now, look at my body. My body is forty years younger than my face," because I had a real tight body. And I said, "I want *this* to go with *this*." And I had a face-lift! And put my boobs in perspective—put them up where they belong. And man, I was in seventh heaven.

But that was one miserable week. And he just lived with me on that. He just stayed by my side and cuddled me and coddled me and, you know, nursed, nurtured me. He was a rock.

When we started selling solar, we went to the school at ARCO, Atlantic Richfield. They have a school for teaching about selling solar panels and stuff. We had to go to school for a week from nine to five. And he was just so bright. Very smart, very, very, very, very smart. Not smart—intelligent. He absorbed everything. I could remember nothing. He was the serious one.

We would travel and it was just marvelous. We spent a summer in Idaho, north of Boise, swap-meeting on the weekends, playing golf during the week. Oh, it was the greatest deal in the world. We just had a great time.

I've got some albums of what we did. This is just a smackeroo of what . . . Okay, here's the old truck. We sanded and painted it. I hand-painted this with sponge brushes.

We were on that road in Juneau.

There's a picture of him. He's such a sweetie. Eddie played the banjo.

This is panning for gold. We never found enough to pay for the books that told us where to find it. This was in '87? '86?

Here we are congratulating ourselves at happy hour. Ed had to have happy hour. I don't care what we were doing at fifteen minutes to five o'clock, it all had to halt.

This place I call Popcorn Ridge, up in Idaho. The only people we saw in three months were two forest ranger ladies and
one old man and his grandson coming to get wood. I ran
around in a baby doll nightgown and Ed ran around naked! It
was just a wonderful life.

Being three months on the side of a mountain with somebody
twenty-four/seven, you better get along. When you live in a
truck . . . I mean, we'd go to bed and one turn over, the other
turn over. That's the way it was. Because the bed was only so
wide.

The people that knew me when I was with Bill, they would
say, "I can't even imagine you out there on the ground in a tent.
I can't even believe that you would do this," because I was with
wigs and false fingernails, five-inch heels—I had the whole she-
bang. And the people that I met when I was with Ed said, "I
can't imagine you being at a cocktail party, doing the executive
life." But you can't call it a different lifestyle. It was two different
meetings of soul and body and mind.

I suppose it's like, it's like having a good bowl of chili and
then having another bowl of chili with jalapeños in it! (laughs)
Yes. One is sturdy and filling and you feel good when you get
to eat it and blah blah blah blah blah. But then you take the one
with jalapeños. It sort of sets you up on your heels a little bit.
Yeah, oh, yeah. There would never be anybody who could live
up to those two men. Never. Never ever, ever, ever. I just know
how to pick them.

I was so lucky. You cannot believe how lucky I was. Yes,
yes. With Ed, it was always exciting. Because Ed was just . . .

that man could turn me on by touching my little fingernail.

We didn't have to be married. He did one time admit that it kind of got to him. I really worked hard so he wouldn't feel like a gigolo. I never gave him a credit card. I never put his name on my checking account. But when we bought the trailer park, I put his name on it.

The kids were having a fit. I said, "Hey, I've been with him for ten years. I've taken him off the job market. He has got to have something for his time." I mean, fair is fair.

And we were together twelve years. When he died, it was because he had a heart attack. I went down and emptied the trash and came back. I looked in the kitchen and called, and when I went to the bathroom, I couldn't get the door open. He'd been sitting on the toilet. He fell over and hit the tub. And then his feet went out and that was keeping the door shut.

It was a crying, shrieking time. I tried never to sleep in our bed again. I couldn't sleep in it. I had to sleep on the couch for the next two years. The thought of him not being there with me—I couldn't handle it. It was just too, too wrong.

Two months after Ed died, I was going to go crazy. I needed something to tend to, because all I had was that stupid trailer park. I went into the animal shelter and got me a cat! She's the only one who put her front paws through the cage. We were meant for each other.

I've been living in this motor home since 1999, traveling throughout the United States. My solar panels that I have on the roof give me independence. I don't have to go into an RV park. From January to September, I stayed in eighty-four different Wal-Marts. Prior to that, I was staying at truck stops.

I only have a cell phone, I don't have a computer. I don't

want any e-mails, jokes and stuff, junk mail, junk calls. I don't want any of that. I don't need it anymore.

People are always trying to set me up. Well, I see the husbands around here. (*snores*)

The kids will say, "Don't you get lonesome?"

I say no. Personally, I find my own company more entertaining than most people I meet.

I've had a varied life and a good life. Another piece of ass isn't worth the problems! No way, no way! No, no, no, no, no, no, no. I love my privacy.

I get into bed at night and I got my electric blanket on, and I'm snuggled down here, and I got my book right in front of me, and I'm reading and I'm at peace. I'm at peace with the world. I don't want to accomodate or do anything for anybody. I only want to take care of me, my cat, and my motor home. I like it.